For Dr. Joe — This is about a country I knew well but the Kemps found a few places that ye editor didn't!

Jeff C. Dykes

Cow Dust and Saddle Leather

Cow Dust and Saddle Leather

by Ben W. Kemp
with J. C. Dykes

University of Oklahoma Press
Norman

Library of Congress Catalog Card Number: 67–24617

Copyright 1968 by the University of Oklahoma Press, Publishing Division of the University. Composed and printed at Norman, Oklahoma, U.S.A., by the University of Oklahoma Press. First Edition.

Dedicated to my wife, Myra Juanita Kemp,
without whose love and devotion
this book would not have been written

Foreword

Ben Kemp ranged over much of Southwest Texas, the Big Bend, southwest New Mexico, and spent his last years in the Tonto Basin in Arizona. The readers of this entertaining account of the life of a lawman and cowman on the frontiers of Texas and New Mexico will meet many old friends—friends they know from other recent books about the Southwest. Captain George W. Baylor, Jim Gillett and Dick Ware were Ben Kemp's associates during his two periods of service with the Texas Rangers. After Ben went to New Mexico in 1885, he knew Montague Stevens, Cole Railston, Nat Straw, Ben Lilly, Elfego Baca, the Morleys, Agnes Morley Cleaveland, and many other pioneer citizens of the southwest section.

The Apache Kid roamed through Ben's country and there is a new (or at least different to your editor) version of how he was killed. Black Jack Ketchum and a pal "borrowed" and used a couple of Ben's horses on a bank job, and Ben was accused of bank robbery.

Ben supplemented his income as a cowman (he was never a big ranch operator) in many ways, but his well drilling rig, the first in that section of New Mexico, was probably the most profitable. Just moving the heavy rig from ranch to ranch over what passed for roads in those days was a real adventure.

Ben W. Kemp, the "Benny" of this book and Ben's first son, now retired from the U. S. Forest Service, tells his father's story and most naturally, since they were close as a father and his first born often are, some of his own. He chose to use the third person approach in writing the book. This seems wise—it certainly helped the editor keep Ben and Benny properly identified.

It would be a miracle if some minor errors in dates and in the spelling of the names of places and some of the characters who appear briefly in the story did not appear. Benny and your editor have done the best we could to eliminate such errors, but we know we didn't find them all. They should not materially hinder your enjoyment of this fine biography of a man whose greatest success in life was being a good father to Benny and his brothers and sisters and a good citizen and neighbor wherever he lived.

JEFF C. DYKES

August 25, 1967

Introduction

This is the story of the life of Ben E. Kemp, my father, as he told it to me. Many of the incidents related about his later years were witnessed by me. Like many another young Texan of his day he served his state as a ranger. He was fortunate in having Captain George W. Baylor as his commanding officer and in having such stalwarts as Jim Gillett among his *compadres* in A Company of the Frontier Battalion. What a job these hard-riding, fast-shooting young hellions did for Texas!

After three years with the Rangers he returned to the range. From boyhood most of his life was spent in the saddle. At one time he was considered the best all-round cowhand in the Big Bend. Cattle on a free and open range drove him ever onward towards a sparsely settled frontier. Like many old-time cowmen, my father passed on when open range days were no more.

During his lifetime he made many friends, some were big ranch owners, some peace officers, but many just the restless cowboys and frontier wanderers he met in his own travels. He was acquainted with a number of the more flamboyant characters of the Southwestern frontier and he knew some of the outlaws, too. Father was a staunch believer in justice and fair play and was ever ready to back his judgment. He lived a full life and his account is without frills or fiction.

Ben E. Kemp was born near old Fort Chadbourne on the Butterfield Overland Mail Route (Coke County, Texas) on September 14, 1860. His father was Jasper Stephen Kemp, a Tennessean who came to Texas in the fifties. His mother was Nancy Jackson Kemp, the daughter of John M. (Humpy) Jackson, a Georgian and cousin of the famed General Stonewall Jackson. Grandfather Jasper, nineteen, and Grandmother Nancy, sixteen, eloped when her father decided they were too young to marry and ordered Jasper to leave and never come back. The young bridegroom got a job at Fort Chadbourne, and my father was born there. At the beginning of the Civil War, the fort was taken over by Colonel Ben McCulloch and Jasper was out of work.

Learning that teamsters were needed at Fort Mason, the young couple with Ben, their four-month-old son, left Fort Chadbourne the latter part of January, 1861. All their worldly possessions were in a wagon drawn by a yoke of oxen. The second night on the road, Indians ran off the oxen and butchered them. The young couple then attempted to finish the trip on foot.

Taking what food they could carry, they headed southeast in the direction of Fort Mason. Their route was through a rugged country, inhabited by wild animals and subject to savage Indian raids. In addition to these dangers they had but a scanty food supply. Game was abundant and Jasper Kemp had his rifle, but he was afraid to fire because Indians could hear the report of a fire-arm five miles away on a still day.

It was not possible for them to carry more than one blanket each for bedding and outside of these the only protection they had against the cold January wind was what they could find in the way of caves or natural brush breaks. With these meager shelters and the small fires they dared build, they kept from freezing, although they suffered severely during the cold nights.

After six days' travel they reached a spring, which Jasper thought was in the neighborhood of Fort Mason. By this time Nancy's shoes were worn out and the soles of her feet blistered. When she bathed her feet in the cool waters of the spring the skin peeled off the soles, leaving her feet so tender she could not walk.

Investigation showed this spring to be a favorite camping ground of Indians, so they were in a tight spot. Nancy could not walk, their food was exhausted, and Jasper was afraid to leave his wife and infant son alone while he made a survey of the surrounding country. If Indians found her and the child in her maimed condition, escape would be impossible. Gathering Nancy up in his arms, he carried her and their infant son to a secluded spot a quarter-mile from the spring and hid them, warning her to keep the baby quiet. He then climbed to the top of one of two small buttes near the spring and scanned the surrounding country until dark.

The next day he resumed his watch, and about noon he saw two men on horseback in the distance. They were so far away he could not tell whether they were white men or Indians, but he was almost sure they were coming to the spring, whoever they were. Leaving his lookout, he hurried to a spot near the spring and hid. If the two men were Indians, he intended to kill them and get their horses. If they were white men, he and his family would likely be safe. When the two men rode up to the spring, he saw they were white, and great was his joy when he learned they were a couple of rangers sent out from Fort Mason to look for him and his wife.

The rangers told h'm his wagon had been found a day or two after it had been abandoned. Jasper and Nancy's tracks had been found leading away from the wagon in the direction of Fort Mason. When news of this reached the fort, all the people in the neighborhood had been alerted and scouting parties were sent out in an effort to find them.

Nancy was now lifted into the saddle on one of the ranger's horses, and her husband rode back of the cantle to steady her, as her feet were too tender to use the stirrups.

The rangers rode double on the other horse, the baby being carried first in the arms of one adult and then another. This was the first horseback ride of the boy who later became one of the best broncobusters in West Texas. Within a few hours after they were found, the little party reached Fort Mason and safety.

Jasper Kemp soon had a job as teamster at the fort, and after working a few months, he bought a few head of cattle and settled on a small ranch near the fort.

During the Civil War, there were thousands of cattle in this section of Texas, most of them wild, unbranded, and unclaimed. Within six years Kemp had increased his small bunch of cattle to a sizable herd. During this six-year period two more children were born to the family, a girl and a boy.

In 1866, Jasper and two neighboring cowmen drove a trail herd from Mason to Eagle Pass, Texas. They sold their steers for ten dollars a head, but their return was delayed by Jasper's illness. When he was able to travel, they stashed their gold in their saddle-bags and on the second night camped on the Nueces. Jasper was having trouble with a young horse the next morning when they were overtaken by outlaws. Jasper, unable to mount his frightened horse, was killed, but the other Mason ranchers escaped. Jasper's body was never found and neither was the $3,000 in gold in his saddlebags. His horse somehow eluded the outlaws and was found three weeks later with a turned saddle and such a badly lacerated back that he had to be destroyed.

Grandmother Nancy married again after a few years. Ben's stepfather was Gilford Chapman, a former Texas Ranger. Chapman was honest and a good neighbor, but a stern disciplinarian who punished the three small Kemp children severely at the least provocation. The family moved to Honey Creek Cove, about twelve miles south of the town of Llano. Most of my father's remembered boyhood was lived in the Cove. He loved the outdoors, and he fished in Honey Creek and hunted along the banks. He had some encounters with mountain lions and on one occasion killed a half-grown cub with a pocketknife. While hunting on the north side of Honey Creek, he found the entrance to an old Spanish mine but never told anyone about it until years later.

Ben Kemp was not quite nine when his grandfather, Humpy Jackson, arrived at the ranch during the night. Humpy had killed a Negro soldier near Fort McKavett and was on the dodge. He was constantly on the go between his home on the San Saba and Honey Creek for the next two years. During this time Humpy was charged with killing thirty-two Negro soldiers, but my father thought that this was a major exaggeration. Colonel Ranald Mac-kenzie, the commanding officer at Fort McKavett, ordered his men to bring Humpy in, but they did not succeed. Soldiers from Fort Concho joined the hunt, but Humpy knew the country and the scattered settlers were his friends. Lieutenants John L. Bullis and George E. Albee were among the officers who led details in the search for Humpy. Colonel Mackenzie's tour of duty at Fort Mc-

Kavett ended on April 19, 1870, but Humpy waited until early in 1871 to surrender, and then to the civil authorities. He made bond at Menard on June 14, 1871, stood trial, and was acquitted. He lived out his life on his land and died of a heart attack.

The visits of his grandfather Humpy during the years he was hiding from the soldiers were not the only exciting events on Honey Creek. There were other visitors—Comanches, and on more than one occasion. Once the ranch house was burned, but fortunately, the family was staying with neighbors at the time. The Indians did not get off scot free, however, and the Pack Saddle fight in which the Comanches were routed took place within hearing distance of the ranch. Young Ben and his stepfather visited the battle site the morning after.

Ben was helping with cow roundups when he was twelve. His first job was carrying the "grub sack"—really two heavy canvas bags sewn together at the top so that they could be swung across the saddle tree. He was on a roundup at the Watson ranch when the Comanches attacked. This was his first Indian fight, and he remembered some amusing incidents despite the seriousness of the situation.

Charley Roberts, one of the young boys on the roundup, had his horse killed while he was trying to bring in the remuda. He reached camp safely on foot, but was pretty badly scared after having his horse shot from under him. He joined the other two boys, who were hiding behind some large liveoak trees. The father of the two Roberts' boys was completely frustrated and kept running from one of his sons to the other, asking "Charley, where in the hell is Bud?" And when Charley would point out the tree that Bud was hiding behind, he would rush over to Bud and ask, "Bud, where in the hell is Charley?" This went on for some time.

Gilford Chapman, Ben's stepfather, ran to where he had a cow pony staked out on a sixty-foot rope, and hastily placing a bridle on the pony, he mounted, forgetting to untie the rope from around the pony's neck. Holding the bridle reins in his teeth, he pulled his two cap-and-ball six-shooters and grabbing the pony with his spurs headed toward the din of battle. The frightened animal leaped forward at a dead run and hit the end of the rope length at full speed. The rope held, and the horse was thrown to the ground with terrific force. Gilford Chapman and his two six-shooters traveled on through space some fifteen feet beyond where the horse fell, hitting the ground with enough force to jar him back to his senses. He then got up, untied the rope from around the pony's neck, and joined his comrades in the fight.

After the fight was over, they all realized that no one had seen Mrs. Watson, wife of the man who owned the ranch. It was feared that a stray bullet might have hit her during the fight and someone went to the house to inquire. But their fears were uncalled for. Mrs. Watson had a fire going in the fireplace, and with a ladle and a mold had run a hat full of bullets. Asked why she was going to all this trouble, she said that she had always heard that dry powder and hot lead was a good way to win arguments with Indians.

The Indians got the horses, but not a man of the roundup crew was hurt. Cow work was over as they were all afoot and never expected to see their horses again. However, a neighbor who had also lost his horses trailed the Indians he thought had them, managing to work the horse herd away from the Indian camp during the night. When daylight came, he was far away, and this time the Indians were afoot. Much to the neighbor's surprise the horses were not his, but he recognized the brands of his neighbors and drove the horses back to the Cove after using them to finish his cow work.

It was shortly after the affair at the Watson ranch that my father's own story really began. Many of the things set down in this introduction were told to him by members of the family. To the best of my ability I have checked for accuracy. The War Department Records of Fort McKavett Special Orders and Reports concerning my great-grandfather John M. (Humpy) Jackson's one-man rebellion against the Negro soldiers during Reconstruction in Texas checked out.

Ben W. (Benny) Kemp

Carlsbad, New Mexico
August 15, 1967

xiv

Contents

	Foreword	*vii*
	Introduction	*ix*
1.	Young Cowboy	3
2.	With the Texas Rangers	13
3.	Pete Slaughter's Cow Detective	35
4.	The Outlaw from Tombstone	41
5.	A Bad Man Backs Down	57
6.	The Starkweather Grizzly	64
7.	Geronimo's Last Raid on the Middle Fork	73
8.	The Tenderfoot	78
9.	The V-Cross-T Wagon Boss Hires a Cowhand	91
10.	The Cow Camp at Nine Points	101
11.	Alpine and Its Citizens	111
12.	Northward Ho	118
13.	Ranching on Beaver Creek	134
14.	The Capture of Black Jack Ketchum	165
15.	A Mining Town and Its Citizens	173
16.	Drilling Water Wells	191
17.	The Apache Kid's Last Horse Wrangle	212
18.	Alamosa Country	225
19.	Mesa Redondo	243
20.	The Adams Story	267
21.	The Last Divide	284
	Appendix	290
	Index	295

Illustrations

John M. (Humpy) Jackson   7
Nancy and Jasper Kemp   8
Ben E. Kemp   9
Captain George W. Baylor   16
Dallas Stoudenmire   17
James Gillett   23
Ed Scotten   43
Bill McFarland   59
John Graham   75
Jack Ward   89
The V-Cross-T Chuck Wagon, 1900   93
Black Jack Ketchum   169
Bill Keene, with his wife and adopted son   213
The Apache Kid   223
The Beaver Creek Homestead   247
The Mesa Redondo Ranch   247

Cow Dust and Saddle Leather

1.
Young Cowboy

When Ben Kemp reached the age of fourteen, he left home. His leaving was occasioned by what he considered unjust punishment by his stepfather, Gilford Chapman. Chapman had hired a Dutchman named Joe Rouse to cut some cedar fence posts, and for some reason he requested that the posts be peeled. One day the boy happened to pass by where Rouse was working and was greeted by the Dutchman, who liked him. Only a few words had passed between the two when the stepfather appeared, and on seeing the boy, he flew into a rage. Snatching up several strips of the heavy bark that Rouse had peeled from the cedar posts, he twisted them together, and grabbing Ben by the shirt collar, he began to beat him unmercifully. Rouse, who feared that the boy would be killed, picked up his chopping ax and, raising it above his head to strike, told Chapman that he would kill him if he hit the boy another time. Chapman released his hold on Ben's shirt collar and let him go.

That night the fourteen-year-old boy told his mother that he was going to leave home and that Chapman had better not try to bring him back. His mother was grieved to see him go, but did not insist on his staying, for she knew the ill-feeling that existed between her son and his stepfather, and she was afraid that the boy might kill Chapman.

After leaving home, Ben got a job with a fence-building crew. He was used to hard work and was determined to make good, so he held his job by doing the same amount of work that the men did. All might have gone well had it not been for a bully in camp. This unprincipled man took a dislike to the boy and did everything in his power to make life miserable for him. One morning after breakfast this bully decided to give young Kemp a whipping, not for any particular reason, he said, but just on general principles. The boy had been brought up in a community where self-defense was a necessary acquirement, and he met the man half-way. Since the man was twice his size and weight, he knew that if he took a punch from him, it would be his finish. His only chance was to dodge the blows aimed at him and watch for an opening. He was more agile on his feet than the camp bully and before the fight had lasted five seconds, he landed a blow on the man's chin, but there was not enough power behind it to knock him down. As the fight raged on, the man began to tire, and shortly his breath was coming in gasps. At this stage of the fight, the bully caught his heel in a tree limb that lay at the edge of camp, and the boy hit him at the same time. The man went down and the boy jumped in the middle of him with all his might. This knocked all of the fight out of the would-be bad man and he begged for mercy.

After working with the fence crew, Ben Kemp got a job on a cow ranch. It wasn't long before the owner of the ranch realized that the boy was a good ranch hand and bronc-buster. Ben had learned to ride when he was only nine years old. His stepfather owned a few head of stock horses and each year broke several geldings to ride. Many of these horses were two-year-olds, and the average man was a little heavy for them. Chapman wanted to break the horses to the saddle as young as possible, so he hit upon a plan of using the nine-year-old boy.

His method was to rope a gelding and pull it up to the snubbing post in the center of the cow corral. He then threw a rope over its withers and tied a large loop around its neck with a knot that would not slip. Then a loop was passed from the remaining rope back through the collar, so that one hind foot was caught and quickly jerked off the ground by pulling on the free end of the rope. A hackamore was now placed on the pony, and a blindfold was fash-ioned from a bandanna handkerchief that was held in place by wrapping the corners under the side ropes of the headstall on the hackamore. Next a saddle was placed on the pony's back and cinched down. Then a saddle rope was tied in the end of the hack-amore reins and all was ready for the boy to mount. This was not hard to do as a rule, for the horse could not see and had to stand on three feet. When the boy was set in the saddle, he was told that he could either ride the pony or get a thrashing. Chapman then untied the trembling horse from the snubbing post and removed the loose rope collar, letting the horse's foot to the ground. He took a firm grip on the rope that was tied in the end of the hackamore reins and jerked the blindfold from the pony's eyes. The frightened animal's only concern then was to get rid of the boy and saddle on its back. Ben Kemp said in later years that he had to do some tall riding to stay in the saddle, and the worst part of it was when the horse pitched to the end of the rope held by his stepfather. The sudden change in direction caused by jerking the horse around would nearly break his neck.

His early training stood him in good stead, for during the three years that Ben Kemp worked on this cattle ranch, most of his time was taken up in riding broncs. He was considered one of the best riders in Southwest Texas, which was some distinction as this section of the state had many good riders at that time. During the time he was working for this rancher, he corralled a bunch of his horses near the headwaters of the Llano. A black gelding weighing about a thousand pounds took Ben's eye, and he decided that he would break him, on the chance that the owner would let him keep the horse in his mount as long as he worked for him. He roped the horse and threw a dally around a corral post. After getting the horse tied up and blindfolded, he unsaddled the horse he was riding and drove him out of the corral with the range horses. Closing the gate, he cinched his saddle down on the black horse, and arranging his rope so that he could turn the horse loose after mounting, he swung into the saddle and removed the blindfold. In cowboy lingo, the horse went high, wide, and handsome. Bucking straight across the corral, he cleared the top rail by two feet, landing on the outside in open country. He pitched for a quarter of a mile, and when this failed to dislodge the rider, he broke into a run. Not being bridle wise, the animal was steered in a general direction by rapping it alongside the head with the end of the hackamore reins. At sundown Ben rode into Fort Clark just as the flag was being lowered and the cannon fired for retreat. He

5

had covered a distance of sixty miles, and both horse and rider had about reached the end of their endurance.

After quitting the first rancher, Kemp worked at several other ranches, and while traveling from one of these to a ranch at the head of the Nueces River, he had an experience that left an impression on him for the rest of his life. He was on his way to the Meyers ranch, which ran both sheep and cattle. En route he stopped in at one of the Meyers' sheep camps and was surprised to find there one of his boyhood friends and a cousin who was known as Pegleg Jackson. Jackson had been nicknamed Pegleg as the result of an accident. He was a gun crank and was always fooling with firearms; one day he discharged a gun accidentally and shot himself through the foot. Blood poisoning developed from the wound, his leg had to be amputated just below the knee. Jackson was forced to use a peg leg, hence his nickname. He had an unreasonably high temper and had killed a friend at a swimming hole because the boy had playfully thrown mud on him. He had killed another man for practically no reason at all. Ben Kemp did not like what he knew of Jackson's reputation, and finding him at the sheep camp, he decided to ride on to the ranch, but his boyhood chum put up such a plea that he finally agreed to stay overnight. Everything went along fine until supper was over and the dishes washed; then the conversation between Kemp and his chum drifted back to their childhood days and the wrestling matches they had had. The friend said that things had changed since those days and bet him that he could throw him two out of three falls. Ben did not want to wrestle, but his friend kept on bantering until a bet was made and the scuffle started. Ben threw his chum for two falls and won the match. All was in fun and would have gone well if it had not been for Jackson. When Ben won the match, it made him mad. He told Kemp he was no wrestler and that he could throw him himself. Kemp replied that he did not care to wrestle with him, but Jackson accused him of being afraid and dared him to try. This was too much. Ben started toward him, and Jackson quickly grabbed up Kemp's six-shooter from where he had left it at the front of the tent and, wheeling, fired. Ben was close enough

6

John M. (Humpy) Jackson "staged a one-man rebellion against Negro
soldiers during Reconstruction in Texas."

Nancy and Jasper Kemp "eloped when her father decided they were too young to marry."

Ben E. Kemp, "the best all-round cowhand in the Big Bend."

to him that he could shove the barrel of the six-shooter to one side, and the bullet missed him by a hair's breadth, hitting his friend, who stood just back and slightly to one side of him. Ben quickly wrung the six-shooter from Jackson's hand and cocked it to kill him, but before he could pull the trigger, his friend fell at his feet saying, "Pick me up, Ben, pick me up." Kemp reached down to help his friend, and Jackson ran out of the tent into the dark night and made his escape.

Ben Kemp's boyhood friend was taken to the Meyers ranch, where he died. Jackson lost no time in putting out the report that Kemp was responsible for the killing, and Ben was soon arrested and placed in jail. Jackson was also arrested and jailed, but his family came to his rescue and soon had him out on bond. Ben, not knowing many people in this section of the state, prepared to remain in jail until district court sat, which was several months off. He was surprised when Meyers put up his bond and took him out to the ranch, where he put him to work taking care of a flock of sheep, a job at which he excelled but, being a cowboy, never bragged about in later years.

When court sat, Ben was acquitted. Testimony was given that Ben Kemp's friend had told what had actually happened at the sheep camp before he died. Pegleg Jackson had good counsel and managed to escape the punishment he justly deserved, but it was not long before he reached the end of his trail. About three years after he killed Ben Kemp's friend, his camp was found in a dense thicket several miles from any settlement. The camp was intact except for what rats, skunks, and coyotes had packed away. Jackson's skeleton was in camp, too, and there was a bullet hole in the bleached skull, centered between the two eye sockets. No one ever knew for sure who had killed him, but the general public gave credit to the brother of the boy whom Jackson had killed at the swimming hole.

As long as Ben Kemp lived, he never took part in another friendly wrestling match.

Predatory animals were raising havoc with Meyers' sheep, and in an effort to stop them he used large quantities of strychnine, placing it in the carcasses of sheep that had been killed. After several months of intense use of this deadly poison Meyers began to have spasms which his family thought were caused by the poison he was handling. They urged him to quit, but he only laughed at their fears and increased his efforts to kill the predators that were about to destroy his flocks. Within a year Meyers died, and the county lost one of its most respected citizens. Ben Kemp was sorely grieved over his death, for Meyers had been more like a father to him than an employer.

Soon after Meyers' death Ben left the ranch and joined a group of men headed for the Pecos River. Among them were two brothers named Brown, who Ben said were the best rifle shots he ever knew. As they rode along, someone in the group began to talk about the expert rifle shots he had known. Someone else mentioned the Brown brothers, and the first man said he would bet five dollars that neither one of them could shoot a bird out of the air, as he had once seen done. His bet was called, and when the two Brown brothers had killed five buzzards on the wing without missing a shot, everyone, including the man who had made the bet, was convinced that they were the best rifle shots in Texas.

Kemp was working for a cow outfit on the Pecos River when the town of Ben Ficklin washed away. A few miles down the river below town he swam the flooding river to get to a watermelon patch and nearly drowned. A few days later some of the cowboys found in a pile of driftwood a barrel of whiskey that had belonged to one of the saloons in Ben Ficklin, and work had to be stopped for the next two days for all the cowboys to sober up.

After quitting this cow ranch, Ben Kemp returned to Llano County, and a man near Fort Mason hired him to haul some equipment from the town of Uvalde on the Nueces River to his ranch. Returning to Honey Creek, Ben talked his brother Steve into going with him. It was nearly a hundred miles through a sparsely settled country that was subject to Indian raids, but the two brothers gave this little thought. They were glad to be in each other's company once again and were enjoying the scenery and having a delightful time camping out. Reaching Uvalde, the boys loaded

11

the equipment on their wagon and returned to Fort Mason without mishap.

After working for two or three different ranchers near Llano and Fort Mason, Steve returned to Honey Creek Cove, and Ben went back to the Mexican border near Laredo and Eagle Pass, where he worked for two years trying to locate some of the men implicated in the killing of his father, but twelve years had passed since the murder, and he was not successful.

2.
With the Texas Rangers

After his search along the Mexican border Ben Kemp returned to
Honey Creek, and while there he called on one of his boyhood
friends, a young man named Will Roberts. He learned that Will
was planning to make a trip to Lake Valley, New Mexico, to ar-
range bail for his brother John, who had been jailed on a trumped-
up horse-stealing charge. Young Roberts asked Kemp to go with
him, and since Ben was out of work, he readily agreed. He knew that
the trip was fraught with danger and the risk of being killed, for
a band of Apache Indians, led by the renegade chief Geronimo,
was on the warpath and making raids throughout southern Arizona
and New Mexico.

Packing a horse with a light bed and camp equipment, Kemp
and Roberts mounted their saddle horses and left Honey Creek
Cove early in April, 1881. Their route was by way of Fort Mason,
to the San Saba River and up the river to Fort McKavett, across
the divide to the head of Devil's River, and on to Fort Lancaster,
where they crossed the Pecos River at the Horsehead Crossing.
After crossing the Pecos, they continued west to Fort Davis, making several camps before they reached there. After reaching Fort
Davis, they decided to stay over a few days and let their horses
rest up since they were pretty well jaded by this time.

While visiting at Fort Davis, the two young men made the acquaintance of Henry Cox and his family. Cox was a true westerner,
tall and slender, standing six feet, four inches, and weighing 190
pounds. He had sparkling blue eyes, with a twinkle that showed
both honesty and kindness. He and his wife had six children, all
girls. During the summer of 1880 they had moved to Fort Davis
from the Nueces River, near Uvalde, where they had lived since
the early 1860's. Henry Cox was a stockman, and he and his broth-

13

er Erwin had trailed about five hundred head of cattle from the Nueces River to the Davis Mountains in search of a better range.

Several members of his family, including one daughter, a brother, and six cousins, had been killed by Indians during the time that the family had lived in the Nueces country. Cox had taken part in several Indian fights and entertained the two young men with stories of his experiences.

After leaving Fort Davis, Kemp and Roberts had to be very cautious, for any Indians who had drifted off the reservation would likely be found in this part of the country. On reaching Eagle Flats (southwest of what is now Van Horn, Texas), they found ample proof that a band of Apache warriors were on the warpath, for they arrived at a ranch that had been attacked only a short time before and the family living there massacred. The ranch house had been ransacked, and among other articles the Indians had found were several bolts of cloth. They had tied the ends of these bolts to their horses' tails and then raced across the prairie unwinding the bolts as they rode. Strips of cloth were scattered over the valley for a mile. Fresh mounds of earth marked the final resting place of the unlucky family. Someone had visited the ranch after the raid and buried the bodies.

The two young men still had to cross the mountainous country between Eagle Flats and Fort Quitman before reaching the Río Grande, and this could easily prove the most dangerous part of their journey. Only a few months before, on August 9, 1880, Ed Walde, a stagecoach driver, left Fort Quitman with General Byrnes as his only passenger in the rear seat. On reaching Quitman Canyon, which was a very crooked and narrow defile with mountains on each side, Walde kept a close watch. The canyon was partly boxed in, making an ideal place for ambush. About halfway up the canyon Walde, driving around a sharp bend, came face to face with Chief Victorio's advance guard of one hundred warriors. Both Indians and white men were taken by surprise, but Walde quickly went into action. He laid the leather on the two little Spanish mules he was driving and headed them back down the canyon towards Fort Quitman. Before he could get started, the Indians

14

opened fire, and General Byrnes was shot through the chest and killed instantly. He fell forward and partly out of the stage, but Walde had no time to pull him back inside. He was busy trying to guide the two little mules down the crooked road, for if ever a man was driving for his life, Walde was. The Indians came after him in hot pursuit, firing as they came. The mules were badly scared by this hail of lead, but they were too fleet of foot for Indians to gain on them. Luckily, neither Walde nor the mules were hit, and after a race of five miles the Indians gave up the chase and turned back towards the mountains.

Walde reached Fort Quitman with General Byrnes's body, and on examination it was found that he had another wound, a rifle ball having passed through his thigh. Jim Gillett, who examined the stagecoach later, said that it was literally shot to pieces. He said that he noticed where a bullet had glanced along the stage's white canvas top, leaving a blue mark a foot long before it went through; three spokes of the coach wheels were shot in two, and there were fifteen or twenty bullet marks on or through the stage. Walde must have had a charmed life; it was a miracle that he escaped without a scratch.

Kemp and Roberts' route took them through Quitman Canyon, and after seeing the ranch house at Eagle Flats, any thought of daylight travel was abandoned. During the day they selected a good hiding place and picked out high mountain peaks which they used as landmarks to guide them in their night travel. They tied their horses to the end of a stake rope to keep them from straying. The two young men reached Fort Quitman without mishap and felt that most of the danger from Indian attack was over for the time being.

There were a number of Mexican settlements along the Río Grande Valley, and Kemp and Roberts started to travel by day, which was much more to their liking. The first night after leaving Fort Quitman, they camped near Fort Hancock and the second night across the river from St. Augustine, Mexico. About noon the next day they met an elderly white man, who stopped and asked them where they were going. They gave him their names and told

15

Captain George W. Baylor, "in command of A Company, was a man of high moral standards and was respected by his men, but he was known to have a fiery temper."

Dallas Stoudenmire, "one of the brave and daring marshals of the southwest."

Rose Collection, Division of Manuscripts
University of Oklahoma Libraries

him they were headed for Lake Valley, New Mexico. The stranger then told them that he was Captain George W. Baylor, in command of A Company, Frontier Battalion, Texas Rangers, which was stationed at Ysleta, a small settlement up the valley near El Paso. Captain Baylor joined the two young men, and while riding back towards Ysleta with them, he told them that he was in need of dependable men and asked them if they would consider joining his company. They thanked him and explained that they were on their way to help out a friend and had to get to New Mexico as soon as possible. Captain Baylor then asked them to come by camp and stay all night, and this they did.

All the men in the ranger camp were young fellows, the oldest being about twenty-five years old, so Kemp and Roberts had an enjoyable evening visiting with them. Within an hour after they had arrived in camp, the rangers began to beg them to enlist in the company. The subject of enlistment was debated until midnight, but Kemp and Roberts were adamant, still maintaining that enlistment was not possible for them. The next morning when Kemp and Roberts prepared to leave camp, their duffle bags were missing, and they were told no enlistment, no duffle bags. Friendly banter was exchanged until finally a compromise was made: if Kemp would enlist, they would let Roberts go on to Lake Valley. Ben agreed, and thus began his service with one of the most efficient law enforcement groups the world has ever known.

A few days after joining Company A, Ben Kemp was on duty in El Paso when one of the most noted fights in the town's history took place. The fight was between the old and new town marshals. The new marshal, Dallas Stoudenmire, was a Confederate war veteran, who had served under General Joe Johnston during the Civil War. He was a handsome blonde, standing six feet, two inches, and weighing 180 pounds. He was a crack shot and occasionally carried two six-shooters. He was a man with steel nerves, well suited for the tough job that the town presented at that time. He had been appointed marshal about a month earlier when the former marshal, George Campbell, had resigned because the city council would not increase his salary. In an effort to force them into meeting his demands, Campbell selected a bunch of the outlaw element to shoot up the town, which they did at 2:00 A.M. one morning, firing several hundred shots. The scheme backfired, for instead of rehiring him, Mayor Magoffin sent a hurry call to Captain Baylor at Ysleta, asking him to send a detachment of Texas Rangers to help police the town. Captain Baylor sent a detail of six rangers, including Ben Kemp, with Sergeant Gillett in charge, to quell the disturbance.

A few days after the rangers arrived in El Paso, two Mexican boys were murdered at a ranch some ten miles up the river north of town. Gillett and his men investigated the murder and brought the bodies of the unfortunate boys into El Paso, where a coroner's inquest was held. John Hale, manager of the ranch where the double murder was committed, was summoned to appear before the coroner. There were indications that Hale and a former ranger named Len Peterson had committed the murders. The inquest was held in a public place, and a large crowd of curious onlookers collected. Besides the rangers, Marshal Stoudenmire, former Marshal Campbell, and his assistant, Bill Johnson, were present. It was customary in those days to have an interpreter at court trials, since a large element of the population along the Río Grande spoke only Spanish. A man named Krempkau was selected to perform this duty.

The trial dragged on till noon, when the proceedings were adjourned for lunch. The rangers left to prepare their meal, and a few minutes later, Krempkau came out of the room where the hearing was being held. A crowd had collected in front of the building, and Krempkau was accosted by John Hale, who had been offended by the way he had interpreted the evidence. After a few hot words were passed between them, Hale drew his six-shooter and shot Krempkau through the head, killing him instantly. Marshal Stoudenmire, hearing the shot and seeing what had happened, quickly drew his gun and shot at Hale. His draw was too fast for accuracy and he missed, killing Juan Pérez, a Mexican bystander. Like chained lightning he fired a second shot, and Hale fell to the ground mortally wounded. Campbell, the former marshal, prob-

19

ably thought that this was a good time to get rid of Stoudenmire, so he drew his pistol and started walking across the street. Turning suddenly, Stoudenmire shot him down. Thus four men were killed within a few seconds. Ben Kemp said later that about all the rangers could do when they got to the fight was to pick up what was left.

A day or two later Stoudenmire met Johnson, Campbell's former assistant, on the street, and in the fight that followed Johnson was killed. Stoudenmire was exonerated of these killings on the grounds that he had committed them in self-defense and in line of duty. The following week a group of law-minded citizens gave him a cane in appreciation of his good work. There were other citizens in El Paso who were not so pleased with what Stoudenmire had done. They were the so-called sporting, gambling, and prostituting crowd, who were friendly toward Campbell and Johnson, who had granted them special privileges during their terms of duty. This element was determined to get rid of Stoudenmire at all costs and kept plotting against him. On September 18, 1882, he was tricked into entering the swinging doors of the saloon. Doc Manning shot at him, but the marshal shot him through the arm, knocking his six-shooter out of his hand. As Stoudenmire backed through the barroom door into the street, someone hit him in the back of the head, knocking him down. Then while one of his assailants held him, another placed the muzzle of a six-shooter close to his head and pulled the trigger. So ended the life of Dallas Stoudenmire, one of the brave and daring marshals of the southwest.

The Southern Pacific Railroad was building from the west into El Paso in the spring of 1881, and the payroll was sent out from town to the railhead some thirty-five miles to the west. The rangers received a tip that two outlaws, who were being harbored by friends up the river from town, were going to hold up the paymaster and rob him on his next trip out to the railroad camp. Having obtained this information, six rangers, including Ben Kemp, laid an ambush for them at the fork of the road, about six miles up the Río Grande northwest of El Paso. The right-hand fork of the road went to Las Cruces and the left-hand to the Southern Pacific Railroad camp. Four of the rangers took a position behind an embankment, within fifteen yards of the road fork, while Kemp and another ranger by the name of Hughes hid behind some rabbit bushes about fifty yards up the Las Cruces fork. There was a full moon, and the roadway was plainly visible.

About ten o'clock that night the rangers sighted two men on horseback approaching from the west along the road that led to the railroad camp. Although Kemp and Hughes were nearly three times as far from them as the rangers hidden behind the barricade, they could see the two riders plainly in the bright moonlight. When the riders had come within thirty yards of the embankment, the rangers called on them to halt, but instead of obeying the command, they spurred their horses into a dead run. Instantly the four rangers behind the embankment opened fire. Ben Kemp, who was already sitting down on the ground, rested his elbows on his knees and started firing his .44-caliber Winchester at the horse nearest him. Nearly fifty shots were fired by the rangers in the next ten seconds, and although nearly all of them were crack shots, the two men they had tried to stop rode out of sight in a cloud of dust.

Quickly mounting their horses, the rangers started after them in hot pursuit and had only traveled a few hundred yards when they discovered a man and his horse standing in the middle of the road. They quickly surrounded him and ordered him to raise his hands which he promptly did. The rangers then received a surprise, for the man they had captured was the Southern Pacific paymaster. When they asked him why the hell he had run when they had called on him to halt, he said he thought they were robbers trying to hold him up, and when his companion ran, he did, too. The other man was one of the two outlaws they were trying to capture. He had joined the paymaster a few miles up the road, with the intention of riding into El Paso with him. He made his escape, and the paymaster would have, too, but one of the bullets from Kemp's Winchester hit his mount just back of the rear cinch strap, forcing it to halt. The wound was fatal, the animal, a fine racing mare, dying a short time later. The paymaster was sorely grieved over the loss and said afterwards that the next time anyone said "halt," he was

21

going to do so, regardless of who it was, for it seemed to him that a thousand bullets had come within a hair's breadth of hitting him.

The eastbound Overland Stage between Deming and El Paso had been held up and robbed several times, and since the robbers had made their escape, there was reason to believe that the act would be repeated. Deciding to put a stop to these holdups if possible, Captain Baylor detailed two men to guard the stage. The men had instructions to ride the stagecoach to Deming. One of them would stay over, while the other made a round trip to El Paso and back to Deming. Then the one who had stayed in Deming would take the stage.

On one of these runs Ranger Frank DeGarnett, who was riding inside the stagecoach, had told the driver that in case an attempt was made to hold up the stage, not to stop, but to ply the leather on the work teams and make a run for it. The stage had reached a point about twenty-five miles west of El Paso when two masked bandits stepped from the bushes alongside the roadway and ordered the driver to halt. Dodging as far as he could to the side of the seat opposite the outlaws, the stage driver yelled at his team and cracked his whip. Simultaneously with the snap of the whip, the night air was rent by the report of two heavy-caliber revolvers, and a bullet whizzed by, a scant inch above the driver's head. The frightened team sprang into their collars and passed the two hold-up men at a dead run. Ranger DeGarnett, moving like chained lightning, had jerked the stagecoach door open and swung out on the side. Holding the door facing with one hand and his Colt .45 with the other, he opened fire on the two outlaws, who were now concentrating their fire on him. The fight was short but vicious. DeGarnett killed one of the outlaws and wounded the other as the stage flew past them. They in turn riddled the coach with bullets, even shooting a fob off of a gold watch chain that was fastened across DeGarnett's vest. It was a miracle that DeGarnett and the stagecoach driver weren't killed, but neither of them had a scratch. The stage drove on to El Paso, and the next morning a detachment of rangers went out to the scene of the attempted holdup.

James Gillett "crossed the river into Mexico and brought back Elfego Baca."

They buried the outlaw on the spot, picked up the trail of his wounded companion, and soon had him in custody.

The rangers' time around camp was usually taken up by such chores as horse wrangling, standing guard, or taking their turn at mess, which called for everything from gathering campfire wood to baking a cake. They also had their share of policing the campgrounds to keep them clean and orderly. Recreation included horse racing, card playing, and target practice.

The state issued them ammunition occasionally, and being short on cash, the rangers used cartridges instead of money in their poker games. The lucky players would accumulate quite a few cartridges at times. Most of the rifles and six-shooters were of the same caliber, and the few cartridges that were different could usually be traded to the men owning the off-caliber arms.

About ten o'clock on a bright, sunshiny morning in the summer of 1881, most of the rangers were lounging around the patio at Ysleta, where they were camped, when they heard a volley of shots off to the southwest in the direction of the Río Grande. There was a pause, and then what sounded like a regular battle broke loose. A couple of months earlier Sergeant Gillett had crossed the river into Mexico and brought back Elfego Baca, who was accused of the murder of A. M. Conklin, a newspaper publisher from Socorro, New Mexico. This had caused a breach of comity with the Mexican population along the river, and there had been threats of violence against Gillett and the ranger force. Knowing that a couple of men from Company A were in the vicinity of the shots, the rangers in camp were almost sure that they had run into serious trouble. Grabbing their rifles and six-shooters, they left camp at a run. Ben Kemp, who was winner in the card games, had a twenty-five-pound sack nearly half-full of cartridges, and grabbing this up, he joined the other men in a race toward the sound of battle. It was over half a mile from camp to the place where the shots were being fired, and when he reached the scene, he was gasping for breath and staggering like a drunk man from lugging the heavy bag of cartridges.

On questioning the two rangers, who were the only persons

24

found at the scene of disturbance, the other members of the company were disgusted to learn that they were only burning up some of the surplus ammunition they had won by trying to kill a bull snake they had found in a pile of driftwood. Captain Baylor, who encouraged a proper amount of target practice by his company but not the kind that caused such a disturbance, lectured the two men on the proper use of firearms around camp.

In the summer of 1881 an Indian raid was reported near the Quitman Mountains. Captain Baylor, reasoning that these Indians would follow the mountainous country north as far as possible, selected ten men of his command and two Pueblo Indian scouts, and leaving Ysleta, he made a forced march to the south end of the Diablo Mountains, where he established camp and sent out scouts in an effort to cut the Indian trail.

A few days before leaving Ysleta, Sergeant Gillett and Ben Kemp had a misunderstanding over some trifling matter, and although they were still on speaking terms, conversation between them was rather limited. Captain Baylor must have noticed this, for he sent these two men on the longest circle from camp.

Kemp had been nicknamed "Wooley" because of his very light beard, which his companions said looked more like wool or peach fuzz than anything else. After he and Gillett left camp, several miles were covered in silence, broken only by the clip-clop of horses' hoofs and the squeak of saddle leather. Finally Gillett said, "Ah, doggone it, Wooley, there isn't any use in this." And from that time on they were the best of friends, and conversation was plentiful the rest of that day. Late that afternoon they cut the Indian trail and hurried back to camp to inform Captain Baylor.

Breaking camp, Baylor immediately took up the trail, which led through some of the roughest country in that section of the state. C Mess had the misfortune of losing their cooking utensils. Their pack mule lost its balance while trying to pass a ledge of rock on a narrow trail and fell over a cliff into the bottom of a dry wash some twenty feet below, smashing its pack flat.

The Indian trail was followed from daylight till dark, and on the afternoon of the third day it reached the foothills of the Guada-

25

lupe Mountains. By this time the Pueblo scouts were positive that the Apaches were less than five miles away. The trail entered a canyon leading back into the mountain, and when night fell, Captain Baylor ordered his men to keep their horses tied on a stake rope and to be ready to break camp before daylight. By 3:30 A. M. the rangers were in the saddle and headed up the canyon, and when daylight came, they discovered the Indians, about twelve in number, camped at the foot of a rough, rocky ridge that led back to the main mountain. From all indications the Apaches did not suspect that they were being followed for they had failed to put out a guard. Baylor and his men were practically in their camp before they realized what had happened. Although taken completely by surprise, the Indians disappeared as if by magic among the rocks on the mountainside and opened fire on the rangers. The rangers quickly dismounted and sought shelter behind the large rocks at the foot of the ridge. It was now every man for himself as they started their advance up the mountainside. The rangers had to think quickly and act quickly as they darted from rock to rock, firing at their enemy and keeping concealed at the same time.

During this advance, one of the rangers jumped around a rock to find himself face to face with two Indians. Without taking time to raise his rifle, he fired from the hip, striking one of them between the eyes. Quickly he levered a second shell into the chamber of his rifle, but before he could fire again, Captain Baylor, who was following him closely, parried the muzzle of the rifle upward by striking it with his own, and said, "Don't kill them. Can't you see they are squaws?"

"No sir," the ranger answered. "They all look alike to me."

It was learned later that the women had taken shelter behind the rock to administer to their wounds. The older of the two, the one who was killed, had a broken arm, and the younger was shot through the palm of the hand. Realizing that Captain Baylor had saved her life, the young woman followed him closely as the advance up the mountainside continued, keeping only a step behind him as he darted from rock to rock.

When the din of battle ceased and the rangers regrouped, Captain Baylor was missing, and it was feared that he might have been seriously injured or killed. He had last been seen chasing an Apache up the mountainside, firing at him as he dodged from rock to rock. The young Indian woman was following in the Captain's tracks, and the rangers were concerned over the possibility that she might have hit him with a rock or stabbed him in the back. Some of the men were in favor of going back up the mountainside to search for him, but others advised waiting for a while. When half an hour had passed, the Captain and the woman returned unharmed. The Captain was carrying a small rock that was spattered with blood, and when someone asked him if he had killed his Indian, he showed them the rock and said, "No, but, by granny, I got some of his dinner." It was evident that he had shot the Apache buck through the stomach, and no one doubted that it would be a fatal wound.

Three bucks were killed and three others badly wounded, as was indicated by the amount of blood along the trail of their escape up the ridge toward the main mountain. All of the camp equipment and all of the horses belonging to the Indians were captured. None of the rangers were wounded during the fight, which didn't seem possible, since the Indians, after reaching the rocks on the mountainside, had a slight advantage.

The rangers were discussing the fight when Captain Baylor returned and were amused over the problem the woman would present, since she followed him so closely he found her almost under foot every time he turned around. She seemed to have a terrible fear of all his men and apparently thought that her life depended on staying within arm's length of him at all times.

The rangers pitched camp near the battleground. They were jubilant over their victory but tired and hungry, having been forced to march for three days on scant rations. Plenty of game had been sighted while they were trailing the Indians, but no one had been allowed to fire a rifle. The report of firearms could be heard for several miles on a still day, and Baylor did not want the Apaches to know that they were being followed. On the afternoon following the fight, Baylor gave his men permission to hunt, and rangers

27

fanned out in every direction from camp. Soon they had killed two deer and a bear, and that night they had a feast.

Next morning they broke camp and started back to Ysleta. On the second day of their return trip they topped out on a rocky ridge and saw a bunch of antelope. One of the rangers quickly dismounted and shot one, killing it. Meanwhile a large rattlesnake bit one of the best saddle horses, and since he was warm from the brisk rate of travel, it was very likely he would soon die unless something could be done to stop the deadly venom from spreading through his body. One of the rangers ran to the antelope that had just been killed, and ripping it open with his pocket knife, he removed the liver. Taking a bandanna handkerchief, he bound the warm liver around the horse's leg where the poisonous fangs had penetrated. Since they had a fresh supply of meat, the rangers decided to wait until the next morning to see if the snake-bitten horse would survive. Everyone expected to find the horse dead the next morning, but outside of being a little sluggish, he seemed to be all right, so the march was resumed.

Everyone was in good humor and a jovial mood, and as Captain Baylor rode along at the head of his command with the Indian woman's pony only a pace behind, one of his men said, "Man, that squaw sure hangs on to the Captain's coat tail, don't she?"

"Hell," said another. "That's the Captain's shadow."

"That might be his shadow," said a third, "but I'll bet you it disappears when we reach Ysleta."

Captain Baylor was a man of high moral standards and was respected by his men, but he was known to have a fiery temper, and the woman was not a joking matter to him. So the conversation was carried on in an undertone, because no one wished to raise his ire. The woman never reached Ysleta, however, for Captain Baylor turned her over to the commanding officer of a troop of cavalry that was stationed at Fort Hancock. A year or so later she married a Mexican who owned a small farm on the Río Grande, where she brought up a large family. If she ever returned to the Indian reservation to visit any of her people, no one ever knew about it.

This was the last fight that Texas Rangers had with Indians. It was fought in the summer of 1881 and involved ten Texas Rangers and twelve Apache Indians. It was not the same fight that Captain Gillett describes in his book, *Six Years with the Texas Rangers* (Austin, 1921), which was fought on January 29, 1881. In the fight that Gillett describes, there were men from two ranger companies and about nineteen or twenty Indians. Although Gillett says there were no more redskins in Texas, he mentions that Captain Baylor's company made several scouts during the summer of 1881 and that these were reported to the adjutant general as scouts after Indians. In actual fact, two of these scouts picked up Indian trails, one of them ending with the fight in the Guadalupe Mountains during the summer of 1881.

It is evident that Gillett kept a kind of diary, for in a letter to Ben Kemp in 1927 he mentioned that he had lost his notes on this fight and therefore had failed to mention it in his book. Through proof that he had taken part in a fight with Indians during the summer of 1881, Ben Kemp, as a veteran of the Indian wars, was eligible for pension in later years.

As mentioned by Gillett, there were scouts out to the Sacramento and Guadalupe mountains that failed to find any sign of the redskins, and these scouts did furnish great sport for the rangers, because they were allowed to hunt on their return trips to Ysleta, and there was an abundance of game everywhere.

Company A, having no more Indians to run down, now turned its attention to the murderers, thieves, and renegades who infested the border between Texas and Mexico at that time. El Paso, being a thriving town into which three trunk-line railroads were building, became a beehive of gamblers, crooks, and drifters, who thought that here was their golden opportunity.

In addition to the regular run of thieves and robbers, there were Mexicans living on both sides of the Río Grande who had been members of a mob which had overrun the valley in 1877 and committed several murders during what was called the Salt War. They had no love for the Texas Rangers and no doubt co-operated with renegades on both sides of the river.

It was soon evident that before Captain Baylor could cope with

29

the situation in El Paso, he would have to purge his own company of undesirables. There were men in his company who had made good Indian fighters, but they were not law-abiding citizens, and their sympathies favored certain shady characters, who they claimed were being browbeaten and persecuted by the law. As soon as these men were weeded out, Company A began to make it decidedly uncomfortable for law violators.

A short time after Company A was purged of these undesirables, Captain Baylor and some of his rangers were called into El Paso to investigate a disturbance. They had just arrived in town and dismounted when they heard a mumbling sound coming from the opposite side of the street. Looking in that direction, they saw six men whom Captain Baylor had discharged a few days earlier walking down the sidewalk in single file, mimicking calling bulls by saying, "Bo-o-o-o, I ain't a gonna be a ranger any more. I'm gonna be a citizen, a citizen, a citizen." Everyone was rather amused except Captain Baylor, who said, "By granny, I ought to put every one of them in jail."

Saloons and gambling halls were the usual gathering places for the rougher element, and El Paso seemed to have one of them on nearly every corner. At one such establishment a gathering of such hoodlums felt powerful enough to send word to the rangers at Ysleta that their presence was not needed in El Paso and to stay out.

On hearing this, Captain Baylor called all his men together and told them to be ready to march into El Paso early the next morning. On reaching El Paso, he marched his men into the saloon that had sent the warning, and aligning them along the bar, he ordered a round of drinks, seeing to it that every man filled his glass to the brim. When their glasses were drained, he marched them out into the street and aligned them into a company front facing the saloon.

By this time word had been broadcast, and a large percentage of the renegade element had gathered on the street near the bar. When Captain Baylor decided the crowd had reached its peak, he stepped forward in front of his company and said, "I have received word from a certain element in this town that me and my men are not welcome and to stay out. Now I want it understood that I am here to enforce law and order, and by granny, I'll do it if I have to shoot this place down to a man." The rangers were ready for whatever might happen and the hoodlums knew it. Within a few minutes the crowd began to disperse and soon vanished off the street.

Some of the undesirables that Captain Baylor had discharged lost no time in joining up with a bunch of cow thieves, who worked on both sides of the Río Grande. Knowing that the rangers were not allowed to cross the border, they established their camp at a small cabin just west of the river on the Mexican side.

One day Sergeant Gillett, with a detail of six men, including Ben Kemp, cut the trail of a bunch of stolen cattle and followed it down the east bank of the river to a point opposite the outlaws' holdout, but the cattle thieves had crossed over to the Mexican side before the rangers could overtake them.

Several men could be seen around the one-room adobe cabin preparing their noonday meal. They paid no attention to the rangers, who they thought would not cross the river after them. Their insolent attitude infuriated Sergeant Gillett, and he declared his intention of crossing the river and capturing them. Picking up a small limb that had fallen from a tree, he drew a line on the ground between himself and his men and said, "I am not commanding any of you men to cross the river, but anyone wishing to volunteer can step across the line to my side." All of the rangers quickly stepped across the line.

The rangers now discussed the best way to reach the adobe building. There was a perpendicular bank west of the river that would furnish them protection until they could reach a point within seventy-five yards of the house. A narrow footpath led from the house to the edge of the water on the west side of the river where a small rowboat was moored, so Ben Kemp took off his clothes and swam the river and brought the boat to the Texas side.

The landing on the Texas side could be seen by the outlaws, but the boat passed out of their sight ten feet off the bank. All of the men except one, who was left to guard the horses, were ferried across safely. Kemp put on his clothes, and the rangers advanced

31

up the slope from the river's edge to the foot of the three-foot bank. Peeping over the bank, they could see an open expanse of ground between them and the building. All agreed that their only hope of reaching the house was to cover this space as quickly as possible. When they were ready to make the charge, one of them said, "Here's where somebody gets cut off at the pocket." No one answered him, but he spoke what all were thinking. When all was ready, Gillett said, "Now!" and every man leaped over the bank at a dead run. Gillett was fleet of foot, but Kemp was only a step behind him when they reached the building. They were fifteen steps ahead of the other men. Gillett said, "Take the window, Wooley." Then, running around to the front of the building, he poked his rifle through the open door and yelled, "Hands up," but Kemp already had the only two occupants of the building covered with his rifle.

By this time the other rangers had arrived, and placing the two men found in the cabin under guard, they searched the building and found evidence that six or eight men had occupied the room; the rangers had counted six before crossing the river. There were enough guns and equipment in the building to have fought off an army, and the rangers were at a loss to understand why the outlaws had failed to put up a fight. On questioning the two men they had captured, they learned that while the rangers were crossing the river, the outlaws had argued over what they should do. They had agreed that they could kill all of them before they could cross the open space between the riverbank and the cabin, but most of them were against killing men who had been their buddies in the ranger force less than a month earlier, so they had decided to make their getaway before the rangers could reach the building.

When the two prisoners were asked why they hadn't escaped with the other outlaws, they said the law had nothing against them. They were just visiting the outlaws with the intention of joining them. But after seeing what had happened, they had unanimously decided against such a move, because they said, no man in his right mind would have charged across an open flat seventy yards wide in broad daylight against a bunch of armed outlaws, and they had no hankering to fight crazy men.

The outlaws had mounted their horses before the rangers could reach the cabin and disappeared into the thick brush that covered the river bottom. With no other choice the rangers were forced to cross the river and make their way back to camp.

On one occasion Ben Kemp and two other rangers were making a scout up the Río Grande near Canutillo in search of cow thieves when they ran into three men who were stealing horses from the Mexican ranchers along the rivers. Thirty years later one of the outlaws, a man by the name of Gann, gave the following account of the fight that followed. He said that about mid-afternoon he and his two companions discovered the rangers at a distance of two hundred yards, and thinking they were some of the local Mexican ranchers, they decided to give them a scare. Without dismounting, they jerked their rifles from their saddle scabbards and fired a volley of three shots in the rangers' direction. At the first volley two of the rangers' horses took fright and started rearing and trying to run.

This left Kemp alone for a minute or two, and Gann said he quickly dismounted, holding on to the bridle reins of his frightened saddle pony while bullets from the rifles of the three outlaws were kicking up white puffs of dust all around him. Taking his time, he sat flat on the ground, and resting his elbows on his knees, he began firing. His first shot cut one of Gann's bridle reins within four inches of his hand, and his spirited saddle horse, already frightened by the shooting, cold-jawed and circled out of the fight. One of the other outlaws quickly dropped down Indian fashion on the side of his horse opposite the ranger. He moved just in time, for a bullet passed through the top edge of the cantle of his saddle, and he would have been killed had he been sitting upright.

The third outlaw was having trouble trying to hold his saddle horse and bring his sights to bear on the ranger when a bullet hit the stock of his rifle and knocked it out of his hand. By this time the other two rangers had joined in the fight. Gann said he and his two companions decided that if they tarried there any longer, some-body was sure to get hurt. So they left without ceremony, riding hell for leather into the thick brush that covered the river bottom. The rangers gave chase, but the outlaws were riding the best horses, and within a mile they split up, each one going in a dif-ferent direction. After several hours of circling and trailing, night overtook the rangers and they were forced to abandon their search and return to camp.

3.
Pete Slaughter's Cow Detective

During the late summer of 1881 reports reached the ranger camp at Ysleta that contractors on the Texas and Pacific Railroad, which had just reached Van Horn station, were paying bullwhackers fifty dollars a month. Kemp was not a full-fledged bullwhacker, but he had broken two yoke of oxen when a boy of thirteen. Fifty dollars was nearly double his ranger pay, so he decided to quit the ranger force and try to get a job at Van Horn.

When he notified Captain Baylor of his intention, the Captain tried to talk him out of it, telling him that it would not be long until he could work his way up in the ranger force if he stayed. Besides, he needed him. Kemp was determined, however, and the next morning he saddled his cow pony and headed for the Texas and Pacific Railroad camp.

Arriving there, he started working for a contractor who was hauling water for the track-laying crews west of camp. He was placed in charge of two heavy tank wagons with six yoke of oxen and was told to keep sufficient water hauled to the labor crews at the end of the rail. At first he was a little doubtful that he could handle the job, but he needed money so badly that he had to make good, so he tied into the job with determination, and by the end of the month he was a first-class bullwhacker. Water had to be hauled from the Van Horn wells, and a halfway camp, which became the main camp, was established about ten miles west of the Van Horn station.

One afternoon Kemp arrived in camp to find everyone there in a state of excitement. The men who were riding herd on the horses and cattle that belonged to camp had reported a band of Apache Indians less than a mile away. A barricade of wagons, scrappers, and other equipment was being placed around camp, and all the firearms were being inspected and readied for the attack which everyone believed was only minutes away. All the cattle and horses were driven inside the main enclosure, and the women and children were placed in a second barricade inside the main one. It was quite an elaborate setup, and from all indications the camp expected an attack from a large band of Indians. When an hour had passed and no Indians were sighted, Kemp became skeptical and began to question the men who had reported seeing them. These men said that while they were out guarding the cattle and horses, they had seen about twenty Indians riding toward some water tanks in the mountainous country north of camp, and it was their opinion that these Indians were a detachment of a larger band. After talking with the men, Kemp came to the conclusion that these herders had been too excited to know what they had seen, and against the advice of nearly everyone in camp, he saddled his cow pony and rode out to scout the surrounding country. In a short time he cut the trail of ten sets of pony tracks leading north in the direction the day herders said the Indians were traveling. He followed the trail north to the water tanks, but instead of Indians, he found six prospectors camped there. They said they were on a prospecting trip to the Sacramento Mountains in New Mexico. After visiting a while with the prospectors, Kemp returned to the railroad camp and told the people what he had found and said that in his opinion there was not an Indian within a hundred miles. The excitement died down, but it was nearly noon the next day before work could be resumed on a normal basis.

When the rail reached what is now Eagle Flat station, Ben Kemp quit the bullwhacking job and went back to Llano County, arriving about the first of May, 1882. On arriving home, he found his family ill with influenza and Edith, his baby sister, seriously ill. For many hours during the next week he walked the floor day and night carrying her in his arms. With such devoted care Edith regained her health, but she was a very sick little girl for a while.

In the summer of 1882, Ben was hired by a rancher on the North Concho. He and an older man were placed in a line camp on the outer edge of the range. There was no other ranch within fifty miles of their camp. At this time the range was a vast expanse of rolling mesas and wide valleys seldom crossed by anyone except an occasional cowhand. One day Kemp and his companion made an extra-wide circle from camp and were forced to bed down on their saddle blankets when night overtook them. His companion, who claimed to know the range thoroughly, said they would reach camp before noon the next day, and when two o'clock rolled around and no camp was sighted, Kemp suspected that they had by-passed camp and were lost. He mentioned this to the older man, who said it was not possible, but when night overtook them and camp was not sighted, Kemp knew they were lost.

Next morning both men were suffering so from thirst they were becoming delirious. Kemp knew that if they didn't find water soon, they would perish. He had heard experienced frontiersmen say that a draw would eventually lead to water, so he decided to try to find water this way. The older man tried to stop him, but Kemp had lost all regard for his opinion and continued to ride. About ten o'clock that morning he rode into Kickapoo Springs, more dead than alive. He fell off his pony and crawled into the water, but he still had the presence of mind to realize that if he drank too much it would kill him. So after drinking a little and bathing his face, he dragged his thirst-crazed horse away to keep him from killing himself. Half an hour later he went back to the spring and drank again and let his cow pony take another drink. After this he crawled under the shade of a tree and lay down to rest. He had only been there a short time when the older man rode up. Reaching the spring, he fell into the water and began to drink, and Kemp had to drag him and his horse away from the water to keep them from over-drinking. When they had quenched their thirst, the older man told him that this was Kickapoo Springs and that he now knew where they were and could find the way back to camp. Kemp was still in doubt, but they made it back without further trouble.

When Ben Kemp quit this cow ranch, he started working for the Schreiner brothers near Kerrville. They raised sheep and were building a rock fence enclosure to hold their rams. Since there was not enough rock on the surface to complete the fence, pits had to

37

be dug to uncover more rock. Kemp was working in one of these pits when the two men on top lost their hold on a large rock, which rolled back into the pit and pinned him against the wall. He was seriously injured and remained bedfast for the next three months. When he was again able to ride horseback, he made his way back to Llano, where he stayed the remainder of the winter.

In the spring of 1883, Kemp hired out to Pete Slaughter, who owned a cattle ranch and was having trouble with cattle thieves. Slaughter knew of Kemp's service with the Texas Rangers and wanted him to catch the men who were stealing his cattle. Kemp finally agreed to do this, provided he was given a ranger appointment when he was ready to bring them in. This was agreed to, and for the first and only time in his life he started work as a private cattle detective.

The leaders of the cow-stealing ring were an elderly man and his married son. Since they were considered dangerous and desperate characters, it was decided that Kemp's appointment should be delayed until the last minute so that the outlaws would not learn his identity. By joining them and taking part in their work, Kemp had collected enough incriminating evidence against them by the last of November to secure a conviction. The cow thieves usually camped in tents so they could change location at will. They always stayed in a remote section of Slaughter's range and therefore were hard to locate. But luck was with the rangers. A few days before they were ready to close in on the thieves, Pete Slaughter located their camp at an isolated spring on his range and offered to guide the rangers to it. The rangers were glad to accept his help and followed him out to within a mile of the spring. They hid in a thicket while Slaughter rode on to a low ridge half a mile south of the spring where he could spot the cow thieves if they were still there. When he saw that they were, he headed back toward his ranch so that anyone who might have seen him would think he was going home. After riding a mile or two, he circled back to the rangers and told them that the old man and his boy were in camp. The rangers asked him to stay and help capture the outlaws, but

38

Slaughter said that was their job and he wanted no part of it. By this time it was nearly dark, so the rangers decided to wait until about daylight the next morning before trying to crawl up to the camp. They knew that the old man and his boy would fight to the finish if given half a chance.

The rangers were not sure how they could reach camp without being discovered. The old man owned half a dozen hounds, which the rangers were almost sure would discover them and start barking. To their surprise, however, they managed to crawl within twenty yards of the camp the next morning without a sound from the dogs.

It was nearly daylight by this time, and the rangers were directly in front of the tent. They could have called on the outlaws to surrender, but they decided that the only way they could capture the cow thieves alive was to get the drop on them before they knew anyone was around.

The rangers decided on a plan: one of them would walk to the door of the tent and call the old man's name while the other two kept him covered. When neither one of his companions volunteered to go, Kemp said he would if Ware and the other ranger would fan out on each side of the tent and make as much noise as possible when he awoke the outlaws. This was agreed to, and when the two men had taken their positions, Kemp walked across the camp clearing to the tent. Pushing the tent flap aside with the muzzle of his .44 Winchester, he called the old man's name. The old fellow immediately sat bolt upright in bed, at the same time bringing a heavy buffalo rifle he had placed alongside him to bear on Kemp. When this happened, the two rangers on each side of the tent started making a lot of noise, swearing that they were going to shoot the tent into doll rags if the old man didn't come out at once. Kemp then discovered that there were three men bedded down inside the tent. Besides the old man and his son, there was a young fellow about eighteen years old, who, on hearing the threats of the two rangers outside, jumped to his feet and grabbed his trousers. But before he could take a step, the old man said, "Damn you, if you try to leave this tent, I'll shoot you half in two." The young man froze in his tracks, dropping his trousers back to the ground.

Then the rugged old outlaw began ranting at Kemp. "Why you yellow-livered skunk," he said, "I might have known that you was spying on me all the time. I have a notion to blow you apart."

Kemp, who had his rifle barrel aimed at the old man's chest, calmly replied, "You could kill me all right, but not before I could kill you."

The old man asked Kemp how many there were in his party. When Kemp told him there were ten Texas Rangers surrounding the tent, the old fellow said, "I guess you've got me," and slowly laid his rifle down. Immediately the young man, who had frozen like a statue when the old man threatened to shoot him, flew through the tent door into the chilly morning air without even taking time to retrieve his trousers. When the old man walked out of the tent with his son and could only see three rangers, he asked, "Where are the rest of your men?"

"Oh, I don't need them now," Kemp answered.

"By George," the old man said, "If I had known there were only three of you I could have whipped you all."

But it was too late for talk, for by this time he and his son were wearing handcuffs. The two prisoners were taken to jail and were later tried and convicted. The court sentenced them to three to five years imprisonment in the state penitentiary. There were no charges filed against the young man who was visiting the cow thieves' camp. He must have stayed clear of people such as the old man and his boy, for there is no record of his being associated with law violators again.

4.
The Outlaw from Tombstone

By the middle of February, 1883, Ben Kemp had finished his work for Pete Slaughter, so one morning he roped his two cow ponies out of the remuda. He packed his bedroll on one, saddled the other, and headed for Ysleta. After several days' travel he reached Ysleta and discovered that Company A had moved to the Marsh ranch three miles below El Paso. He rode out to the new location and received a hearty welcome from Captain Baylor. Most of the men he had served with in 1881 had resigned. Sergeant Gillett left the company in December, 1881, to take a job as captain of guards on the Santa Fe Railroad. It was from this service that he was known in later years as Captain Gillett. At the time Ben Kemp returned to Company A, Gillett was employed as marshal of El Paso. While serving in this capacity, he was credited with saving former Marshal Stoudenmire's life. Stoudenmire, who drank too much at times, got into a drunken brawl with a former deputy sheriff by the name of Page and tried to shoot him, but Page was close enough to parry the weapon upward, and the bullet went into the ceiling of the Acme bar, where the row started. Page was about to get the upper hand when Marshal Gillett arrived at the scene with a double-barreled shotgun and arrested both of them.

In the spring of 1884, Kemp and a ranger friend, Ed Scotten, were convinced that one of the bars in El Paso, where a collection of riffraff held out, was harboring a fugitive. The man in question had frequented this bar for a month or two, drinking and gambling. Kemp and Scotten had seen him several times, but he disappeared just after the rangers received a poster from the authorities at Tombstone, Arizona, giving his description and calling for his arrest. The two rangers came to the conclusion that someone was keeping him in hiding and were probably carrying meals to him.

Behind and adjacent to the bar was a small one-room adobe building that had only one door and one window. The window, which was in the back of the building, was boarded up, and the door was padlocked from the outside. It appeared to be nothing more than a storeroom, but the two rangers were almost positive that this was where the fugitive was hiding. There were several problems involved in getting him out of the building. The man was reported to be a killer, and unless they managed to take him by surprise, he would probably put up a fight, and they would have to kill him. They didn't want to do that unless they were forced to it. The bar personnel presented another problem. If they discovered what the rangers were trying to do there would be a dozen men to contend with instead of one. With all this in mind, the two rangers decided to try to reach the building without being seen and then watch to see if meals were being carried to anyone inside.

Leaving the ranger camp before daylight one morning, Kemp and Scotten worked their way to within fifty yards of the suspected hideout and left their saddle horses hitched to a board fence on a side street. From here they walked to the back of the small building and hid.

A few minutes after daylight a man carrying a covered plate came out of the back door of the bar, and on reaching the front of the small building, he pulled a key out of his pocket and unlocked the door. At this moment the rangers stepped around the corner of the building with cocked Winchesters and motioned him to stand aside. The outlaw, hearing the door unlock and thinking that his breakfast had arrived, pulled the door open and found himself looking at the muzzle of a cocked rifle. The man behind it told him that if he made one false move, it would be his last. The rangers, knowing that the men in the bar would stop them if they could, hastily searched their prisoner for weapons, and then Kemp took him to where the saddle horses were hitched.

Ed Scotten, warning the man who had brought the outlaw's breakfast to stay outside and keep quiet, hurriedly stepped through the back door of the saloon and closed it behind him. Covering the men in the bar with his Winchester, he backed to the front door,

Ed Scotten. "Kemp and Scotten were convinced that one of the bars in
El Paso was harboring a fugitive."

Rose Collection, Division of Manuscripts
University of Oklahoma Libraries

which opened onto the main street. He warned them he would kill the first man who made a move or tried to leave the room. The men were so taken by surprise that for a moment no one seemed to realize what was taking place.

On reaching the saddle ponies, Kemp forced his prisoner to mount his horse, and then, taking the reins of Scotten's horse, he swung up behind the outlaw. Guiding his horse with one hand and leading Scotten's horse with the other, he galloped around to the front of the bar. When Scotten saw him turn the corner, he started running to meet him, and before the men in the bar could get outside, the two rangers and their prisoner were headed down the street at a dead run. No shots were fired at them, probably because the men in the bar were afraid that they would kill the prisoner. They also knew that Captain Baylor and the rest of his rangers would be on their necks in no time if they started a gun fight.

A safe distance out of town, Kemp and Scotten halted long enough for their horses to catch their wind, and during this short rest their prisoner tried to bribe them into letting him escape. He offered them three hundred dollars if they would let him run. He said they could shoot over his head so that they could claim later that they had tried to stop him. When neither of the rangers answered him, he raised the ante until it reached fifteen hundred dollars, which he said was all he had. But the rangers were not interested and flatly told him that, as far as they were concerned, no amount of money could buy his freedom and that if he ran, they would kill him surer than hell. This sobered the outlaw, and after a short pause he said. "You fellows have about as much sympathy for a poor guy as that damned Wyatt Earp and his bunch of murderers."

The two rangers, who had not been sure that they had the right man, became convinced he was the man they wanted when he mentioned the Tombstone deputy's name.

On reaching camp, they wired the sheriff at Tombstone. But before he arrived, some of the outlaw's friends in El Paso applied for a writ of habeas corpus, and it was feared that they might obtain it and have the prisoner released. As a safeguard he was removed from the ranger camp and taken to a secluded spot, where two rangers stood guard over him day and night until the sheriff from Tombstone arrived. On his arrival the nature of the charges against the outlaw was revealed. A year earlier he had been hired as a cowhand by a widow who owned a ranch between Benson and Tombstone, Arizona. After he had worked for her several months and gained her confidence, he robbed her of two thousand dollars and disappeared.

A short time after the arrest of the Tombstone outlaw, Kemp and two of his ranger friends were returning to the ranger camp on foot after making a trip to El Paso. It was about eleven o'clock at night and there was no moon, but it was clear, and a star-decked sky gave them enough light to follow the narrow trail that led to camp. It was summertime and weeds waist-high grew along each side of the trail. Kemp was about twenty steps ahead of his two companions when, on reaching a point about a mile from camp, two men raised up from the weeds alongside the trail and fired their rifles at him point blank. They were not more than five feet away, so close, in fact, that the two rangers who were following Kemp could see his body plainly outlined by the light from the powder flashes of the two rifles. They thought he had been killed, because the men who had fired at him were so close that a miss seemed impossible. Realizing that they would be the next targets of the would-be assassins, Kemp's two companions dived for cover. One of them sought protection between two rows of a nearby cornfield, while the other hid behind a small bunch of bushes. By this time four more rifles had joined in, and plenty of lead was flying in their direction. In a few seconds a bullet hit the top of the row where one of the rangers had hidden and knocked a spray of dirt over his body. Figuring he would be killed if he stayed there any longer, he sought shelter farther away. The other ranger abandoned the bush he was hiding behind after a bullet passed through it, cutting off several limbs and barely missing his body.

Because Kemp was walking and it was dark, the two shots fired at him missed, passing just behind him. Knowing that an *acequia* (irrigation ditch) ran parallel and about ten feet to one side of the

45

trail, Kemp jumped for it, pulling and cocking his six-shooter at the same time. The ditch, which was about five feet deep, had no water in it, but soft mud about a foot deep covered the bottom. Misjudging the distance, Kemp tripped and fell into the ditch head first, ramming his six-shooter into the mud and accidentally discharging it. A less sturdy weapon would have burst or jammed, but the .45 Colts could take a lot of rough treatment and still come up shooting. When Kemp regained his feet and raked the mud out of his eyes, he peeped over the top of the ditch and counted the flashes from six rifles. His would-be murderers had quit firing at him when he fell into the ditch and were firing in the direction taken by his two pals. Since he could not see the sights on his six-shooter or skylight any of the men who were hidden in the tall weeds, he pointed his six-shooter by guess and fired at one of the powder flashes of the rifle nearest him. Immediately all six of the enemy began firing at him, knocking a hatful of dirt off of the bank above him into the ditch. Kemp ran a great risk of being killed under this hail of lead, but he continued to return their fire, and at his third shot a yell rent the air, and a voice screamed in Spanish, "My God, I am killed." He then realized that the men who had waylaid him were Mexicans.

The Mexicans now broke and left on a run. Scrambling from the ditch, Kemp started in pursuit, but after he had chased them a hundred yards, they ran into a small adobe building. Realizing he had little chance of dislodging them, he walked out to the Southern Pacific Railroad's right of way and followed the track down to a point opposite the ranger camp. When he reached a point near the adobe wall that enclosed the patio where the ranger company was quartered, he heard voices, and guessing that it was his two ranger pals, he whistled. There was a prompt response. The two men were overjoyed to see him. They thought he had been killed and were in a quandary about what they should do. If they reported the fight to Captain Baylor, he would likely reprimand and discharge them for leaving the fight before they found out what had happened to Kemp. On the other hand, if they returned to where the fight had taken place, they might run into an army of Mexicans and get killed themselves. They were sure there was a large band, judging by the number of shots fired during the short time the fight lasted. After discussing what had happened for a few minutes, Kemp and his two companions entered the patio without disturbing anyone and went to bed.

The next morning six rangers visited the spot where the fight had taken place and, on making inquiry, found that the Mexican who had yelled that he was killed was only shot through the calf of the right leg and during the early morning hours had made his way back to the Mexican side of the Río Grande.

The rangers were riled over the attempted murder and kept a close watch. A few weeks later Kemp, who had been promoted to corporal, was leading a patrol along the Río Grande below El Paso when he ran into some of the men implicated in his attempted murder. The Mexicans jumped into the water and started swimming for the opposite shore. The rangers opened fire and wounded two of them, but they made their escape to the Mexican side and disappeared.

On Monday, September 8, 1884, Captain Baylor received word from Irvin and Company, a mercantile establishment in El Paso, that one of their employees had disappeared and they suspected foul play.

On inquiry Baylor learned the man's name was J. T. Stevens. He had borrowed a saddle horse from a Colonel Marr and left town with a man named Hall, headed for the Munday brothers' ranch, eight miles above El Paso on the Río Grande. The purpose of this trip was to purchase some cattle. Stevens had five hundred dollars in his pocket and was wearing a fancy Mexican hat, a gold watch, and a three-hundred-dollar diamond ring. He was due back in El Paso on the first or second of September, but no one had seen or heard from him since he left.

Captain Baylor took Corporal Kemp and a squad of rangers to the ranch, where they met Munday, who told them that he had ridden from El Paso out to his ranch to see what had happened because Stevens had failed to return. He had found the cattle scattered, the saddle horses gone, and the two men, Hall and Delaney, and a Mexican boy who was staying at the ranch missing.

47

The rangers began a search near the small ranch house and found Stevens' body buried in a shallow grave a short distance away. His hat, his watch, his ring, and his money were missing. While circling for the murderers' trail, the rangers stopped in at Alton station on the Southern Pacific Railroad, and the section boss told them that two Anglos and a Mexican boy had come into the station driving ten thirst-crazed horses. They had watered their horses and eaten breakfast at the station. They had told the section boss they were horse traders from Old Mexico, but the section boss's wife and children described Hall and Delaney exactly. The outlaws had evidently gone towards the Portello and failed to find water, for the rangers found their tracks, which led back to the railroad, on an old wagon road half a mile west of Alton station.

Leaving Alton station, the rangers followed the outlaws' trail to Aden, where the stationmaster and his wife described Delaney exactly. He was wearing Stevens' hat. Hall and the Mexican boy had not dismounted. After Delaney had filled their canteens, they had gone on towards Cambray.

In an effort to head the outlaws off, Baylor left Kemp in charge of the ranger detail at Aden and took the westbound train for Deming. There he met a man named Woods, who told him that a white horse had been on his ranch at Tres Hermanas for a week. Since the horse was branded "O" on the neck, it was Baylor's opinion that it was one of the horses stolen from the Munday brothers. If so, the outlaws had turned off at Cambray and taken a trail through Tres Hermanas Mountain.

On the strength of this information Captain Baylor telegraphed Kemp that he was going on to Tombstone, Arizona, in order to head the outlaws off if they tried to cross the border to Guaymas, Mexico. He told him to come up to Cambray station and try to pick up the trail from there, and if it went towards Tombstone, to follow it, and if not, to wire him.

At Cambray, Kemp picked up the outlaws' trail and followed it towards Deming. Four miles out from Cambray station the rangers found a dead horse that had been one of the horses the outlaws were driving.

On reaching Deming, which was a small town, they were surprised to be met by the town marshal, a man named Tucker, carrying a sawed-off, double-barreled shotgun. Kemp told him they were Texas Rangers, and the abashed marshal told them he was sorry. He was having trouble with Curley Bill's gang of outlaws and had mistaken them for some of his men.

The rangers learned later that Tucker had killed seven of the Curley Bill gang one evening when they had left their hideout in the Chiricahua Mountains and come into town with the express purpose of killing him. Tucker had killed one of the gang a month earlier, and they were bent on revenge. When they reached Deming, the outlaws had gone directly to a bar to wash the dust out of their throats from their long ride. After several drinks they walked out onto the street, and when they could see nothing of the marshal, they decided to coax him out by shooting up the town. They succeeded. Tucker appeared at a street corner and blasted them down in a hail of buckshot.

The trail of Hall, Delaney, and the Mexican boy was lost at Deming. When they heard about the white horse, the rangers made a forced ride to reach the Tres Hermanas ranch. Finding no sign of the outlaws, they rode on to a ranch in northern Chihuahua, Mexico, with the same results. Convinced that the outlaws had not come this way, they turned back to Separ station, west of Deming.

By this time their saddle horses were jaded from the continuous hard riding, so the rangers wired Captain Baylor at Tombstone, informing him that their horses had broken down. He wired back that they should rest until further orders. But before his wire reached them, they received word that the outlaws had been seen at a ranch near the east foot of the Burro Mountains, some twenty-five miles north of Separ.

Without delay the rangers saddled their weary mounts and rode to the ranch. They picked up the tracks of the outlaws' horses there and trailed them to the head of Mangas Creek. On the trail the rangers found Munday's white horse killed, and near an old mining shaft they found the pony the Mexican boy had been riding tied to a tree, where he had evidently been held for three or four days. Since they also found the rigging used by the boy, they suspected that Hall and Delaney had murdered him and thrown his body into the shaft.

The tracks of the outlaws led down Mangas Creek to the Gila River and up the river to the Red Barn, a stage stop on the Silver City–Mogollon route. Their horses gave out a second time, and they were forced to call a halt until they could rest up.

On the second day after their arrival at the Red Barn, Captain Baylor arrived on the stage. He had ridden out the country along the border from Tombstone to Deming before he found which way his rangers had gone. On the day of his arrival word was received that Hall, Delaney, and the Mexican boy had been seen riding north on Duck Creek three days before the rangers arrived at the Red Barn. When Baylor heard this, he said it would be impossible to overtake the outlaws on their broken-down horses, and it was doubtful that they had enough money to pay expenses back to El Paso.

Kemp had left El Paso with three hundred dollars in his pockets, but this had dwindled to a few dollars. He had made an all-out effort to overtake and capture the murdering robbers. To abandon the trail at this point was a bitter pill to take, so he begged Baylor to let him take the best horse in the command and follow the outlaws.

"I am opposed to just one man following these outlaws," said Captain Baylor.

Private Atkison, who was listening to the conversation, said, "Let me go with him, Captain. I'll make him holler calf rope."

Captain Baylor agreed to this, and taking the two best horses, Kemp and Atkison bade their comrades adieu and headed towards the rugged mountainous country to the north.

The trail of the outlaws led up Duck Creek and along the western foothills of the Mogollon Mountains to Big Dry Creek, where Kemp and Atkison stayed overnight at the Siggins ranch. The next day they made a short ride to the WS Ranch on the San Francisco River above the little village of Alma. The cowboys at this ranch told the rangers that the outlaws had only five horses left, including the ones they were riding, all of which were in a badly jaded condition.

From the WS Ranch the trail swung west and crossed the New Mexico–Arizona border into Blue River Valley. On the divide between the San Francisco and Blue rivers the rangers found another horse the outlaws had left. The trail led up the Blue River, and the rangers felt sure they would soon overtake the outlaws. About 11:00 A.M. the morning after leaving the WS Ranch, the two rangers rode around a sharp bend in the Blue River. They saw a man working in a small garden and decided to question him. When the man saw them, he started running toward a small cabin on the east side of the river. Spurring his horse, Kemp ran between the man and the cabin. The man, realizing he could not reach the house, raised his hands above his head and started walking backwards, saying, "Well, I guess you've got me."

"Hell stranger," Kemp said, "all I want of you is a little information."

"I sure thought I was a gonner that time," the man said.

It was learned later there was serious trouble among the ranchers in this section of the territory and several men had been killed. Kemp and Atkison questioned the man, and he told them that the outlaws and their horse wrangler had passed his place about three days earlier. The rangers were close enough to the outlaws that they could easily follow their horse tracks, and it was evident that the outlaws had only four horses, including the ones they were riding. At a ranch several miles up the river from where they had questioned the scared gardener, they found another horse that the outlaws had left. From this ranch the tracks of the outlaws left the Blue River and turned up a canyon on the east side. A few miles up this canyon the tracks led into a smaller side canyon. The rangers noticed, on reaching the mouth of this side canyon, that three sets of horse tracks had entered the canyon, but only two had come back down. Suspecting foul play, the two rangers continued up the side canyon, and before they had reached a point half a mile from its mouth, they found the bodies of the Mexican horse wrangler and his horse. Both of them had a .45-caliber bullet hole centered be-

51

tween the eyes. The rangers did not have anything with which to dig a grave, so they returned to the main canyon where they discussed what they should do. If they returned to the last ranch they had passed on the Blue River, they would be delayed in overtaking the two murdering scoundrels. Since the unfortunate Mexican boy was dead and past anyone's help, they decided to follow after the murderers until they met someone to whom they could tell what had happened and where to find the body.

The two outlaws were trying harder than ever to cover their trail. They had committed another murder and knew there was a possibility the rangers were still following them. They worked their way to the top of the San Francisco Mountain divide and followed it to the head of Legget Canyon, then down Legget Canyon from its head to where it quit the main mountain. Then they left the canyon and swung east towards Milligan Plaza on the San Francisco River. It was evident they became lost after leaving Blue River, because no man in his right mind would have undertaken the route they did with horses that were already jaded. They were trying to cover their trail, but it was only a matter of time before they would have to leave the rough and broken country between the Blue and San Francisco rivers. Their wandering around over this rough divide had only served to cut down their rate of travel. After leaving Legget Canyon, the outlaws rode on to the SU Spring, later owned by Montague Stevens. There they learned that they had dropped off the wrong side of the mountain to reach Luna Valley, and after inquiring about the trail leading from the San Francisco Valley to Luna, they headed in that direction.

To men who were less skilled in following tracks, the trail of the outlaws would have been lost in the rough terrain along the San Francisco mountain divide. But Ben Kemp was one of the best trailers in Southwest Texas and kept steadily on until he and Atkison reached the SU Ranch. After telling the cowboys at the SU where to find the Mexican boy's body, they hurried on, and when they reached a saddle through which the trail passed on the San Francisco Mountain divide between Milligan Plaza and Luna Valley, they stopped to let their horses rest. There was a grove of large, quaking aspen trees near the grassy glade where they stopped, and the rangers inscribed their names on two of the trees. Kemp inscribed "Corporal Ben E. Kemp, Co. A, Frontier Battalion, Texas Rangers, October 3, 1884." After resting an hour, Kemp and Atkison saddled their horses and rode on to Luna Valley, where they stayed overnight at a Mormon rancher's house. There they talked with a man who had seen the outlaws, and he told them the two horses the outlaws were riding had about reached the end of their endurance. It was his opinion that the horses could not travel another ten miles, and he showed the two rangers where the outlaws had crossed Luna Valley.

The rangers took up the trail immediately, and before they had followed it ten miles, they found one of the outlaw's horses in a small valley where they had unsaddled it and left it to die. This slowed down the two outlaws to the speed of a man on foot since their last weary animal could not possibly carry them double. They would have to change about, one of them riding while the other walked.

The outlaws had stayed away from ranches after they had killed the Mexican horse wrangler. They were out of provisions and hungry. For the past five days they had subsisted on a few wild berries and what small game they could kill. The rangers, knowing they would probably stop to purchase food soon, had hopes of running them down within the next few hours. Their trail led up a tributary of the San Francisco River to a saddle northeast of Escudilla Mountain and over a divide onto the southwest drainage of the Little Colorado River in Arizona. Several miles north of the divide the outlaws reached the Magdalena-Springerville road, later Highway 60. They camped for the night at a deserted ranch cabin near the Crosby Spring, six miles east of Springerville, Arizona. Because they had been forced to walk part of the time for the past two days, their hunger had increased, so in desperation they killed a jack rabbit and ate it for supper.

When the rangers reached Crosby Spring, the outlaws were gone, but the blood puddle left where they had dressed the rabbit indicated that it had not been more than twelve hours since the rabbit had been killed. From Crosby Spring, the outlaws turned west toward Springerville, and the rangers were almost sure they would find them in this small Arizona town.

When the rangers reached Springerville, their first thought was for their tired and leg-weary saddle horses. They were directed to Gustave Becker, who ran a feed yard and drove the stagecoach between Springerville and St. Johns, Arizona, at this time. When their horses were cared for, they struck up a conversation with Becker, telling him who they were and describing the two men they were following. Becker told them that the two men had been passengers on his stagecoach to St. Johns the day before. This was discouraging news to the two rangers, for they had hoped to over-take them in Springerville. Though their disappointment was great, it did not upset their appetites. They had been without food for the past two days and were exceedingly hungry. When Becker pointed out a house where they could purchase meals, they immediately started for the place. Before they reached there, Kemp pulled a ten-dollar bill from his pocket and told Atkison it was the last of their money. Atkison stopped short in his tracks and wanted to know what they were going to do.

"Well," said Kemp, "we will sell our saddle horses and take the stage for St. Johns in the morning."

"Whoa!" said Atkison, "them horses don't belong to us. We have no right to sell them."

"Oh, we will make it all right with the boys when we get back to El Paso," said Kemp.

"What will happen when we use the money that we get for the horses?" Atkison asked.

"We are both cowboys by occupation," Kemp replied, "and there are cattle ranches all over the country. We will keep our saddles, and when we run out of money, we will stop and work until we can save up enough to get back to El Paso."

"No sir-e-e," said Atkison, "I'm turning back. You are not going to get me out on a limb like that."

"What about calf rope?" Kemp asked.

"Hell! You are crazy," Atkison yelled. Then they both grinned and walked on to the house, where they ordered their meals.

The next morning they headed for El Paso, three hundred miles to the southwest. They made every penny of their ten dollars count but ran out of money before they reached the ferry landing on the west bank of the Río Grande near El Paso. The ferryman knew them, but he said that he could not take them across gratis and as far as he knew, the only way they could cross the river without paying was to swim their tired horses, which was next to impossible because of the treacherous quicksand. The ferryman kept arguing until he was convinced they were taking him seriously, then he yelled, "All aboard for the eastern shore," telling them he was only rawhiding and was only too glad to ferry them across.

An hour later the two tired rangers rode into their quarters at Marsh ranch, much to the relief of Captain Baylor, who had worried to some extent over the two men, who, according to rules governing Texas Rangers, were working outside their jurisdiction. Sergeant Gillett's venture into Mexico to make an arrest had almost caused an international disturbance. Baylor had been sorely grieved over this incident and was opposed to his men working outside the boundaries of Texas. Only under extreme circumstances would he follow criminals into another state.

Two or three days after returning to camp, Kemp and some of his ranger friends made a trip into El Paso. During their rounds they happened to visit the store owned by Irvin and Company. The owners were wealthy and prominent businessmen in town. When someone mentioned that Kemp and Atkison had failed to capture the outlaws who had murdered J. T. Stevens, they wanted to know why the two rangers had turned back when they were so close on their trail. When they were informed that it was a lack of funds, Irvin said, "We would have wired you money."

"Why didn't you mention this when we started out after them?" Kemp asked. "We would have caught them if you had."

It wasn't long until the two men who murdered Stevens reaped their just reward. They robbed a bank in Colorado, and a posse gave chase, wounding one outlaw's horse. The outlaws met a farmer on his way into town with a wagon and span of horses. They held him up, slashed the traces on one of his work horses and rode him away. All this took time, and the posse overtook and killed them within five miles of the bank they had robbed.

On his return from chasing the two murderers, Ben Kemp had a surprise visitor, a lawyer who had driven all the way from Austin to El Paso in a buckboard to see him. The lawyer was searching for heirs to the estate of Joseph Kemp, a resident of the state of Tennessee, who had died a year earlier. Joseph Kemp knew that some of his relatives lived in Texas and requested that his lawyer locate them before he died. The lawyer had come to Austin after a lengthy search and found Ben Kemp's name in the ranger files. After rechecking the names of Joseph Kemp's relatives, he came to the conclusion that Ben Kemp was the legal heir to the estate. He offered to file suit in Ben Kemp's name, but Kemp told him he did not have the money to hire counsel. The lawyer told him he would not need any, because he would pay all expenses incurred in filing suit for the estate. He was taking the case, he said, with the understanding that he would retain a fee of sixteen thousand dollars, which was 10 per cent of the estimated value of the estate.

For some reason Ben Kemp had a foreboding that there was something wrong with this man's claims. After several days' meditation, he told the lawyer he had no desire to go to Tennessee on a gamble of obtaining an estate from a relative he had never heard of.

The lawyer stayed in El Paso a month, pleading with Kemp to file a claim, but Kemp was adamant and flatly refused. Finally, the lawyer gave up in disgust and left, wondering no doubt what kind of man would turn down a fortune so easy to obtain.

5.
A Bad Man Backs Down

During the winter of 1884 to '85 there seemed to be less work for Captain Baylor and his rangers. Except for a few minor arrests and a patrol of the Río Grande Valley, the company was practically inactive. On April 15, 1885, Company A was disbanded.

Ben Kemp was offered a lieutenant's commission to transfer to Captain McDonald's company, stationed near Del Río, but he had had his fill of ranger work and refused. The adjutant was disappointed and told him he would not accept his resignation, but Kemp quit anyway, riding away from the ranger camp with his papers in his pocket.

Thirty-five years later these treasured papers were still in his possession, but they were lost in 1919, when saddle strings that held a coat containing them came untied and the coat fell to the ground. The papers were lost within a few miles of Kemp's ranch, and he backtracked the entire circle, but neither the coat nor the papers were found.

After quitting the ranger force, Ben Kemp returned to Llano County where he gathered his cattle, the increase from a few head his mother had given him several years before. He intended to move them to the Big Bend, south of Alpine. When his brother Steve heard of his plans, he insisted on going with him and taking the few head of cattle he owned. Between them they had about three hundred head, so they hired a sixteen-year-old boy by the name of George Page to help trail them through. Because Page had grown up in the hill country south of Llano, he had never seen a railroad, so when the herd neared the Southern Pacific rails, he rode three miles just to see the track. That afternoon he insisted they pitch their camp where he could see the train when it came by. No trains ran before they went to bed that night, and since he was tired, Page was soon fast asleep. About 2:00 A.M. a freight train roared by, and Page sat bolt upright in bed, asking, "What's that?"

Ben Kemp, who was sleeping with him, was afraid he would stampede and said, "Lay down, you damn fool," and tried to grab Page, but he was gone in a flash. Fifty yards below camp there was a pool of water, and Page hit it, running full tilt. After he changed into dry clothes and went to bed, he could not find his pillow, and the next morning after daylight they discovered it floating around in the pond, where he had dropped it when he ran into the water.

The trail herd reached a spring near the foot of Nine Points Mountain about the last of May. The two Kemp brothers turned their cattle loose on the open range and paid Page in cattle for helping them trail the herd through.

Because he was short on cash, Ben Kemp decided to ask for work with his old ranger friend, Jim Gillett, who was general manager of the Estado Land and Cattle Company. Gillett decided to quit the police force at El Paso when the company owners had asked him to manage their cattle herd and ranch south of Alpine in April, 1885. Gillett knew that the cattle range was rough country and decided he would need the best cowhands he could find. Before leaving El Paso, he had told Ben Kemp that he would have a job waiting for him whenever he quit the ranger force, so Kemp was hired immediately. Kemp knew most of the men Gillett had hired. Among them were several of his old ranger pals, including Dick Ware, who was in the fight at Round Rock on July 20, 1889, when Sam Bass was killed. As a whole they were a jolly and carefree group, but as sometimes happens, there was a bad man among them. This man, Dick Duncan by name, posed as a gun slinger, fast on the draw and a dead shot. Kemp had been working with the outfit less than a week when Duncan began nagging him. He tried to ignore him, but the situation only grew worse, until one evening at the chuck wagon during supper both of them started to take a helping of beef steak out of the Dutch oven at the same time. With an air of contempt Duncan jerked his fork back and made a slurring remark about a dog sticking its nose in the oven. Kemp was already fed up with Duncan's abuse, and this insult threw him into a rage.

58

Bill McFarland ("Bill Mac"), "a friendly and jovial sort of fellow, liked by all who knew him."

Turning on the man, he called him every abusive name he could think of and dared him to make a move, but Duncan backed down completely, never to cross him again.

After Duncan quit the Estado Land and Cattle Company, he joined a family traveling from the Río Grande near El Paso to Del Río. This family included a man, his wife, and mother-in-law. En route they camped near a pond on the Río Grande, and during the night Duncan murdered the entire family by splitting their heads open with an ax. He was later tried and convicted of this terrible crime and paid for it with his life.

In the early summer of 1885 one of Ben Kemp's ranger friends, a man named Bill McFarland, was hired by the company. A native of Georgia, he was a friendly and jovial sort of fellow, liked by all who knew him. McFarland, or "Bill Mac" as his friends called him, was a few years older than Kemp but had not been old enough to serve in the army during the Civil War. He had been a member of the Ku Klux Klan directly following the Civil War and claimed that during Reconstruction years he and others of his Klan had got rid of several undesirable characters of his community without having to kill them.

Kemp and McFarland quit the Estado Land and Cattle Company about the tenth of August and rode to Alpine. Kemp had told McFarland about his trip from the Red Barn to Springerville, Arizona, a year earlier. Kemp had been intrigued when he heard cowboys discussing the vicious grizzly bears that roamed the mountain ranges near the WS Ranch and had decided then that he would return to hunt some of these bears. McFarland, who was considered an ardent hunter, was not interested in grizzlies as much as he was in smaller game, but when he heard Kemp tell of the abundance of game he had seen on his trip, he wanted to go with him.

Since he could leave his brother Steve and Page in care of the cattle while he was gone, Kemp decided this was the best chance he would have to kill a few grizzlies. After buying a team and wagon, he and McFarland loaded the wagon with supplies and headed for Fort Davis, where they hunted for two or three days in the Davis

Mountains. After they broke camp at Fort Davis, they drove to Toyah, a watering station on the Texas and Pacific Railroad.

Before leaving Alpine, they had ordered two Winchester hunting rifles to be expressed to them at Toyah. Bill Mac ordered a .45–.70 caliber which he said would kill anything he wanted to shoot, but Kemp, after hearing the WS cowboys tell how hard a grizzly was to kill, decided to buy a .50–.110 caliber. When they reached Toyah, they were forced to wait for the rifles which had not arrived.

While waiting for the rifles, they made the acquaintance of a man named Washie Jones. Jones and his family were on their way to California, but when Kemp described the country on the head-waters of the San Francisco River, which was beautiful at the time he passed through there in 1884, and told Jones that he and Mc-Farland were going to Milligan Plaza (now Reserve, New Mexico), Jones decided to go with them. W. J. Jones, his oldest son, was working for the Red River Land and Cattle Company, which had ranches on the headwaters of Gila River about fifty miles east of Milligan Plaza.

Traveling with the Jones family was a young English doctor by the name of Pounds, and he was very much interested in what the WS cowboys had told Ben Kemp about the grizzly bear and other game that roamed through the Mogollon, San Francisco, and other mountain ranges near Milligan Plaza. There were two other families camped at Toyah, and when they heard of Jones's decision, they asked if they could join the party.

With all settled, the small caravan left Toyah on August 15, 1885, and headed northwest towards El Paso. Since Ben Kemp knew most of the country, having traveled over most of it during his service with the Texas Rangers, his wagon took the lead. At first there were some adjustments necessary for traveling in a caravan, but most of them were made within the first few days. One of the men in the party had a problem before they started: whether to bring his hounds or his wife's cookstove. The problem was solved by leaving the cookstove.

The weather was fine, and each night the party enjoyed sitting around the campfire to discuss the day's travel and points to be reached the next day. Because water was scarce on this stretch of their trip, camps had to be planned so that there would be no undue suffering from thirst. Water barrels helped solve this problem, but if there were two dry camps between waterings, the work teams suffered. No trouble was encountered, however, until they reached the Río Grande.

One morning at a camp on the Río Grande, about halfway between El Paso and Las Cruces, two of their work horses were missing. Kemp and McFarland circled the camp and cut the trail of three horses. When they discovered that two sets of tracks belonged to their work team, they knew the horses had been stolen. After following the three sets of tracks for a few miles, they found their work team tied to a tree. They hid and watched the two horses for an hour, but no one came to get them. They knew that if they didn't return to camp within a reasonable length of time, someone would come to look for them, so Kemp left Bill McFarland to watch the horses while he returned to the wagons. He told Jones what had happened and that he and Bill Mac were going to watch the horses until someone came to get them, and then they would either capture or kill whoever it was. Jones maintained that some of the Mexicans living along the river had probably stolen the horses and if they killed them, they would have a fight on their hands. Kemp argued that a horse thief should be killed regardless of who he was, but Jones said they didn't have time to stop and fight a war. The younger man finally agreed and reluctantly brought Bill Mac and the horses back to camp, but he was so mad at Jones for not letting him settle with the horse thieves that he barely spoke to him for the next four days. The caravan was not troubled with horse thieves again, but the treacherous Río Grande had to be forded. They accomplished this with less trouble than they had anticipated, and the caravan continued towards Deming, New Mexico.

The man who owned the hounds was having trouble. Continuous travel made his dogs' feet so sore they could barely walk. He had anticipated this problem before leaving Toyah and had bought a large bull hide from a rancher. He stretched this under the running gear of his wagon. The dogs soon learned to ride on the bull hide when their feet were too tender to walk. The man was a fine rifle shot and kept his hounds supplied with fresh meat by killing rabbits, running or not. Killing a running rabbit at fifty yards with the slow-velocity rifle of those days was a feat anyone could have been proud of.

For days the four wagons rolled across open plains with nothing in sight but rabbits, weeds, and sagebrush. There were no convenient rest stations as there are now, and at times this presented a problem for the two young men whose wagon led the caravan. However, all of the wagons were equipped with bows and sheets, and among the equipment in Kemp's wagon was a large cowbell. He said afterwards that he often wondered if the people in the other wagons wondered why he or McFarland rang the bell now and then during the day's travel.

When the caravan reached Silver City, two wagons camped, but Kemp, McFarland, and the Jones family went on to Milligan Plaza, arriving there on September 8, 1885.

Washie Jones was pleased with the new location and decided to make his home there, but Kemp, McFarland, and the English doctor had their minds set on hunting. So loading their wagon with equipment and a fresh lot of supplies, they drove to the west end of the Plains of San Agustín and established camp about three miles northwest of a ranch owned by a man named James A. Patterson. Nearby they found plenty of fresh water, the result of recent rains, and plenty of good grama grass for their work team and saddle horses.

6.
The Starkweather Grizzly

One morning a few days after pitching camp, Ben Kemp and Bill Mac decided to ride over to the Wagon Tongue Mountains to hunt for bear. The mountain range was southwest of camp, and they decided that the easiest way to reach it was to ride back to the top of the Continental Divide, which was west of camp, and then down the divide to the main mountain. As they followed the Socorro–San Francisco Plaza road down the western slope of the divide towards a little Mexican settlement called Aragon, they saw a covered wagon drawn by four horses approaching them from the west. This was nothing out of the ordinary since they were on the main road to Socorro, which was the nearest railhead and trading center for all the people throughout this section of the country. As they approached the wagon, however, the two young men realized that something was wrong. A woman was driving the team, and she was weeping bitterly. When they reached the wagon, Ben Kemp raised his hand, and the woman stopped the team. He asked her what was wrong assuring her they would help if they could. The woman, whose name was Bradberry, said that her husband, who was in the wagon, was seriously ill and she was trying to reach Socorro and find a doctor before he died. McFarland and Kemp told her that there was a good doctor in their camp, and reining their horses around, they struck a trot back down the road with the woman following them. When they reached camp, Dr. Pounds examined Bradberry and said that he had a bad case of cholera morbus. He administered medicine, and within a short time Bradberry was much better. The Bradberrys stayed in camp until the husband was fully recovered, and during this time they explained how they happened to be in this part of the country.

They had moved from Texas to Georgetown, New Mexico,

64

during its boom days. Work was plentiful, and they had lived there several years. After a time the rich silver deposits began to play out, and they were forced to move to another location. They came up the Río San Francisco, thinking that there might be a suitable locality where they could file a homestead. Finding nothing that suited them, they had continued to Milligan Plaza, where Bradberry had become ill.

They felt quite indebted to Kemp and his party, for it was doubtful that Mrs. Bradberry could have reached Socorro with Mr. Bradberry alive. Dr. Pounds would accept no pay for his service, but the Bradberrys were determined that they were going to leave something in token of their appreciation. They owned a map showing the location of the lost Bowie, or Mission San Saba, mine in Texas, and they insisted that Ben Kemp take it. They explained that while they were living at Georgetown, they had befriended an ancient Mexican miner. This old man was more than a hundred years old, and no one would hire him. He was on the point of starvation, and the Bradberrys, feeling sorry for him, had taken him into their home as a kind of chore boy. He had lived with them until he died, and on his deathbed he had called for pencil and paper. When they gave it to him, he drew them a map showing the location of the mine in relation to the old Mission San Saba and the San Saba River. He explained that he had worked there as a water boy, carrying water to the miners in 1792. He told them that this was, in his estimation, the richest silver mine in the world. The last white man to see the mine was James Bowie in 1836. The mine is known throughout West Texas as the lost Bowie mine. Ben Kemp was well acquainted with the San Saba country and many times had ridden over the ground where the mine was supposed to have been located. His grandfather lived on the San Saba River not more than five miles from the mine. His sister Mary, who married a man by the name of William Bradford, lived within three miles of the mine's supposed location. He tried to talk the Bradberry's into keeping the map, but they wouldn't listen. They told Kemp that they would probably never go back to Texas, whereas he would, and if he didn't locate the mine, it would probably never be found.

65

Finally, to please them he accepted the map, and the Bradberry's went on their way to eastern New Mexico.

The English doctor was having the time of his life hunting antelope. He loved to watch them playing on the prairie near camp. On one occasion he threw an antelope hide and horns over his back and shoulders and crawled out to where about twenty-five were grazing. He was having lots of fun watching the antelope caper around him, but a range cow saw him and gave chase. He lost his antelope hide and barely saved his own by outrunning the cow to camp.

After a month of hunting the trio had their fill. There were thousands of antelope on the Plains of San Agustín at this time, and another group of hunters, headed by two brothers, were killing them by the hundreds, hauling them to Socorro, and shipping them by rail to St. Louis, Missouri.

After leaving their camp near the Patterson ranch, Kemp, McFarland, and Pounds moved down the north fork of Negrito Creek, about a mile above where it joins the south fork. They found a nice spring of sparkling water and plenty of grass for their horses. At this time there were large numbers of deer and turkey in this section, and there was seldom a morning when deer couldn't be seen from their camp.

During the time that they were camped on the Negrito, Ben Kemp made a trip to Milligan Plaza. He always stayed with Washie Jones on such visits, and on this trip Washie told him about a grizzly bear that had scared the man who brought the mail from Luna Valley to the San Francisco Plaza. The mail carrier said the bear, an extra-large grizzly, had stopped him on several occasions by standing in the trail on the divide between Luna Valley and the head of Starkweather Canyon and refusing to let him pass. He said that when the bear stood up on its hind legs, it was taller than a man on a horse. He did not shoot the bear, fearing he would only wound it.

This was the bear that Kemp was looking for. His only experience had been with the Texas black bear, and he couldn't visualize a bear such as the mail carrier described. The next day he saddled his horse and rode to the divide between Luna Valley and the head of Starkweather Canyon, timing his ride so that he would arrive in the middle of the afternoon. He tied his horse to a tree to keep him from straying and started out on foot. There had been a good mast and he could see plenty of signs where the bears had been. About an hour before sundown he spotted not one but two bears. They were on a ridge too far away for an accurate shot, so he started working his way toward them. The bears were traveling from tree to tree, lapping acorns, and paid little attention to Kemp. When he got within range for a long-distance shot, he decided to take a chance.

The large grizzly was standing on his hind legs lapping acorns from the upper branches of a small tree. Kemp placing his rifle against the side of a pine tree to steady it, took careful aim, and pulled the trigger. The distance was greater than he had thought, and the heavy 50-caliber bullet hit the grizzly through the stomach. Instantly the large bear tore the small tree to pieces and gave a bellow of rage and pain that fairly shook the air. The smaller bear, frightened by the shot, now started running towards Kemp. Between Kemp and the bears was a small swale of comparatively level ground where there were several large pine logs. When the smaller bear had reached a point about fifty yards away, Kemp yelled, "Hey there, where are you going?"

The bear stopped short in its tracks and raised its head to look. Figuring that the bear was close enough to shoot through the head, Kemp took quick aim and fired. At the crack of the rifle the bear, which was standing just beyond a falling tree, dropped out of sight behind the log. By this time, the big bear had started galloping off in the opposite direction, and levering another shell into his rifle, Kemp started running after him. Reaching the log where the smaller bear had fallen, he jumped over the log and bear and kept on running. He had run about a hundred yards when he heard a noise behind him, and looking back, he saw the smaller bear following him only a few feet away. Not having time to shoot, he quickly swung around a pine tree, and luckily, the bear galloped by. He had only creased the bear; the heavy rifle ball had merely stunned it. Both bears were now traveling in the same direction, and he followed after them.

By sundown the bears had reached the breaks of Legget Canyon. They had gone into a brush thicket and were making quite a bit of noise, grunting, snuffing, growling, and breaking twigs. Having seen what had happened to the oak tree, Kemp decided that it wouldn't be wise to get too close to such bears, so he started to return to his horse.

He was just topping out on the north side of the canyon when he saw the large bear just ahead of him. The bear was pretty sick and did not pay him much attention. Before it had traveled fifty yards up the mountainside, it crawled under the branches of a juniper tree. By this time is was almost dark, and Kemp couldn't see the sights on his rifle. Thinking that he might get close enough to kill the bear with one shot, he worked his way up the side of the mountain within fifteen feet of the bear, which lay hugged up around the juniper tree. He picked out a large rock a few yards away to climb upon for an escape, and trained the rifle on the grizzly as well as he could, then pulled the trigger. The heavy report of the .50–110-caliber rifle was followed by a bellow of pain and rage that shook the ground. When Kemp looked for the rock he had intended to run up on, he could see nothing but a white puff of gunpowder smoke that hung in the still air. When the smoke cleared away, he saw that the bear was between him and the rock and coming after him. In an effort to dodge the bear he jumped back, caught the heel of his boot on a rock, and fell backward down the mountainside. In one lunge, the grizzly was on him, bawling and trying to bite him through the head at the same time. He would have been killed if the bear had not been so badly wounded. The heavy rifle bullet had passed lengthwise through the animal's body and broke its right front leg. It could neither hug nor slap while standing on three feet.

Kemp was young, active, and badly scared. In less time than it takes to tell about it, he had flounced from under the huge grizzly and was running at top speed around the side of the mountain. He had run about fifty yards when he ran into a slide of

68

small loose rock and fell down. At first he thought that the bear had caught him, but the bear was fifty yards behind, still trying to catch him. When he regained his feet, Kemp made record time racing to a dead oak tree that he could see a few yards farther on and scrambled up into its branches like a squirrel. He had barely climbed to safety when the grizzly reached the foot of the tree and started circling the base, looking up at him and growling viciously. Somehow Kemp had managed to hold on to his rifle and had carried it with him when he climbed the tree. He now readied it for another shot at the bear, but a dense growth of oak bushes around the foot of the tree kept him from seeing the bear well enough to get a shot at him.

On the upper hillside about fifteen yards from the tree was a small open spot, and in a short time the grizzly entered this opening and stood looking up at him. Since Kemp could not see the sights on his rifle, he pointed it by guess and fired. When the echoes of the discharge had faded out in the canyons and the white puff of powder smoke had cleared away, there was still a black spot in the small opening, indicating that Mr. Grizzly was still there. After sitting in the tree and watching the grizzly, which never moved or uttered a sound for the next half-hour, Kemp decided that he would either have to come down from the tree or freeze. He was in his shirt sleeves and had lost his hat when the bear ran over him. The nights were pretty cool at this altitude, which was around eight thousand feet, and he was chilled through. Although he thought that the grizzly was dead, he wasn't sure, so he stayed up in the tree as long as he could. As he sat watching the huge bear, he decided on a plan that might be his last. He would slowly climb down the tree, watching the bear closely. If nothing happened, he would cock his rifle and creep up to the bear and poke him with the muzzle. If the bear moved, he would pull the trigger and run. Following his plan, he climbed down the tree and quickly eased his way up to the huge grizzly. When he poked him with the muzzle of the rifle, nothing happened, and he knew the bear was dead.

His next concern was to build a fire and warm his chilled body.

When his teeth had stopped chattering from the cold and he was comfortably warm again, he examined the bear and found that his last shot had hit the huge animal between the eyes, killing it instantly. He decided to skin the bear, and putting a keen edge on his pocketknife with a whetstone, he ripped the hide down the back of one of the bear's hind legs.

Suddenly from the mountainside above him, where he had lost his hat, he heard a terrible commotion. Evidently the smaller bear which he had wounded earlier in the day had found his hat and was doing a lot of growling, snuffling and rock-rolling. Kemp was about ready to climb back into the tree when the noise died down and the bear apparently left. By then he decided that he had had about all the grizzly bear he could stand for one day and started back to his horse some three miles away.

Kemp had knocked the heels off his boots while running from the grizzly, and this made travel through the mountainous country awkward. About halfway back to where his horse was tied, he was coming down a rather steep slope covered with pine needles and was having trouble trying to keep his footing with his heelless boots. When he had worked his way to a point about halfway down the mountain, both of his feet suddenly slipped from under him, and he hit the ground on the seat of his trousers. At the same instant something hit him with a whack on his back. His first thought was that the wounded bear had caught him, so he flopped flat on his stomach, cocking his rifle at the same time, but all he could see was the limb of a tree he had just passed, swaying back and forth. He then realized that he had pulled the limb with him as he passed the tree, and when he fell, the released limb had swung back and hit him. He reached his horse about eleven o'clock that night and rode back to Milligan Plaza. He said afterwards that every black tree stump he saw on his way back to town that night appeared to be another grizzly.

On reaching town, he told no one what had happened, and the next morning he rode back to where he had killed the grizzly and removed its hide. Since the English doctor had asked him to save

70

the gall bladder if he killed a bear, Kemp decided to cut the gall bladder off the liver. It was more of a job than he had bargained for. The bear had been dead for several hours before its stomach was opened up, and the odor was distinctly nauseating. Several attempts were made between gagging spells before the gall bladder could be removed. This was the last gall bladder that Kemp ever collected for the doctor. After he had skinned the bear, he placed the hide, which weighed about eighty pounds, on the tree of his saddle. He was riding a horse that stood seventeen hands, and the grizzly's hide, when draped over the saddle horn, touched the ground on each side of the horse.

Kemp attracted quite a bit of attention when he rode into Milligan Plaza, and Washie Jones said, "Well, I see that you have got old bruin." He then started asking questions and kept on until he had the whole story. Then he laughed and said, "And so you ran; that's the way with a boy."

"Yeah, and an old man would have run, too," replied Ben Kemp sarcastically.

After his first experience with grizzlies, Kemp decided that they were dangerous critters to fool with, and he was careful not to take any unnecessary chances with them again.

Someone located a spot that a grizzly was using on the mountain just west of San Francisco Plaza, and a group of men decided to go on a bear hunt. Among them were Ben Kemp, Montague Stevens, Washie Jones, and Milligan. Stevens and Milligan had some young dogs that they wanted to train as bear dogs. Ben Kemp only had one hound, and he was considered a good dog. All told, there were nearly twenty in the pack, for the other men had brought their dogs, too.

Within a very short time after reaching the spot that the grizzly was using, the dogs picked up his trail, and the chase was on. It lasted throughout the day, but the dogs could not tree the bear. Three dogs were killed by the grizzly, and several others seriously injured. By sundown the bear, traveling in a western direction, had reached the breaks of the Blue River in Arizona, and all the

71

dogs had quit the trail except Kemp's. At dark he could still be heard in a deep canyon east of Blue River, but the chase was abandoned, and the hunters returned to Milligan Plaza. Ben Kemp never expected to see his dog again, but after three days he returned, footsore and weary, but otherwise unharmed.

7.
Geronimo's Last Raid on the Middle Fork

Whereas Bill McFarland liked to hunt deer and turkey, Ben Kemp liked to hunt bear. He killed six grizzlies during fall of 1885. Their camp was established near a small log cabin that stood on a bench above the creek bottom. A spring as pure as snow and as clear as a crystal bubbled from the foot of the bench. This spring was on the north fork of Negrito Creek about a mile above where it flows into the south fork. The ridges along the north side of the canyon at this spot are partly open, and there was seldom a morning when turkey and deer could not be seen from camp. It was a hunter's paradise. Kemp and McFarland furnished the ranchers living along the creek and the residents of Milligan Plaza with all the wild game they wanted. They kept the cabin hanging full of dressed turkey, deer, and bear meat, and anyone was welcome to take all he could use.

There were several families living along the creek at this time. The Kiehnes owned a cow ranch about half a mile down the creek from their camp. The Wylies lived on the south fork about a mile and a half away, and Jack Russell lived about a mile below the fork of the creek. Henry Cox lived on what is now known as Cox Canyon, a tributary of the north fork, and his son-in-law, John Collins, lived at what is now known as Collins Park. There were two or three other families living in the neighborhood, and the two young hunters made the acquaintance of all these friendly ranchers. Ben Kemp renewed his acquaintance with the Cox family, which he had met at Fort Davis in the spring of 1881. During the intervening years he had not heard from them and was surprised to find them living in this isolated section of the territory.

They told him that after leaving Fort Davis, they had moved to White Oaks, New Mexico, where they had lived for two years.

73

During this time Henry Cox's daughter, Tibitha, married a cowboy by the name of John Collins. Later the family learned that Collins had been a friend of Billy the Kid. He had warned the Kid against going to Pete Maxwell's house in Fort Sumner on the night of July 14, 1881, when Sheriff Pat Garrett supposedly killed him. Collins claimed that the next day he helped bury the corpse of the man Garrett killed, and it was not Billy the Kid.

In the spring of 1883, Henry Cox and John Collins trailed their cattle and stock horses to the head of the north prong of Negrito Creek. Erwin Cox did not come with them. He moved to Capitan, New Mexico, where he lived several years. After moving to Negrito Creek, Collins was hired as a scout by the United States Army. He put in many days of hard riding through the rugged mountain ranges at the head of the Gila, Blue, and San Francisco rivers. He usually traveled light, carrying his camping equipment in a bag tied to the back of his saddle. The troop of cavalry he rode with dubbed him "Gunnysack Johnny," a nickname that stayed with him until he resigned.

Josephine Cox had grown from a child of eleven years into a robust and pretty girl of sixteen since the first time Ben Kemp had met her. Within a few months they were in love, and when he left for Alpine, she promised to write him regularly.

The southwest corner of the territory of New Mexico was still Indian country in 1885. A few months before Ben Kemp arrived at Milligan Plaza, Geronimo, the renegade Apache chief, and his band made a raid on the Middle Fork of the Gila River and killed three men. The morning after the killing a runner on a sweat-soaked, foam-caked saddle horse galloped into Henry Cox's ranch and told him the Apaches were on the warpath. Cox had heard so many false alarms of Indians on the warpath that he was skeptical, and he said, "I've heard these wild rumors before, and it's my guess there is not an Indian in a hundred miles of here."

"Well, you are mistaken this time," the runner said. "I was down on the Middle Fork yesterday when they killed Baxter, and they would have killed me if I hadn't jumped my saddle horse over a thirty-foot cliff into the river bottom to get away from them."

John Graham (alias John Collins) "claimed he helped bury the corpse of the man Pat Garrett killed and it was not Billy the Kid."

Reining his horse around, he said, "I am going to warn the other neighbors. If you and your family want to get out of here alive, you had better get to rolling." With this final warning he left on a run, disappearing around a bend down the creek in a cloud of dust.

Henry Cox realized that he and his family were in grave danger, and he lost no time preparing to leave. He called his nearest neighbors, and they quickly decided on a course of action. Protection depended on the number of people and the proper location. Their fighting force was small, and the ranch house was certainly no place to fight off an attack. It was in the bottom of a canyon whose sides were covered by large boulders, behind which an enemy could hide and kill anyone spotted at the house. After a short discussion the settlers decided to try to reach the Y Ranch on the west edge of the Plains of San Agustín. This ranch, owned by a large cattle company, kept a number of cowboys hired and was located in an open draw away from the main mountain, about seventeen miles east of the Cox ranch. It would require about six hours of travel through rugged country with boxed canyons to reach it.

Placing their families and supplies in three wagons, the small caravan left Henry Cox's ranch about noon, and when they reached a point about three miles east of the ranch along the north edge of the Valle Bonito, a bunch of stock horses, running full speed, came out of a draw to the north and crossed the road a hundred yards ahead of the wagons. Henry Cox and his friends thought that Indians had been chasing the horses, so they stopped and prepared to fight, but no Indians appeared, and the caravan drove on to the Y Ranch, expecting to be attacked any minute.

By noon the next day sixty people had arrived at the Y Ranch, and it turned from a peaceful cow ranch into an armed camp of hard-riding, hard-shooting frontiersmen. Scouting parties were sent out in all directions, but only once was Geronimo's trail cut—at the mouth of Cottonwood Canyon, about four miles east of the Y Ranch. The Indians, contrary to their usual mode of travel, had crossed the west end of the Plains of San Agustín at night and entered the mouth of Long Canyon. The scouting party followed their trail for some distance, but the wily Apaches made their escape. After staying a month at the Y Ranch, all of the families returned home. Most of them expected to find everything destroyed, but to their surprise all was just as they had left it.

By the first of January, 1886, General Miles had troops stationed at several locations over the Southwest, and it looked as though the ranchers would be reasonably safe, but when Ben Kemp reached Alpine, he received a letter from Josephine stating that a detachment of the Eighth U. S. Cavalry had been ambushed by a band of Apache Indians at the Siggins ranch on Dry Creek and seven of the troop had been killed. The Indians had escaped into the Mogollon Mountains within twenty-five miles of Henry Cox's ranch. This was disconcerting news, but a month later he received a letter stating that Henry Cox was moving his family to Fairview, a small mining town in the east foothills of the Black Range, where they would live for the next few months. This was good news, for they would be safer at this small hamlet.

Geronimo surrendered to General Miles at Skeleton Canyon near Bowie, Arizona, during the early part of September, 1886, and he and his band were sent to Florida. For the first time white men felt reasonably safe while traveling through mountain ranges of the Southwest.

8.

The Tenderfoot

It was about the first of February when Kemp and McFarland returned to Alpine, and since it would be more than two months before the cow work would start, they wondered how they were going to pass the time.

Kemp first tried his hand at quirt-making, then at poker-playing. Although his winnings were not spectacular, he managed to win enough to pay for his board and lodging. A man named Darling, his wife, and three teen-age daughters owned and operated the hotel where he stayed. Since he had met these people a year earlier, they were friends as well as host, and he was treated more as one of the family than as a hotel guest. By the time the cow work started the next spring, Kemp had made the acquaintance of almost everyone around Alpine. When Gillett was ready to start the cow work, at the G–4 Ranch, he moved his chuck wagon to a spot about two miles outside of Alpine. He told all the men he had hired to meet there and have their mounts cut out to them.

The Estado Land and Cattle Company was a syndicate, and one of the owners, a widow who lived in Philadelphia, was the mother of a teen-age son who wanted to become a cowboy. So she placed the boy on a train and sent him to Alpine with a letter of introduction, asking Gillett to give the boy a job at the ranch.

The boy had been in school most of his life and had seen very few cattle before reaching Alpine. He arrived at the chuck wagon one afternoon wearing his city clothes and a hard-boiled derby hat. There was an exchange of glances and grins among the cowboys, but no one paid him much attention until the cook called chuck. Not knowing what else to do, the boy followed the men to the chuck-box, and after he filled his plate with food, he sat flat on the ground like the other men did, removing his derby hat and placing it on the ground beside him.

Dick Ware, who was still working for the company, was the last man to start for the chuck-box, and as he passed by the boy, he jumped to one side and yelled, "What's that?" Jerking his .45 like a flash of lightning, he sent three bullets through the crown of the derby. Gillett, who usually was not in favor of such tomfoolery, said "Aw, doggone it Dick, what did you want to ruin the boy's hat for?"

"Hat?" said Ware. "Is that a hat? I thought it was some kind of snapping turtle, and I was only trying to kill it before it snapped the lad."

Everyone laughed except the boy, who evidently wondered what kind of ruffian he had run into. The next day he went back to town and bought a complete cowboy outfit, from sombrero to boots.

A month or two later Gillett sent a wagon into Alpine to get supplies for the ranch. There were practically no roads in those days, and the supplies had to be hauled over a very steep hill along the route. This hill was only a few miles from camp, and since Gillett feared that the teamster would have trouble descending it. he and four cowboys, including Kemp and the easterner, went out to meet the supply wagon.

It was almost dark by the time the wagon reached the hill, and the teamster unhitched the lead team so that he could handle the wheel horses better while sliding down the mountainside. As a further precaution two cowboys tied their saddle ropes on to the endgate of the wagon and then took a dally around their saddle horns to help the team hold the wagon. When all was ready, the teamster urged his team over the brow of the hill and started down the incline. By the time the wagon had reached a point halfway down the mountainside, the team was sitting down in their breeching and sliding on their haunches, trying to hold the wagon. The two cowboys who had tied their saddle ropes onto the back of the wagon were trying to keep it from running over the team, but their two saddle ponies were being literally dragged down the steep mountainside. When the teamster realized there was no chance of holding the wagon, he threw the lines at the team and jumped for his life. The cowboys, seeing what had happened, released their dallies, and the wagon turned end over end down the mountain side, miraculously passing over the team's backs without seriously injuring them. When Ben Kemp saw that the wagon was gone, on impulse he drew his six-shooter and, giving a war whoop, fired two shots into the air. The young easterner, who was watching him, drew a double-action Smith and Wesson revolver that he had purchased with his cowboy regalia and fired six shots in rapid succession.

The next morning Gillett returned with the teamster and two other men to repair the wagon and gather up the supplies. Several cases of canned goods were scattered down the mountainside for two hundred yards. When he returned to camp Gillett singled out Kemp and said, "Doggone it Woolley, why did you shoot up the wagon? There are several cases of canned goods with bullet holes in them, and a lot of good chuck has been ruined."

"Why, I only fired two shots into the air," Ben Kemp said. "It must have been the easterner; he emptied his sixshooter."

"If that's the case," said Gillett, "I guess it's all right. His mother owns a fourth interest in the outfit."

During the time that Ben Kemp worked for the G–4, a young man by the name of Bill Isacks came to work at the ranch. Isacks was a know-it-all kind of fellow and a big blowhard.

One day in the autumn of 1886, Ben Kemp, Bill Mac, and Isacks were riding the range, branding calves that had been missed during the summer roundups. In their circle they came to what was known as Croton Oil Spring. The water in this spring was as clear as crystal and almost as cold as ice, but it was highly im-pregnated with gypsum, which is a strong cathartic. The three men had started out early, and it was afternoon when they arrived at the spring. They all were thirsty, and Isacks dismounted to get a drink. When he did, Bill Mac said, "Bill, you had better not drink any of that water; it will sure upset your belly."

But Isacks went right ahead, saying, "It won't hurt me. I've got a man's stomach that can stand more than kids' stomachs, like yours and Ben's."

Ben Kemp then tried to warn him, too. "He's right, Bill, that stuff will beat you to the bushes every time." But Isaacks paid him no heed, and, lying down at the edge of the spring, he drank his fill.

The three cowboys then started their return ride to camp, when an hour later they ran onto a bunch of cattle. Among the cattle was a large unbranded calf, and Isacks slipped the horn string that held his saddle rope and built a loop. For all his braggadocio, Isacks was a good roper and rider. He was riding a good horse, and before the calf had run a hundred yards, his loop settled neatly around its neck. When it did, he pulled his horse to a sliding halt and braced himself for the quick jerk that he knew was coming. When the calf hit the end of the rope at a dead run, there was a sudden and violent jerk, and a mile away you could have heard Isacks yelling, "Damn that Croton Oil Spring!" Realizing what had happened, Kemp and MacFarland fell off their horses and rolled on the ground with laughter.

Once on a circle from the ranch Ben Kemp roped a mountain lion, and after stunning it by running on the rope and jerking it around bushes, he dismounted and shot it through the head with his .45 six-shooter. Jim Gillett, who had lived on the frontier most of his life, had never killed a lion, so he wanted to take it into camp to show the other boys. He placed the lion behind the cantle of his saddle and tied it down with the saddle strings. They started for camp, and after a few minutes Ben Kemp happened to notice that the lion was still breathing and said, "Jim, that damn thing ain't dead."

Gillett, who had watched him shoot it, said, "Aw, doggone it, you're just imagining things," and he rode on, but kept looking back at the lion. When they had ridden only a few yards farther, the lion drew in a deep breath and let it go with a wheeze. Gillett flew into action, untying the saddle strings with unbelievable speed. When they were untied, he grabbed his horse with the spurs and the surprised animal jumped from under the lion, letting it fall to the ground. Kemp then dismounted and shot the lion a second time, killing it. He had only stunned it with his first shot. If it had regained consciousness while still tied to Gillett's saddle, there would have been more excitement than anyone could imagine.

Working for the company at this time was a Mexican horse-wrangler by the name of Juan Sanchez, who had the habit of getting drunk whenever he had enough money to buy liquor. Gillett sent Ben Kemp and two other cowboys with Sanchez as interpreter across the Río Grande into Mexico to inquire about cattle belonging to the Estado Land and Cattle Company. The range on the south side of the river was controlled by a wealthy rancher, Don Ignacio, who showed them every courtesy, inviting them into his home and showing them around his farms and other properties, which included two distilleries and a wine press. Sanchez had never seen so much free liquor in his life, and he proceeded to get gloriously drunk.

Don Ignacio was branding calves at the time of their visit and invited them out to the branding corral to watch his *vaqueros*. At that time few Mexican cattle owners used a running iron, and Don Ignacio's *vaqueros* were using a stamp iron, which would make an ugly scar rather than a smooth brand if it was too hot or was held to the skin a little too long. In the course of conversation the G–4 cowboys asked the Don why he had never used a running iron so that his *vaqueros* could brand cattle on the range instead of having to bring them into the home ranch. Don Ignacio was somewhat puzzled about how an animal was branded with such an iron and asked for a demonstration. Kemp always carried a running iron on his saddle, so he got it and placed it in the branding fire. When it reached the proper temperature, he removed it from the fire and ran the Don's brand on a large calf that his *vaqueros* had tied down.

Don Ignacio was fascinated and immediately offered Kemp three times his wages to stay and teach his *vaqueros* the use of the running iron. The Don was determined to hire him if he could and finally offered him a job as general manager on his ranch. But Kemp explained to the Don that he could not speak Spanish, and since he had experienced some trouble with Mexicans while he was a Texas Ranger, he was afraid that he might run into some of his former enemies on the Don's ranch and cause serious trouble. Don Ignacio told him that it would not take long for him to learn Spanish since he would provide special tutors and that every night he would stay at the hacienda where he would be absolutely safe. But Ben Kemp couldn't forget a certain night when he had miraculously escaped from a band of treacherous Mexicans who had waylaid him near El Paso. So he turned down a job that probably would have made him wealthy.

Since the G–4 cowboys had obtained the information they needed about the cattle, they bade the good Don *adios* and forded the Río Grande back to the American side.

Sanchez was drunk by this time and, as usual, had become quarrelsome. He had dropped to the rear where, as he rode along, he would take an occasional shot at cattle or horses that showed up along the roadside. Night overtook the G–4 cowboys before they could reach camp. There was a full moon that made it almost as light as day. They rode along at a jog trot, and the two cowboys with Kemp were riding fifty yards in the lead. Sanchez, who was riding to the rear of the other men, charged a bunch of cattle they had just passed and fired several shots at them as they ran away. The other men paid little attention to him and continued riding at a steady gait. For about thirty minutes after Sanchez had fired his revolver at the cattle, the silence of the still night was broken only by the creak of saddle leather and the steady clip-clop of the horses' hoofs as they trotted up the dusty road. Suddenly Ben Kemp heard Sanchez riding like the wind to overtake them, swearing as he rode and fighting his horse. When he got within a few yards of Kemp, he mentioned that he hated all gringos, and riding up to his side, he shouted, "I want to fight!"

"I don't want to fight," Ben Kemp answered. "If you want to fight, go hunt somebody else."

Sanchez replied, "No, I want to fight you!" He shoved the muzzle of his .44 revolver against Kemp's ribs and pulled the trigger, but fate played in Kemp's favor. Sanchez had missed reloading one of the empty chambers of his revolvers after shooting at the cattle, and the hammer fell on a fired shell. As a result, Kemp was unhurt, except for a bruise on his ribs. Before Sanchez could pull the trigger of his revolver a second time, Kemp jerked his Colt .45 from his leggings pocket and fired. Instinctively, Sanchez leaned forward in an effort to dodge under the muzzle of Kemp's six-shooter, but the heavy .45-caliber bullet hit him in the top of the shoulder, knocking him from his saddle onto the dusty road. The dust kicked up by the frightened horses almost obscured sight of Sanchez for a few seconds. Kemp reigned his horse to where Sanchez lay watching him closely. The other two cowboys, hearing the shot, looked back and saw a riderless horse. Knowing that something serious had happened, they reined their horses around and galloped back. When they reached Kemp, they asked him what had happened, and he told them what Sanchez had done and said that he had killed him. By this time the dust had settled so that they could see Sanchez plainly, and one of the cowboys saw him move. Sanchez still had his revolver in his hand, and the cowboy yelled, "Hell, look out, he ain't dead!"

Kemp, seeing the glint of the moon on the deadly weapon, said, "Well, I'll dead him," and fired a second shot at Sanchez's head. He missed and the bullet passed between the Mexican's head and the ground. Then Sanchez flipped forward and sprawled face down in the dusty road, losing his revolver at the same time. Kemp raised his .45 for a third shot, but one of the cowboys jerked the weapon from his hand and saved Sanchez's life. One of the men retrieved Sanchez's revolver and stuck it inside his own belt. Then they lifted Sanchez back into his saddle.

When they reached camp, Sanchez's wound was examined. The .45 bullet had entered the top of his shoulder and come out in the middle of his back. Since it was almost a hundred miles to the nearest town, there was no chance of obtaining a doctor. Sanchez was in terrible pain, for shock had caused the effect of the liquor he had drunk to wear off. There was no medicine in camp, and the cowboys thought that Sanchez would soon be dead. Knowing that they were going to have to take their chances on him dying, they put him to bed.

The next morning Sanchez was still alive, but his body was so swollen from the gunshot wound that the blue army coat he was wearing had to be cut from his back. As several days passed, Sanchez improved, and the cowboys came to the conclusion that the bullet from Kemp's .45 must have passed along his shoulder blade just under the skin, causing only a flesh wound.

During Sanchez's convalescence both he and Kemp had been deprived of their six-shooters, but the other men in camp must have decided to let the two men settle their dispute for good. At sunup one morning about three weeks after the shooting, while the cowboys were sitting around the campfire, Sanchez on the opposite side of the fire from Kemp, they were both handed their six-shooters at the same time. Kemp immediately cocked his, but Sanchez broke open his Smith and Wesson, throwing all of the cartridges onto the ground. This apparently settled the trouble between them, but Ben Kemp never trusted Sanchez after that. A few years later Sanchez was killed by the town marshal at Shafter while on a fighting drunk.

During one of Jim Gillett's visits to the camp where Ben Kemp was staying, someone discovered a bee cave. The cave was about halfway down the face of a fifty-foot cliff, and the only way that it could be reached was by letting someone down on a rope. They all decided that a little honey would taste good, so Kemp volunteered to go down on the rope and rob the cave. Gillett and two other men were to stay up on top and pull him back up when he finished gathering the honey. They let him down, and he had just started gathering some honey into a pail when he heard a commotion up on top. Gillett yelled, "Come back on top, Wooley. We're pulling you up." Grabbing his pail and swinging clear of the cliff, he was hauled to the top in record time. Then he discovered what the trouble was. The bees had attacked the men that were holding him suspended on the rope, and Gillett's curly hair was black with them. As soon as Kemp was safe on top of the cliff, his helpers broke into a wild stampede. They managed to get rid of the bees, but not before they all became victims of many stings. That evening they had honey for supper, but Gillett didn't enjoy it much because of his painful bee stings.

After supper the men hung their honey pail in a stooping live oak tree at the edge of camp, and that night after everyone had gone to bed, they heard a fox trying to get into the honey. Several of the cowboys got up and started walking around in their bare feet, trying to get a shot at the fox. Among them was a man by the name of Fowler, who was scared to death of vinegarroons. He was sure he would die if one ever bit him. The men had been walking around the tree for only a minute when Fowler gave a yell and grabbed one foot in his hands. He went hopping back towards the tent where he slept, screaming, "Vinegar bug bit! Vinegar bug bit! Vinegar bug bit, my God!" and on reaching the tent, he fell inside onto his camp bed, moaning pitifully. By this time the whole camp was aroused, and when Fowler's foot was examined, there was a white welt where something had bit or stung him. The sweat was running down Fowler's face, and it was evident that he was in pain and scared to death. He looked as though he would die if something wasn't done soon. Someone lighted a lantern and started trailing around where the men had been walking in their bare feet and soon found what had stung Fowler. It was nothing more than a crippled wasp that someone had slapped off of the honey pail earlier in the evening. Fowler's pain was now reduced, and within an hour he was asleep and out-snoring any man in camp.

Imagination can play odd tricks on people as was proven by an elderly man a short time after Fowler was stung by the wasp. This man, with Ben Kemp and another cowboy, made a circle out from the main camp and had to stay out overnight. They were forced to use their saddle blankets for bedding, and since these blankets furnished little more than just a pad to lie on, a campfire had to be kept burning in order to keep warm. The men agreed to take turns tending the fire so that all of them could get a little rest. After Ben Kemp and the older man took their turn, they laid down and went to sleep. About two o'clock in the morning there was an explosion that sounded like the report of a rifle, and the older man immediately began to roll on the ground, crying, "I'm shot, I'm shot." His two companions were startled into action and grabbed their firearms to protect themselves against an unseen enemy. Then there was a second explosion, and to their great relief they discovered that the explosions were caused by heated rocks upon which the fire had been built. The fire had died down, allowing the rocks to cool off. As a result, the rocks had contracted quickly, and small fragments had broken loose, making a popping sound. Evidently one of these fragments had hit the older man between the shoulders, and his two companions told him so. But he was positive that he had been shot, and was not convinced otherwise until they removed his shirt, looked for a bullet wound, and then rubbed a hand over his back to show him that there was no blood.

In 1886 part of the Big Bend country southwest of Alpine was a wild and unsettled section. There was evidence of wild people living there, but no one ever saw them. Many times when the cowboys returned to camp, they would find their tracks, which were especially interesting. The tracks in one set, evidently that of a male, were over eighteen inches long; the other tracks were much smaller, about the size of a number five shoe. Sometimes the two wild people wore moccasins, but usually they were barefoot. The cowboys set all kinds of traps to catch them, but they never so much as got a glimpse of them. Who they were and how they lived is as much a mystery today as it was then. When these wild people visited the cow camps, they never molested anything; a camp could be left for a month at a time, and not one item would be missing. Although their tracks would show that they had visited camp a number of times, they would never enter a tent or touch a thing. The one with the large tracks became known as "Old Big Foot" by everyone in the Big Bend, but who he was, what he looked like, or what became of him, no one ever knew.

Ben Kemp and Bill McFarland worked for the G–4 from the time the spring work started until work stopped that fall. Then Bill Mac quit for the winter, but Kemp worked on, staying at a line camp on a remote part of the company's range. He lived in a dugout in the side of a hill. It was not a fancy habitation but afforded good protection against the cold wind and snow. He had a good corral and lean-to shed. He caught a range cow and broke her to milk, so he had plenty of milk and cream. On mornings when he started a day's ride, he would fill two air-tight quart jars with cream and place them in his saddle pockets. At night when he returned to camp, the cream would be churned and the butter ready to remove from the jars. Kemp stayed in this camp for five months without seeing a soul. He saved his wages, and during the summer of 1887 he formed a partnership with Bill Mac and a man by the name of Tarvin. They bought another bunch of cattle, and Steve Kemp, who thought the range was getting too crowded, moved the cattle to a new location.

Ben Kemp continued to work for the G–4, and that fall Bill Mac and a cowboy by the name of Jack Ward went to work for the company and helped Kemp with a shipment of cattle to Chicago. The company paid their expenses, and they had the time of their lives. When they reached Chicago, they made the rounds—visiting stores, going to shows, and calling on photographers where they had their pictures taken.

Jack Ward was annoyed by people yelling, "Hello, Texas." He had made the mistake of wearing his buckskin suit and Mexican hat; therefore, people he met on the street assumed he was from Texas.

At one of the large, dry-goods stores Ben Kemp noticed what he first thought was a beautiful woman standing at the top of a stairway leading to the second floor. As he neared the top of the stairs, he realized that it was a mannequin, and he walked up to it, lifting the hem of its skirts as he said to Jack Ward, who was following him, "Jack, ain't this a pretty thing?"

Ward had never seen one before, and he almost fell back down the stairway, exclaiming, "Lay that down, you damned fool. Somebody will shoot your head off!" The joke was on Ward, and he bought a round of drinks at the next bar.

During the winter of 1887, while Ben Kemp was working for the G–4, a neighboring rancher named Guage hired two cowboys who were exceedingly homely. These men liked to joke about their homeliness. One of them claimed that after he grew up, an old neighbor told him that everyone had been sure he would have to grow up as a dogie, because when he was born, his mother had taken

88

Jack Ward—"people assumed he was from Texas."

one look at him, then had to be tied to the bedpost for a month before she would claim him. The homely man said that when he heard this, he had become discouraged and had wandered into the heat, hell, and cactus of the Big Bend country in a despondent mood, thinking he was the ugliest man in the world. But lo and behold, when he reached Guage's ranch, he found a man working there who was uglier than he. So he applied for a job immediately, and Guage hired him.

In a short time these two individuals were arguing about who was the ugliest, and one day while they were on day herd they got into a fight. One of them, whose name was Bill, got the other down and was sitting astride him, pommeling him with his fists. Another cowboy on the other side of the herd saw them and rode around to see what was happening. Bill claimed that the cowboy who rode up thought he was killing a snake and had told him, "Be sure and kill him, Bill, that's the meanest-looking damned snake I ever saw." This ended the fight, for Bill said any man that ugly was welcome to be his partner. So they shook hands and were the best of friends from that day on.

When Guage needed a couple of men to stay at a line camp on the outer edge of his range, miles from any other habitation, these two men asked for the job. They lived in a dugout on the side of a hill and proclaimed themselves the ugliest varmits in all West Texas. They were known throughout the Big Bend as Guage's Boogers.

Evidently Booger Ed, one of Texas' noted bronco riders, had a lot in common with Guage's two cowboys. It was said that he had a friend purchase a saddle for him and leave it at a certain store in San Antonio. Several months passed before Booger Ed went after the saddle. The proprietor of the establishment where the saddle was left had never seen him, but when he walked into the store, the merchant threw the saddle upon the counter and said, "Here's your kack." Booger Ed was taken by surprise and asked the merchant how he knew who he was. "Why that was easy," he answered. "Your friend just told me to give the saddle to the ugliest damn man on earth."

9.
The V-Cross-T Wagon Boss Hires a Cowhand

By January, 1888, Kemp and his two partners had their range around the spring at Nine Points heavily stocked, so Kemp decided to go back to Milligan Plaza, get a job on some cow ranch, and look the country over for a better range.

The Red River Land and Cattle Company, or the V + T as the local ranchers knew them, were running two chuck wagons at this time. One, called the Datil wagon, with headquarters six miles up the canyon north of the Datil post office, worked the north half of their range. The Gila wagon, with headquarters at the V + T Ciénaga, worked the south half, which included the headwaters of the Gila River and the south side of the Plains of San Agustín, extending west from the Magdalena Mountains to the San Francisco River.

A man named Charley Woodley was wagon boss for the Gila division. Since the Ciénaga ranch was only thirty-five miles from Henry Cox's home, Ben Kemp rode to the V + T Ciénaga and asked Woodley for work. Woodley was a little particular about whom he hired and wanted to know if Kemp had any experience as a cowboy. Kemp showed him a letter of recommendation, stating that he was one of the best all-around cowhands in Southwest Texas. The letter was signed by the district judge and the county clerk of Brewster County, Texas. Jim Gillett and other friends had advised him to get the letter before he left Alpine. Although he had never intended to use it, he was glad that he had it to show Woodley. Woodley was impressed and hired Kemp immediately, paying him five dollars more per month than any other cowhand on the ranch. This favoritism displeased the other cowboys, and three or four months later Kemp's letter of recommendation was stolen. He suspected that it was stolen by one of the cowboys Woodley had fired, but he had no direct proof.

91

Among the men working at the ranch were Billy Jones, Nat Straw, Sam Martin, Bob Lewis, Johnny Monday, Frank Holliday, and Billy Wilson. Most of them were the ordinary run of cowboys, but a few days after Kemp started work, they had a visitor at the ranch who proved to be an exception. This young fellow, a boy in his late teens, rode into the Ciénaga ranch house late one afternoon on a jaded horse and asked Woodley if he could use another cowhand. Woodley did not need anyone, but, as was customary in those days, the boy was invited to stay at the ranch a few days until he and his horse could rest up.

When the visitor unsaddled his horse, he threw his saddle, a badly used-up old kack, on the top rail of the pole horse corral. No one paid it any attention, but one morning when Ben Kemp went out to the barn to grain the saddle horses, he noticed that the saddle had fallen to the ground. The saddlebags had come open and four large bull hoofs had rolled out of them onto the ground. Kemp examined them and found that they had been removed from the dried carcass of a bull that had died a year earlier. They were trimmed so they could be fitted to a horse's hoofs. Kemp suspected that their visitor had been in some kind of trouble, but it was not until after the boy had left the ranch that he learned the part the bull hoofs had played.

In the spring of 1888, a bank at San Marcial was robbed. A posse picked up the robber's trail and followed it to the east foot of the San Mateo Mountains, where they found a spring where many cattle were watering. At this point the bank robber had evidently nailed the bull hoofs to his horse's feet, for no horse tracks could be found leaving the spring. After he had reached a point far enough away from the spring that he could be reasonably sure the posse would not find his horse's tracks, he must have stopped, removed the bull hoofs, and placed them in his saddle pockets, probably with the thought that he might have occasion to use them again. This boy was an expert quirt-maker, and during the time he stayed at the ranch he made several fine quirts for the other cowboys.

One morning when Woodley was ready to make a circle out from the ranch, some of the cowboys decided to have a little fun, so they

The V-Cross-T Chuck Wagon. *From left to right*: High Pockets, Jerry Kelly, Bill Bodenhammer, Ben Kemp, Benny Kemp, Ab Alexander, Jack Bean, George Foster (wagon boss), and Bill Keene asked the newcomer if he would like to make the circle with them. When the boy said he would, one of the cowhands picked up a rope and roped out the most outlawed horse in the entire remuda for him to ride. This horse was a notorious bucker and had thrown nearly every man who had tried to ride him. The outlaw horse would stand still to be saddled but would break in two as his rider swung into the saddle. When the horse was saddled, he was turned over to the boy, and the cowboys stepped back to watch the fun. When Kemp noticed the boy jerk a hank of hair from the horse's mane and wrap it around his spur rowels, he knew the boy was not the greenhorn they had thought he was. As the boy swung into the saddle, the outlaw horse went high in the air, using every trick he knew to dislodge his rider, but the boy kept his seat without pulling leather, and when the horse finally gave up and quit, he was scratched from neck to rump as though two bobcats had caught him.

As the group of cowboys rode away from the ranch, Woodley asked the boy if he would like a job breaking broncos for the company. When the boy told him he would like to have the job, he was hired. He was an expert rider and enjoyed working with the broncos. When he arrived at the ranch, he told the cowboys his name was Bill, so they nicknamed him Bronco Bill. It was evident that he was a drifter. The people at the bank he robbed must have had a poor description of him, because he stayed at the V + T Ciénaga ranch, less than 150 miles from San Marcial, for seven months without being recognized. When the steers were ready to be trailed into Magdalena that fall, Bronco Bill told Woodley he was ready to quit, and he rode away from the ranch without anyone ever knowing his legal name.

After Bronco Bill left, Kemp took over his string of horses. One day when he was by himself on a circle near the Monica Tanks ranch, west of Magdalena, he was nearly killed by a bronc that stepped in a blind prairie-dog hole and fell on him. When he regained consciousness, he was lying on a bed in a house, and strangers were staring down at him. They told him that a rancher who had found his riderless horse had backtracked to where it had fallen on him. The rancher had gone for help, and he and his friends had carried Kemp to the ranch house. Kemp had been unconscious for four or five hours, but luckily no bones were broken, and within a week he was back in the saddle.

During the summer of 1888 sheep from the northern sheep ranches ventured onto the V + T range near the Ciénaga ranch headquarters. It was all open range, but the company had bought up the patent land that included watering places. One of these waterings was Black Springs, about five miles north of the ranch on Railroad Canyon. To the east of the springs there was a bend in the canyon, which formed a valley nearly a mile wide. Half a mile south of this valley the canyon was boxed in by cliffs nearly a hundred feet high on the east side. The canyon was about two hundred yards wide, with a comparatively level floor.

Woodley saddled his favorite saddle pony one morning and headed for Black Springs. When he reached the upper end of the box below the springs, he saw a large flock of sheep in the valley. He had told sheepherders on several occasions to stay out of the valley and away from the spring. Finding sheep there in defiance of his orders made Woodley furious, and he rode up to the herder and asked him what he was doing there. The sheepherder told him that it was none of his damned business, whereupon Woodley untied the rope from his saddle horn, formed a loop, and then whipped the sheepherder for a quarter-mile. After taking care of the sheepherder, he made a circle towards Coyote Peak, about ten miles to the north, then headed back to the ranch. He never wore a gun on a belt, but carried his .45 in a *morral* swung from the horn of his saddle.

It was almost sundown when he reached the upper end of the box below Black Springs. He had ridden only about a hundred yards into it when the still mountain air reverberated with the report of a heavy buffalo rifle and a bullet whizzed past the brim of his hat. Instinctively, he grabbed his mount with the spurs, and the frightened horse leaped forward in a run. Woodley glanced to his left and could see the white puffs of powder smoke from eight or ten rifles along the east cliff of the canyon. Bullets were kicking up dust all around him, and he knew that if he continued down the canyon, he

95

would be within rifle range of his enemies for more than a quarter-mile. He realized that his only means of escape was to find a break in the west wall of the canyon, which led into a small gorge that entered the main canyon. Woodley reined his horse to the right and headed for the west wall, where he found a crack just wide enough for his horse to pass through. He was now unarmed, because his six-shooter had bounced out of the *morral* during his wild race to safety.

He finally reached the ranch around sundown. When he arrived, he told no one what had happened, and after supper he retired to his quarters. When half an hour had elapsed, he called Ben Kemp and Bob Lewis into the room and said. "Damn it to hell's fire, this company has got to hire some fighting men." Then he told them what had happened.

When he finished talking, Ben Kemp, who had his fill of gun fighting during his ranger service, said, "Count me out. I'm not drawing any fighting wages."

Then Bob Lewis, who stuttered, said, "B-b-b-by God, me neither." They told Woodley that they would quit before they would fight sheepherders. They figured that he would fire them, but he didn't.

On November 20, 1888, the V + T chuck wagon reached North Water Spring, on Corduroy Draw, with a thousand head of five- and six-year-old steers. This was the last bunch to be trailed into Magdalena that year; these steers were to be loaded into stock cars at Magdalena and shipped to the eastern markets. At North Water there was a holding trap, an enclosure of about two hundred acres. Most of this was pole fence, strong enough to hold the steers providing they did not stampede, which was not likely since they could scatter out and there was plenty of feed. The cowhands decided to use the holding trap since they would have to stand guard every night the rest of the way to Magdalena, a distance of sixty miles.

Clouds had been piling up in the east all afternoon, and the weather looked stormy, so Ben Kemp, Bob Lewis, Billy Jones, and Frank Holliday decided to put up a tepee tent they used for bad weather. This tent was large enough to hold two camp beds, one on each side of the center pole that held the tent up. The two beds furnished sleeping accommodations for four men, though somewhat crowded. They turned in early and slept soundly until daylight the next morning. When they awoke, the first thing they noticed was the saging tent and the bowed tent pole. They could also see the outline of the snow that had fallen during the night on the tent wall. Lying on their backs, they could just reach the top edge of the snow with the tips of their fingers. Everything was covered; beds that were built down in the open showed scarcely a bulge in the snow. The cook had got up early and shoveled out a place to build his campfire. He had also put a tarpaulin over the chuck-box to protect it from the snow that was still falling. There was much yelling and cursing by the boys who had made their beds down on the ground in the open, because every time one of them tried to push the tarpaulin that covered his bed back from over his head, a tubful of snow would fall into his face.

After breakfast the horses were wrangled in from the small pasture where the steers were being held, and the mounts were roped out and saddled. Since the snow was so deep that it would be practically impossible to trail the herd into Magdalena, the cowboys were all wondering what Woodley was going to do. Although there had not been much talk about it, it was evident that the cowboys didn't intend to go any farther. When everyone had saddled and mounted, Woodley took the lead and started out to take the steers out of the enclosure. After they had ridden a short way, Sam Martin rode up alongside him and said, "Woodley, what are you figuring on doing?"

Woodley answered, "Well, I guess we will turn them loose and go back to the ranch."

"In that case," Sam Martin said, "we'll go back with you."

It was quite a job hauling the chuck wagon back through the heavy snow to the headquarters ranch at the V + T Ciénaga. Then the question was whether any of the cowboys should try to leave the ranch or not. It had snowed nearly all day the twenty-first and still looked stormy. After a day or two at the ranch, Kemp and Holliday decided to ride up to the Datil headquarters ranch, since

97

they could catch the stagecoach into Magdalena from the Datil post office. This sounded preposterous to the other cowboys, who vainly tried to talk them out of going. After saddling two of the largest and strongest grain-fed horses in the remuda, Kemp and Holliday headed north up Railroad Canyon, crossed over the Prairie Mountain divide into the head of Shaw Canyon, and down Shaw Canyon to the Crawford ranch on the south edge of the Plains of San Agustín. They stayed there the next day to let their horses rest up.

Early on the morning of the twenty-sixth they left the Crawford ranch and headed north across the plains toward Sugar Loaf Mountain. They hadn't traveled far from the ranch into the open plain when it began snowing again. There was no object that could furnish them a marker to keep them on the right course, only a curtain of snow all around them. Kemp was leading and Holliday was following, because Kemp's horse was the larger of the two, standing nearly seventeen hands. The snow on the level plain was so deep that it was dragging his stirrups. When they started out from the ranch, Kemp had noticed that the wind was from the east, and he reasoned that if he could keep the snow hitting his right cheek, they would be traveling in a northerly direction, providing the wind didn't change. It was a risk they had to take, so they rode on.

As they rode, they kept noticing small round holes in the snow near rabbitweeds and chamiso bushes. After passing several of these, their curiosity got the best of them, and they stopped to investigate. When they cleared the snow away from the foot of a chamiso bush, a rabbit jumped out. After one jump into the soft snow, all he could do was flounder around until they caught him. After several miles of breaking trail, Kemp's horse began to tire, and Holliday took the lead. In less than a mile he was heading into the wind and back to the open plain, so Kemp took the lead again. Several miles farther on they hit the edge of the timber between Nester Draw and Datil. They turned northeast up the road, which was visible only as a cleared streak through the brush. It was extremely hard to follow in places.

At nine o'clock that night they rode into the Datil post office.

98

which was also a store. Baldwin, the proprietor, was surprised to see them and was inclined not to believe them when they told him where they had come from. They were almost frozen when they reached Datil, but Mrs. Baldwin cooked them a hot meal with plenty of hot coffee, and they were soon back to normal. Baldwin's two boys, Lee and Fred, were just small youngsters at that time and were very interested when the two cowboys told about the rabbits. Baldwin insisted that they stay overnight, but they wanted to ride on to the ranch since it was only about five-and-a-half miles up the canyon. They arrived at the ranch at eleven o'clock, having covered about thirty miles through snow that averaged around two feet on the level. The cowboys at the ranch could hardly believe they had traveled so far in that weather.

The weather cleared on November 27, and the snow melted enough to form a crust on top. The stagecoach from Magdalena could not reach Datil, so Kemp and Holliday were forced to stay over at the Datil headquarters ranch.

Living near Datil was a Norwegian by the name of Olson. Olson was an expert on skis, having learned how to use them in Norway. One morning about ten o'clock, Ben Kemp noticed a man on top of an untimbered ridge west of the ranch, and as he watched, the man came sailing down the side of the ridge like a bird. At the foot of the ridge was an arroyo about eight feet deep and ten feet wide. Kemp expected to see the man break his neck, but when he reached the arroyo, he sailed across as though it had not been there. When Olson arrived at the ranch house, his skis interested the cowboys, who had never seen a pair before. They asked him a lot of questions about them: how far a man could travel in a day's time, how fast he could go, and various other things. Olson told them that skiers had been known to cover a distance of eighty miles in one day and attain speed on downgrades of better than forty miles per hour.

Kemp and Holliday were elated when they talked to Olson, because they thought that by using skis, they could reach Magdalena. Kemp bought the skis Olson was wearing and got his promise to make Holliday a pair. Kemp started practicing right away, and by the time Holliday's pair was ready, he had learned to ski fairly well.

As soon as Holliday could learn, they would be ready to start for Magdalena. Holliday learned slowly, but after several days he could shuffle around fairly well and thought that he was better than he really was.

The south end of ridge west of the ranch house was steeper than the east side, and Holliday, feeling cocky over learning to ski, bantered Kemp for a race down the steep face of this slope, which was covered with a sparse stand of pine timber. Because Kemp doubted Holliday's ability to ski down this steep incline, he warned him to sit down on his brake stick if he began going too fast. The brake stick was a green Gambel oak pole, about eight feet long and trimmed down to about one-and-a-half inches in diameter. It was heavy and practically unbreakable. When all was ready, they eased up to the brow of the hill and over the crest. Then the race was on, and Kemp was kept busy watching his way through the scattering trees. When he reached the bottom of the hill, Holliday was missing, and looking back up the slope, he could see just the tip end of Holliday's skis sticking out of the snow. He worked his way back to where Holliday was lying and asked him what had happened. Holliday said he had gathered too much speed and forgot to ride his pole. Instead he had stuck it into the snow ahead of him and turned a somersault down the mountainside, landing on his back. When Kemp had regained his composure from a fit of laughter, he helped Holliday out of the hole he had made in the snow. Holliday would not try to stand up again until he had unstrapped his skis, and no amount of pleading would induce him to put them back on.

This canceled all thoughts of a trip to Magdalena on skis, and it was twelve days before the stagecoach reached Datil. When it arrived, the two cowboys lost no time purchasing a ticket to Magdalena where they could board the train for Alpine. They were thankful to be headed for a country where they would not have to wade in snow up to their waists every time they stepped outside the house.

10.
The Cow Camp at Nine Points

Olson, the Norwegian who made Kemp's skis, saved the lives of several families who were snowbound on Nester Draw west of Datil, during the winter of 1888. The snowfall in this area reached a depth of six feet, and it was impossible to travel over or through it on horseback, because the snow never crusted over with a sheet of ice strong enough to support a horse.

Olson owned a horse that was a natural pacer, so he devised a set of snowshoes for the animal. After several days of training, the horse could travel over the crusted snow on these snowshoes. Olson hitched him to a sleigh and hauled supplies from Magdalena to Nester Draw, a distance of seventy miles. His ingenuity saved many settlers from starving to death during that hard winter.

When Kemp reached Alpine, he met his partner Bill McFarland, who had come to town to get someone to stay at camp with him. Mexican cattle thieves had been reported stealing cattle and raiding camps, and McFarland did not relish staying in camp alone. He had succeeded in getting a man named Phelps to return to Nine Points with him. McFarland was glad when Kemp decided to go back to camp with them. It was a long ride from Alpine to Nine Points, and they didn't reach camp until late afternoon. When they arrived, they found their cook tent was a shambles. At first they thought the camp had been raided by Mexicans, but on closer examination they discovered the damage had been done by a mother bear with two cubs. The bears had turned over a barrel of honey in the tent and destroyed other provisions.

Kemp and McFarland were almost sure the bears would return that night, so they decided to watch for them. They didn't tell Phelps about their plans, because he was an elderly man and they knew he was tired from the long ride and would want to go to bed early.

101

As soon as they had finished supper, the men lighted their pipes and settled down to discuss the cattle situation. If there were any raids at the tip end of the Big Bend, their camp would probably be one of the first raided since it was only a few miles from the Mexican border. When they had finished smoking their pipes, Phelps rose to his feet and announced that he was a little saddle-weary and ready to go to bed.

The camp consisted of three tents set in a triangle. Besides the cook tent there were two tipis, which contained the bedrolls. Phelps's bedroll was in the tent farthest from the front of the cook tent. Taking his .44-caliber Winchester carbine with him, he retired into the tipi and was soon asleep and snoring.

It was a beautiful night. The air was still and a full moon made the camp almost as light as day. Ben Kemp took first guard, which was to last until midnight, then McFarland was to take over. As Kemp watched for the bears, he suspected they would never come to camp, because Phelps, besides snoring, would flop over in bed every fifteen or twenty minutes and say, "Oh, Lordie." When midnight came and no bears had appeared, Kemp was sure they were not going to visit camp that night.

At midnight McFarland took over, and after watching for about two hours, he was ready to give up, when suddenly the bears appeared in front of the cook tent. The two cubs, thinking only of honey, were a few steps ahead of the mother bear and went directly into the tent, but their mother, an extra-large black bear, was more cautious. She stopped a few feet short of the cook tent entrance and began to sniff the air.

McFarland raised his rifle, took aim, and pulled the trigger. The still night air was shattered by the report of the heavy rifle, which was immediately followed by a bellow of pain from the mortally wounded mother bear, so loud that it seemed to shake the earth. The two cubs bounded through the back of the cook tent splitting it wide open. Phelps emerged from his tent into the bright moonlight, and, holding his Winchester by the end of the barrel, began running around and around his tipi, yelling, "Lordie, Lordie, Lordie!"

By the time Phelps had quieted down, the mother bear was dead, and the cubs had made their escape, their taste for honey from this particular spot cured forever.

Captain Jim Gillett told about his visit to the Nine Points camp, and according to his story, Ben Kemp's partner, Jim Tarvin, who was an Australian by birth and knew nothing of western ranch life before coming to Alpine, must have acquired a knowledge of camp life a little on the rough side.

Gillett said that he and another man rode into the Nine Points camp around noon one day and found Tarvin preparing a meal. There were several hungry-looking hound dogs sitting around the camp watching him closely. Tarvin had to fry bacon to get grease to use as shortening in the biscuits he was making. When he had rendered the grease, he removed the frying pan from the fire and set it on the ground beside him. One of the hounds sitting behind Tarvin sneaked up and lunged for the bacon. The sizzling hot grease seared the hound's nose, and he howled long and loud. Tarvin looked around and said, "Oh yes, damn you, I guess you will," and went right on with his biscuit-making, using the rendered grease for shortening.

Kemp stayed at the cow camp during most of the winter of 1888, but as soon as the cow work started in the spring of 1889, he returned to Milligan Plaza. From there he rode to the V + T headquarters where he asked Woodley for a job and was promptly hired.

While Kemp was working for the Red River Land and Cattle Company, he met a cowboy by the name of Jack Bess. This man was a "claybank," standing six feet, four inches, and weighing about 190 pounds. He wore a long droopy mustache that would have matched Wild Bill Hickok's. This man, who was a character and a prankster, loved his whisky and usually went on a drinking spree at shipping time.

On one occasion when the trail herd reached Nine Mile Hill, west of Magdalena, one of the cowboys rode on into town and returned with two quarts of whisky. After Bess had taken several swigs from the bottle, he got happy and reckless. While he was chasing an unruly steer that had a habit of straying from the herd, his

103

whisky-befogged mind caused him to ride his saddle horse into a cedar tree, and a limb on the tree gouged a four-inch streak down the side of his face, which bled profusely.

When the herd reached Magdalena and was safely corralled in the stock pens, all of the cowboys went to the hotel to clean up and get something to eat. Mrs. Chisholm, the proprietress of the hotel, knew Bess, and when he stepped into the lobby with clotted blood on his face and clothes, she said, "My goodness, Mr. Bess, what in the world has happened to you?"

"Madam," said Bess, "a rattlesnake bit me."

"Terrible," said Mrs. Chisholm, "and what did you do to the rattlesnake?"

"Madam," Bess replied, "I got right down off of my horse, and I stomped every pellet out of his hide, as big as a buckshot." At this point further explanation was cut short by two husky cowboys, who hustled Bess upstairs to a room.

At times when Bess went on a spree, the chuck wagon would return without him, and his money would run short, but not his craving for liquor.

Early one morning he was standing on the sidewalk in front of the Hilton Bar in Magdalena, trying to bum a drink, when one of the town's leading citizens came by. This man was a shrewd dealer, who either owned or had a lien upon a sizable amount of property in town. He had little regard for Bess and started to walk by without speaking, but Bess stopped him, saying, "Just a minute, Mr. Bartlett, I want to tell you about a dream I had last night."

Just to humor him, Bartlett said, "Yes, Jack, what was it?"

"Well," said Bess, "I dreamed I died and went to hell, and when I got down there I noticed thousands of iron pots all turned upside down. I suspicioned there was something under them pots, and finally my curiosity got the best of me. The largest one of all these pots was near where I stood, so I got a crowbar and started to turn it over. Just as I got the end of the crowbar wedged under the edge of the pot, I saw the old Devil coming on a high run, yelling, 'Don't do that Jack, don't do that.'

" 'Why?' I asked.

" 'Because old Bartlett is under that pot,' said the Devil, 'and if you turn him out, he will have a mortgage on hell in less than twenty-four hours.' "

Bartlett got the drift and said, "Aw hell, come on into the bar and I will buy you a drink."

While Bess was working at the AL Ranch west of Magdalena a few years later, he and a cowboy by the name of Hardy rode to San Marcial to attend a three-day celebration. When they reached town, they rode to the livery stable where they left their horses. Then they registered at one of the best hotels where they were assigned to room 12 on the second floor.

The next morning before leaving for breakfast, Bess placed a chair on its back in bed and drew the quilts up over it. About 10:00 A.M. the chambermaid came upstairs to tidy up the rooms and noticed through the partly open door that someone was lying in bed with the covers drawn over his head. She passed the room by and about three o'clock that afternoon returned to complete her work. When she reached the door, she saw the object in bed lying in the same position it had been that morning. Alarmed, she rushed downstairs to tell the landlady there was something seriously wrong with one of the cowboys in room 12.

The landlady went to investigate and found the object in bed as the maid had described it. She called one of the men who worked at the hotel, and he went into the room and turned the quilts down on the bed, exposing the chair. Everyone had a good laugh and rawhided the maid the rest of the evening about finding a dead man in number 12.

The next morning after a day and night of celebrating, Bess and Hardy slept until nearly noon. Finally Hardy got up and dressed. He was trying to get Bess out of bed when they heard the chambermaid on her way to their room. Hardy hid behind the door. Bess, instead of getting up, lowered his garments and raised to his knees. Laying his chest flat on the bed, he pulled the covers over his head and waited. When the maid reached the door, she peeped into the room and could see what she thought was another chair in bed. Saying aloud to herself, "Oh yes, you can't fool me this time," she skipped across the room, grasped the quilts at the head of the bed, and threw them clear to the foot. There was quite an exposure, followed by a loud shriek from the maid, who flew through the door and down the stairway, with Hardy only a step behind her. As Hardy left the room, Jack yelled, "Wait for me, Hardy."

But Hardy answered, "Go to hell, you crazy son of a bitch," and kept running. As he turned the corner a block down the street from the hotel, he looked back and saw Bess following only a few yards behind, with his Levi's in one hand and his boots in the other. The two of them ducked into a bar, where Jack put on his clothes. Then they went to the livery stable, quickly saddled their cow ponies, and left town, Hardy cursing Jack all the way back to camp for ruining their trip to the rodeo.

Contrary to some movie versions of the old Southwest, respectable liquor establishments did not cater to women, and most proprietors forbade them to enter their bars. There were bars in red-light districts, usually run by madams or their paramours, where drinks were sold at twice the regular price, the red-light girls getting a percentage on all the drinks their customers bought. These brothels were located in an isolated part of town, and during the day there was little activity around them. The average cowboy refused to be seen in the company of a harlot on the open street, a fact that was amply demonstrated by an incident that happened in Magdalena one fall during shipping season.

The morning after the V + T cowboys arrived in town with a shipment of cattle, a group of them were making the rounds of the different bars—buying drinks, playing cards, and having a good time in general—when they were joined by one of the red-light girls. She was promptly told that she wasn't welcome and was asked to leave. She became angry and told the men she would do as she pleased, and if they didn't like it, they could go straight to hell. Then she started picking on one of the cowboys and got so abusive that he became furious. He grabbed her, threw her to the sidewalk, and tore off every stitch of her clothing. When he turned her loose, she needed no further persuasion to go home. She flew up the street in the direction of the red-light district as fast as her

106

legs would carry her. Even the cowboys admitted this was rough treatment, but it stopped prostitutes from trying to accompany them along the town sidewalks.

When Ben Kemp quit the V + T in August, 1889, Woodley offered to raise his salary if he would stay, but he turned the offer down. He went out to the corral and roped out his own two horses, saddled one, packed his bedroll on the other, and mounted. He headed for Milligan Plaza, where he intended to sell his saddle horses and squatter's rights on Negrito Creek to August Kiehne.

Kemp and Josephine Cox had been engaged to be married for more than a year and had set their wedding date for the nineteenth of September. Josephine was willing to follow the man of her choice to the end of the world, but Ben knew it was only natural for her to want to live close enough to her family that she could visit them, so he decided to buy a building in Milligan Plaza and establish a grocery store.

As usual, he stayed at the Washie Jones residence, and the next morning while he was looking for a suitable building for his store, Jones asked, "Young man, just what have you got in mind?" Kemp told him, and then Jones said, "Why, that is what the boys and I intended to do."

"If that is the case," said Kemp, "I'll withdraw."

"But the trouble is," said Jones, "we haven't enough money to swing the deal and were intending to borrow from you."

"O.K.," said Kemp, and he loaned Jones three hundred dollars to help establish the first grocery store in what is now Reserve, New Mexico.

After Kemp made arrangements with a parson at Milligan Plaza to perform the wedding ceremony, he rode to the Henry Cox ranch (now the Trujillo place on Cox Canyon) and told Josephine what had happened. She told him that regardless of where they lived, she would be happy as long as she could be with him, so they decided to go to the little cow camp at Nine Points.

When the parson arrived, Martha Cox, Josephine's older sister, who was engaged to a young German named Nat Emmerick, decided to be married at the same time. So on the night of September

107

9, 1889, the two young couples stood in the main room of Henry Cox's log cabin, which was lighted by a bright fire burning in the fireplace, and the parson performed the double-wedding ceremony.

The next morning Henry Cox hitched his team to a wagon and Josephine bade her mother and sisters a tearful good-by. She took her place on the wagon seat between her father and her husband, and the wagon headed for Magdalena, which at that time was the nearest railroad town, one hundred miles east.

After five days' travel they reached Socorro, where Henry Cox bought a wagonload of supplies. He left the next morning on his return trip home, and the young couple bought tickets for El Paso. When they boarded the train, the young bride was all aflutter, for she had seen very few trains and had never been a passenger on one. When they arrived at the Grand Central Railroad station in El Paso, she was aghast because Negro porters from the Hotel Paso del Norte picked up their luggage and carried it away. She insisted that they be reported to the police, but her husband assured her that the porters were employees of the hotel where they were going and their luggage would be safe.

When they arrived at the hotel, they were met by Jim Tarvin, who had come to El Paso to meet them. He was glad that they were going out to the cow camp at Nine Points and suggested that they celebrate the occasion by visiting the dining room, where he ordered an excellent dinner.

The next day they stayed over in El Paso and visited Juarez, Mexico. Mrs. Kemp was amused when Tarvin bought a nice woolen suit of clothes and wore it back across the river under his old suit to keep from paying customs duty. He almost suffocated before they could reach the hotel.

After a couple of days in El Paso, the Kemps bought tickets to Alpine, where they registered at the Darling Hotel. Mrs. Darling and her daughters were excited about meeting Mrs. Kemp, since they had known her husband for several years. They tried to make her feel at home. They toured the town with her, showing her the stores and introducing her to their friends.

After a week's stay in Alpine, Ben Kemp bought a team and a

wagon which he loaded with supplies, then he and his wife headed for the cow camp at Nine Points.

Mrs. Kemp had lived on the frontier all of her life, but this section of Texas was still wild. The camp was only a few miles from the Mexican border and she was terrified of Mexicans. This fear had been caused by several events. One of them was a ghastly murder that had been committed near her father's ranch in Uvalde County by a sixteen-year-old Mexican boy. The boy, whose parents had been killed by Indians, had been adopted by a neighboring family when he was twelve, and he had been treated as one of the family. One day, without any apparent reason, he murdered the entire family of five. It was several days before anyone visited the ranch and found them. The Texas Rangers were notified and went to the scene of the murder. By this time the bodies of the ill-fated family were badly decomposed, so one large grave was dug and the entire family placed in it.

Then, Ike Cox, one of Mrs. Kemp's uncles, had fought with the Texas volunteers during the Mexican War in 1846, and his vivid description of what happened to some of the men captured by the Mexican army had increased Josephine's fear of Mexicans. Furthermore, her father had trouble with Mexican cattle thieves when he lived on the Nueces River and lost several hundred head of cattle that were run across the Río Grande into Mexico.

One morning shortly after they arrived at the Nine Points cow camp, Ben Kemp found some tracks in the soft dirt around the cow corral, which were made by the Big Bend's mystery people, and told his wife about the strange habits of these wild people. He explained that they visited cow camps but never molested anything and that no one had ever seen them. In his opinion they were harmless, but Josephine was not convinced and insisted on accompanying Ben every time he rode out from camp. For days she rode the range with her husband, and thus became the first white woman to ride this section of the Big Bend.

The camp at Nine Points was kept free of rodents by a family of skunks that took over the duties of a house cat. These skunks were so tame that they would search for morsels of food that dropped from the dining table. They never harmed anyone, but Mrs. Kemp never became accustomed to having them run around under the table while she was trying to eat dinner.

Only once during the time they lived at Nine Points did Josephine have to stay overnight by herself. Ben had to make a trip to Presidio, Mexico, to buy a string of saddle horses. After he left, she felt terribly alone and deserted in this isolated cow camp, and about mid-afternoon the next day she had a real scare when a desperate-looking character rode into camp and dismounted. Mrs. Kemp selected a solid chunk of firewood and watched him warily. Although the man looked like a ruffian, he spoke politely and began asking about some of the neighboring ranchers about whom she knew practically nothing. Before she had finished trying to answer his questions, she saw her husband approaching camp with the horses he had bought. She ran to meet him, almost hysterical with joy. Ben Kemp knew the man, and after he had left, he laughed at his wife for getting so scared. But it was not a laughing matter with her, and from that time on he never left camp without her, regardless of where he went.

Although Kemp and his two partners had a fairly good range stocked with nearly three hundred head of cattle, they were heavily in debt. Bill McFarland had tired of staying at the cow camp alone and had gone to St. Louis, Missouri, where he was having a gay time and spending money right and left. Tarvin knew little of the western method of cattle-raising, and he had gone to Alpine, where he took up living quarters at a hotel.

11.
Alpine and Its Citizens

When Kemp learned what his partners had done, he was both angered and grieved, but this would not pay bills, so he sold enough cattle to pay the indebtedness. Only a small remnant of the herd was left, not enough to provide income even for living expenses.

Jim Chastain, a rancher near Alpine, was having trouble with cattle thieves and hired Ben Kemp to catch them. Within a short time Kemp caught two Mexicans butchering one of Chastain's steers within a few miles of Alpine. He captured both of them and took them to town where they were placed in jail. Later they were tried, convicted, and sentenced to the penitentiary. This put a stop to cattle-stealing on Chastain's range.

During this time Kemp and his wife lived at the Chastain ranch, where on the morning of June 8, 1890, their first child was born. The baby boy was named Benjamin William after his father and his uncle William Bradford.

When Ben Kemp quit work for Chastain, he moved his family to Shafter, where he worked in a silver mine for two months. The ore from this mine was shipped by stagecoach, drawn by a frisky team of four half-wild Spanish mules. Two Texas Rangers were assigned to guard the stage on its run to the nearest railhead.

The rangers rode horseback, and at times the stage traveled faster than they did and got out of their sight. On one such occasion the rangers met a rancher in a wagon, coming from the direction the stage had disappeared, and stopped to pass the time of day. They asked the rancher if he had met the stage, and he said, "Nope, I don't believe I did." The rangers were badly worried and started to leave on a run. "Now wait a minute," said the rancher, "back down the road a ways I saw a hell of a dust and smelt mule sweat. That must have been him."

111

From Shafter, Kemp moved to Marathon, where he worked as a section hand for the Southern Pacific Railroad. After leaving the railroad, he worked as boiler-tender at one of the first well rigs in West Texas.

During the late summer of 1891, Kemp moved his family to Llano County, where on the fourteenth of September another baby was born. She was named Julia Jane after her two grandmothers.

Work was scarce in Llano County, so the family moved to Menard, where Ben's sister Mary and her husband William Bradford lived. They found conditions there the same as they were in Llano County, so in the fall of 1891 the family moved back to Alpine, where Kemp gathered the remnant of his cattle at Nine Points and sold them to a butcher, who ran a meat market in Alpine.

Meanwhile Jim Gillett was elected sheriff of Brewster County. When Ben Kemp finished gathering his cattle, Gillett appointed him first deputy. The deputation papers (now a souvenir of the Kemp family) show the date as June 25, 1892.

While Ben Kemp was deputy under Gillett, two men named Bennett and Gaoud got into a shooting scrape at the Darling Hotel. Darling had died a year earlier, leaving his widow and three daughters the hotel. On his deathbed Darling had called Bill Gaoud, who was a close, trustworthy friend and asked him to act as guardian of his family until the estate was properly settled.

Bennett started courting one of the Darling girls, and Gaoud, who disliked him, exceeded his authority and objected. Bennett was several years younger than Gaoud and was considered a fairly good gun slinger. He was also inclined to be somewhat over-bearing with Gaoud, which was bound to lead to trouble. The riffraff element in any town is always ready to promote trouble, and Alpine had its quota. With the backing of these ruffians Bennett boasted that he was going to kill Gaoud the first time he met him. The troublemakers broadcast this over town, and Gaoud soon heard it.

One Sunday, Bennett had been at the Darling Hotel all morning, and Gaoud, who was seething with rage, took a position on the sidewalk, just outside the hotel entrance.

At a quarter-past twelve Bennett stepped through the hotel door

112

onto the street, and the first man he saw was Gaoud. Bennett drew his six-shooter and fired, hitting Gaoud through the left side of the stomach, just below the ribs. The impact from the bullet staggered Gaoud, but did not knock him down. Pulling his six-shooter, he stepped towards Bennett, who, after firing the first shot, ran a few steps, then wheeled and fired again, but missed. Gaoud fired at the same time but also missed. Bennett now started to run again and reached the middle of the street, nearly thirty yards from Gaoud, who realized that he would be out of pistol range in a few more steps.

Gaoud stepped from the sidewalk onto the street. Standing spraddle-legged to steady himself, he grasped his Colt .45 with both hands and took careful aim. At this instant Bennett turned to shoot a third time, but as he did, Gaoud squeezed the trigger, and Bennett fell to the ground with a bullet through his hips.

Ben Kemp had just sat down at the dining table in his home for lunch when he heard the first shot. He had a good idea of what was taking place, since he had heard the talk around town. So he buckled on his belt and gun and lost no time getting to the Darling Hotel.

When he reached the hotel, he found some of Bennett's friends gathered around him in the middle of the street. They had called a doctor and were excitedly discussing the shooting. Gaoud was leaning against the wall of the hotel, his six-shooter in his hand. Kemp walked up to him and said, "Bill, give me your gun." Without a word, Gaoud handed it over.

Kemp noticed that something was wrong and asked, "Bill, are you O. K.?"

"Oh, just nicked a little," Gaoud answered. But when he tried to step away from the wall of the hotel, his knees buckled, and he sank to the ground.

The doctor was called, and after examining the wound, he said that unless complications set in, Gaoud ought to be well in a month. Bennett's wound was more serious, and the doctor was not sure that he would survive.

When Bennett's friends heard this, they were wild with rage and threatened to lynch Gaoud. To prevent such an act, Gaoud was

113

placed in a cell at the county jail for protection, and Kemp stood guard. Everything was quiet until after dark. Then a mob gathered in front of the jail and demanded that Gaoud be turned over to them. When this happened, Kemp said, "Bill, if that mob attacks this jail and I hand you a rifle, I guess you know how to use it."

Grinning, Gaoud replied, "Yes sir-ee, I sure do."

Kemp went to one of the jail windows and called out to the mob, "The first one of you that tries to break into this jail is going to die on the spot. Gaoud is my prisoner, and I intend to protect him with my life."

The mob knew the deputy and his reputation and realized that this was no idle threat. They also knew that the sheriff would back his deputy to the end as long as he was in the right. They milled around for a few minutes, then grew silent and left. Kemp maintained a close guard through the rest of the night, but no one returned to bother him or his prisoner.

After about six months Bennett recovered from his wound and married the Darling girl. This must have cured Gaoud from interfering where he had no business, because nothing more was heard from him.

Alpine had its rough elements during the early days. The town was divided into two sections, the Anglos living on one side of the Southern Pacific Railroad tracks, and the Mexicans on the other. Occasionally cowboys from the Anglo side would make trips to the Mexican section, where they attended *bailes* and flirted with the *señoritas*. Usually they were half-drunk, and the Mexican men resented their visits. This resulted in brawls and fights that sometimes ended with a killing.

On one such occasion a Mexican man was killed during the night and left directly across the railroad track from the Holland Hotel. Early the next morning Holland, the proprietor of the hotel, walked onto the front porch. A moment later he called back to two men who were sitting in the lobby: "Come out here, you fellows. I want to show you a good Mexican." Wondering what he meant, the two men walked onto the porch, and Holland pointed to an object across the tracks. The two men soon realized that it was the corpse of a Mex-

114

ican man, which had been discovered by a sow intent on a meal. Because the Mexican was fully dressed, the hog was having trouble finding a place to take a bite. Since the head was almost the only unprotected part, the sow had grabbed an ear and was yanking and dragging the body around in a circle.

The three men watched the hog for a few minutes, then walked back into the lobby. One of them said, "That hog won't eat the Mexican. He will taste too strong of chili." A few minutes later they heard the chatter of Spanish from across the tracks. Some of the dead Mexican's *amigos* had found his body and were carrying it away.

When Kemp's deputy appointment at Alpine expired, he decided to go back to Menard County. He hitched four half-wild Spanish mules to a light wagon and tied his favorite saddle horse to the endgate. Then he helped his family aboard and headed east.

In those days there were very few fences in West Texas, and Ben knew the entire country, from the Río Grande to the Colorado River, like the palm of his hand.

After leaving Nine Points, he followed the old Comanche war trail a few miles and then headed for the Buffalo Crossing on the Pecos River. After crossing the Pecos, he cut across country to the divide between the draws of Oak Creek and the Middle Concho.

At a point about twenty miles southeast of Big Lake, the left rear wheel of the wagon gave way, breaking all the spokes. The nearest habitation was a cow ranch some twenty miles away, and the problem was how to reach it. Mrs. Kemp did not relish the idea of having to stay overnight with her two small children on this isolated plateau while her husband went to the ranch for repairs.

Kemp thought about the situation for a few minutes, then unhitched the lead team and tied them to the right rear wheel of the wagon. He untied the pony from the endgate and saddled him. Taking an ax, he mounted his horse and rode off down a draw to the north, leaving his wife sitting on the wagon seat, holding the reins of the wheel team.

Before long the wheel team became restless. Mrs. Kemp was afraid they might turn the wagon over if they managed to cut the

115

wheels to the left, so she held onto the reins for dear life, pleading with the mules to whoa, but the mules paid no attention. Luckily, the wagon was too heavy for them to pull, with one wheel broken and the hub buried in the soft earth. But they kept lunging, and every time they did, the two mules that were tied to the right rear wheel would pull back on their ropes, causing the wagon to rock back and forth.

Finally the wheel team managed to twist out from under their breeching and turn to face the wagon. The traces to their harness were still fastened to the singletree and the breast yoke to the end of the wagon tongue, but the harness collars were pulled up on the back of the mules' heads. The more Mrs. Kemp pulled on the reins, the more they tried to back through their collars. She was afraid they would pull their blind bridles off and get away, but there was nothing she could do but cry and plead with them to whoa. Once the mules had turned in their harness, they settled down to a steady pull, with their long ears protruding from under the top of their collars, which were sitting on the backs of their heads.

After what seemed an eternity, Mrs. Kemp saw her husband returning to the wagon, dragging a hackberry pole on the end of a saddle rope. As soon as he was within hailing distance, she began to plead with him to hurry, telling him that the mules were about to get away. He hurried towards the wagon, but when he had reached a point close enough to see what had happened, he fell off his horse in a fit of mirth and rolled on the ground with laughter. This changed Mrs. Kemp's fright to anger, and she told him what she thought of a man who would act in such a silly manner when his wife and little children were in danger.

When he had regained his composure, Kemp set about repairing the wagon so they could continue their trip to the cow ranch. Using the green hackberry pole as a lever, he raised the rear left axle of the wagon, while Mrs. Kemp placed rocks under it to hold it up. When the axle was raised high enough, he placed the pole under the hub of the broken wheel and tied the upper end to the top of the wagon box. Then he lashed the hub securely to the pole, making a kind of sled runner to replace the wheel. When the wagon was repaired, they traveled on and reached the cow ranch the next afternoon. They found a complete blacksmith outfit there, and the wheel was soon repaired.

In due time the family reached Menard, where Kemp soon had a job hauling freight from Ballinger. He hauled all the steel and cement that went into building the Menard County jail.

After finishing the freight-hauling job for Menard County, Ben Kemp moved his family to Ozona, where on April 30, 1893, a third child, a girl, was born, and the Kemps named her Beulah.

Kemp's half-brother, Jim Chapman, was running a bar at Ozona at this time, so Ben tried his hand at bartending for a few months.

When he left Ozona, he moved his family back to Menard where he bought a half-interest in a well rig with a man named Bill Ellis. It was the first rig of its kind in the San Saba Valley. During the time Kemp worked on this rig, the family lived first at one ranch and then another. For a while they lived at the Vinegarroon ranch owned by Jim Calahan, then at the Jenkins ranch, and later at the Bill Bradford ranch.

In the fall of 1894, while the family was living at Bill Bradford's, Kemp sold his interest in the well rig and started working for a man who had contracted to paint a group of buildings in Menard. When this job was finished, Kemp moved his family to Midland, where he joined a man by the name of John Damron. In the winter of 1894 they trapped quail by the thousands. Later they bought a well rig and drilled a number of water wells near Midland, never dreaming that this would one day be a rich oil field.

On October 15, 1895, another baby was born to the Kemp family. She was named Mary Lily after her aunt Mary Bradford.

12.
Northward Ho

From Midland, Ben Kemp moved his family back to Marathon, where he met his old partner Bill McFarland. They formed a partnership and trapped quail until the first of March, 1896.

During the latter part of February, Mrs. Kemp received a letter from Julia, her youngest sister, which stated their father, Henry Cox, had been seriously injured when he was caught in a cave-in while digging a pit at a placer gold mine near Hillsboro. After the accident Henry Cox had been taken to the Santana place, on the head of Cuchillo Creek, five miles west of the mining town of Grafton, where his small herd of cattle was located. He was unable to walk, Mrs. Cox was sick in bed with influenza, and the two young girls, Sarah and Julia, were at a loss about what they were going to do.

Mrs. Kemp was deeply worried by the letter and read it to her husband. He had been debating about returning to New Mexico anyway, so they decided to start for Grafton as soon as possible.

Kemp loaded two wagons, a lead and a trailer, with the family possessions, which included a coop of chickens that was fastened to the endgate of the trail wagon. Both wagons were equipped with bows and sheets. The lead wagon had a forty-gallon barrel lashed to the side for hauling water. Kemp decided to ride the off-wheel horse, which would make it easier to handle the six-horse team.

Two brothers, Buck and Gail Miller, who owned a small bunch of horses near Marathon, wanted to make the trip north with Kemp, and this was agreed to.

When all was ready, Ben Kemp hitched his team of two horses and four mules to the wagons, swung into the saddle on the off-wheel horse, and the journey north began.

From Marathon their route led through the east foothills of the

118

Glass Mountains, then north to the Toyah station of the Texas Pacific Railroad. From Toyah, the wagon continued north towards the Guadalupe Mountains and the old Butterfield Stage route. Following the old stage route, they turned west towards the Organ Mountains.

There were many points of interest which Kemp pointed out to his family and the Miller brothers. Among the most interesting was the dripping springs, or Tinajas, at Las Cornudas. The mountain rising above these springs was virtually a rockpile. No dirt was visible on the mountainside, just rocks of all shapes and sizes. The Kemp family camped overnight at Las Cornudas, pitching their camp within fifty yards of the grave of a Russian nobleman, who was killed there when six men in Lieutenant Tays's command had galloped ahead to get a cool drink of water. Ben Kemp pointed out the bullet marks where the Russian had shot at the Indian who was trying to climb up the face of a high rock. The bullet marks were still plainly visible. There were many Indian drawings, which indicated that this must have been one of their favorite camping places.

After leaving the Las Cornudas, they traveled west through a low saddle between the Organ and Franklin mountains, then into the Río Grande Valley a few miles below Las Cruces. Turning north up the river, they passed New Mexico State College, and Mrs. Kemp remarked on the scandalous attire of the girls playing basketball on the campus. They were wearing full black bloomers that fastened below their knees. She would have been horrified if she could have seen what the play suits would be seventy years later.

From Las Cruces the wagon road ran east of the river to Rincón, then it turned west and crossed the river about two miles east of the Hatch station. The crossing was just below and within fifty yards of the Atchison, Topeka and Santa Fé Railway bridge.

At the crossing they found the water rising in the river. At this time of year snow melting in the high mountain ranges along the Río Grande drainage caused the river to flood. This, however, was only part of the trouble. The crossing looked like it might be boggy, and there was too much quicksand. Kemp begged his wife

119

to take the children and cross over on the railroad trestle, but since they didn't know when the trains ran, she was afraid to try.

Buck and Gail Miller drove their remuda across to test the crossing. Apparently there was a little soft sand on the east side, but within thirty steps there seemed to be a fairly solid bottom.

Mrs. Kemp was sitting on the wagon seat in front with Mary Lily, the baby, in her arms. The three small children, Benny, Julia, and Beulah, had crept up from their bed in the back of the wagon and were peeping from under the wagon seat at the muddy, turbulent water, which both awed and terrified them. When all was ready, Ben, who had stopped his wagons fifty or sixty yards from the river, whipped up his team and hit the crossing at a trot. The wagons had traveled less than twenty-five yards from the bank when the off-wheel horse bogged and fell. When Kemp realized that the horse was going to fall, he jumped off his back into the river, but in doing so, he tripped and fell into the icy water up to his chin. Seeing their father practically submerged in the muddy water was too much for the three small children, who were peeping from under the wagon seat, and with a screech they dived for the bed in the back of the wagon, yelling "Papa's drowning" at the top of their voices. They fell on their faces and pulled pillows across the backs of their heads to shut out the awful sight.

When Buck Miller saw what had happened, he jumped his horse into the river and splashed back to the wagon. Kemp quickly unhitched the lead and swing teams and handed the lines to him. Miller drove the two spans to the bank without getting off his saddle horse and quickly returned to pick up the three frightened youngsters who were hidden in the back of the wagon. Placing them behind his saddle, he took the baby in his arms and rode to dry land, which looked mighty good to the three scared children.

Mrs. Kemp was at a loss about how she was going to get to shore without wading through the icy water. The horse Gail was riding was a bronc, and no woman had ever ridden the one Buck was riding. The question was settled by her husband who carried her on his shoulders to the riverbank.

The wheel team then had to be pulled out of the quicksand.

Everything in the wagons had to be unloaded and packed to the bank on the west side of the river. This included the cookstove, which was pretty heavy, and the coop of chickens that was fastened onto the endgate of the trail wagon. By the time the chickens reached shore, they were almost drowned, and had to be turned out of the coop so they could dry.

The next job was to get the wagons out of the river, and any minute the river might flood and wash the wagons away. Ben Kemp mounted a saddle horse and rode to the little Mexican town of Colorar, about two miles down the river, where he hired a Mexican who owned a yoke of oxen to come help pull the wagons out of the river.

The next morning the wagons were loaded, and the chickens had to be put back in the coop. When grain failed to coax them in, the two oldest children were elected to run them down and catch them. After chasing them through the mesquite brush for half an hour, all of the chickens were caught, except one rooster. He was a large Plymouth Rock, and his endurance and speed were too much for the children. After the children had failed, everyone in camp tried to catch him, but he outran and outdodged all of them. When everyone quit chasing him, the rooster returned to where the work team had tossed some grain out of their *morrals* and started picking corn off the ground. He was keeping an eye on everyone, except the work horses, among which he walked with little concern. When Buck Miller noticed this, he mounted his saddle horse, removed a lariat from the saddle horn, built a loop about eight inches in diameter, and eased his horse among the work team. When the rooster raised his head to look around, Miller dropped the loop around his neck and dragged him to the chicken coop—an exhibition of rooster-roping much appreciated by the tired children.

One of Mrs. Kemp's sisters, Martha Emmerick, and her husband were living at Hermosa during this time, so the Kemps decided to pay them a visit.

From Hatch they traveled up the Río Grande to the mouth of Las Animas Creek, then up Las Animas Creek to Hermosa. The children saw their first Ponderosa pine along Las Animas Creek

121

and also their first mine tunnel. The first night camp was pitched directly across the canyon from an open tunnel. Benny was standing at the back of the wagon looking at the tunnel when Buck Miller rode into camp. When he noticed the boy's fascination, Miller told him, "See that hole over there, young fellow? That's where old Robinson Crusoe lives, and after dark he comes out and catches bad boys. You sure better watch your step."

During the month of April nights are pretty cool at this altitude, so several dry cedar limbs were piled near the lead wagon for firewood. After dark the baby began to complain, and Mrs. Kemp, thinking she was cold, told Benny to fetch a shawl that was hanging on the brakelock on the opposite side of the wagon. This side of the wagon faced the tunnel, and the first thing the boy thought of was Robinson Crusoe. Although he had no idea what Crusoe was like, he did have a feeling that some hideous monster might pounce on him when he reached the shadow on the opposite side of the wagon. Mustering his courage, he started around the wagon and had almost reached the shawl when he thought he saw something move among the rabbit bushes at the bottom of the canyon. He jumped around and ran back to the campfire as fast as his legs would carry him. Buck Miller, who was watching the boy, yelled, "Run, he is about to catch you."

As Benny came around the front of the wagon, he ran into the firewood and tripped. He fell forward on his face, screeching at the top of his voice, for he was sure Robinson Crusoe had caught him.

All of the men laughed uproariously, but Mrs. Kemp was angry, and she told Buck Miller what she thought of a grown man who would scare a little boy like that for no reason. This raking over the coals must have cured Miller, because he never tried to scare Benny again.

After visiting the Emmerick family for a week, the Kemps and Millers continued their trip to Grafton and arrived there on April 6, 1896.

As soon as Kemp found living quarters for his family, he began to make plans to move Henry Cox and his family to Grafton. Both Mr. and Mrs. Cox were sick in bed, and the round-about road to

122

their ranch was so rough it was doubtful that they could survive a trip by wagon. Since it was only five miles from the Santana place to Grafton, Kemp suggested they carry them out by stretcher. He and the Miller brothers accomplished this by making two trips up and down the almost impassable canyon.

When Kemp entered Grafton, he had only seven dollars in his pockets. Work was scarce, and it was necessary that he find employment soon. He saddled a horse and rode to the Gila headquarters of the Red River Land and Cattle Company. He met Tom Henderson, who was V + T wagon boss at this time, and asked him if he needed any freight hauled out from Magdalena. Magdalena was the nearest railroad station that could be reached by wagon. It was ninety-five miles east, and the roads were so rough that the V + T had trouble finding anyone to do their hauling, so Henderson hired Kemp immediately.

When Kemp returned to Grafton, he hitched his teams to his wagons and headed for Magdalena. When he arrived in Magdalena, he found a celebration in progress. A crowd had gathered at the Hilton Bar and was drinking a toast to a Colonel Eton. After a few rounds of drinks the Colonel remarked that he would have to hurry out to the race track north of town and pick up Frank Sellman or they would miss their train to Socorro.

Ben Kemp introduced himself to Colonel Eton and said, "I used to know a Frank Sellman, but he was killed by the Texas Rangers in a gun fight near the Río Grande."

"Now maybe he wasn't," said Colonel Eton. "Frank has been in some pretty tight spots and is packing a lot of lead, but he is still kicking."

This aroused Kemp's curiosity, so he returned to the race tracks with Colonel Eton and received the surprise of a lifetime. There was Frank Sellman, a man he was almost sure had been dead for the past twelve years.

Sellman was glad to see Kemp and insisted on buying him a round-trip ticket to Socorro so they could visit. He told Kemp how he had escaped from several law officers. One of them was a county sheriff who had arrested him and was taking him back to the county

123

seat to stand trial. En route they were forced to stay overnight at a small Texas town. The town did not have a livery stable, so they were forced to place their saddle horses in a feed lot. Then they went to the town's bar, where the citizens bought a round of drinks, congratulating the sheriff on the capture of Frank Sellman. Sellman was always a jovial fellow and drank with them, celebrating his own capture.

There was no water in the feed lot, so when the sheriff and Sellman had finished eating their supper, they returned to the lot to water their horses. Sellman was riding Button, his favorite saddle pony. Although Button did not look it, he had the speed of a race horse and could compete with the best hurdle-jumpers.

When Sellman placed the rope around Button's neck, he also threw a half-hitch around his nose and gave the rope a couple of jerks. The cow pony was alerted immediately. When the sheriff started leading his horse towards the only gate in the lot, Sellman jumped onto Button's back and headed for the opposite side of the corral at a dead run. When they reached the fence, Button cleared the top rail by two feet and landed on the outside. Sellman rode into the darkness of the night and made his getaway.

Sellman told Kemp that he and his partner ran into real trouble a few months later when they were jumped by the Texas Rangers near the Río Grande. In the running fight that followed, both he and his partner were badly shot up. They finally reached the banks of the river, where they hid in some bulrushes. By this time it was night, and the rangers were trying to trail them by lamplight. Once they came within thirty steps of where Sellman and his partner lay hidden. The fugitives heard one of the rangers say, "Man, they sure did lose a lot of blood, didn't they?" Sellman said he whispered to his partner that somebody else was going to lose some blood if they came any closer. But the rangers, who had already lost their trail, turned back. Later that night Sellman and his pal made their escape across the river into Mexico, where Sellman stayed for eighteen months before venturing back into the United States.

Finally he returned to the United States and went to Socorro, New Mexico, where he bought a bar. The bar made money, and after a few years he decided to go back to Llano, Texas, on a visit. It was a poor decision. On the train near Toyah station he met someone who recognized him, and he was seriously wounded in the gun fight that followed. The fight occurred at night, and Sellman jumped off the train. By daylight the next morning he had hired a Mexican with a team and covered wagon. Sellman lying on a blood-soaked bed inside the covered-wagon box, was brought back to Socorro. He was more dead than alive, and it took him eighteen months to recover from his wounds.

At the time Kemp met him, Sellman was running a saloon at San Marcial. He died a few years later of cancer. From the general public's viewpoint, this man had been dead for thirty years before he actually died.

By the end of June, Kemp had saved enough money from his freight-hauling to move his family from Grafton to the Moore place on Taylor Creek, one-half mile northeast of the present Wall Dam. Henry Cox had not recuperated enough from his injury to ride horseback, so Buck and Gail Miller volunteered to drive his cattle to the location.

A few days after moving to Taylor Creek, Kemp found a plot of land on Beaver Creek and decided to file a homestead. This tract of land was five miles west of the Moore place, along the bottom of a partially boxed-in canyon, a thousand feet deep. A road would have to be built into the location before any work could start on a house. This presented a problem, because the road would have to lead down the rough and rugged canyon.

Before starting such a project, Kemp decided to visit his brother Steve, who lived on Blue Creek, west of Cliff, New Mexico. Steve was keeping about thirty head of cattle that were Ben's share of the bunch Steve had taken with him when he left Nine Points.

Ben hitched Molly and Coalie, two small Spanish mules, to a light wagon, and the Kemp family climbed aboard and headed for Blue Creek. Their route followed the old Captain Cooney trail, which left the North Star road at the mouth of Kennedy Canyon and ran west up Houghton Canyon to Cooney Prairie, then to the Cooney mines on Mineral Creek.

125

Little had been done to this so-called road, except to blaze trees along the right of way, and travel was very difficult. From the Cooney mines on, the roads were better. Near Pleasington the children noticed the first mesquite trees since leaving the Río Grande Valley; somehow, it seemed that they were back in Texas.

The family visited Steve Kemp's ranch until the following September. During their stay Ben Kemp worked as chuck-wagon cook for a pool that had been formed when Tom Lyons had barred small ranches from the LC chuck wagon.

Ben feared that weather conditions might interfere with the trip home, so he decided to start back to Taylor Creek around the first of September. Knowing that Ben would have trouble crossing the Mogollon Mountains if a storm hit, Steve Kemp and his daughter, Ollie, insisted on going along to help with the cattle and wagon.

Before leaving, they loaded extra supplies into the wagon for the coming winter. There was a forty-two-gallon barrel of butterball ducks packed down in salt water, and two pigs were placed in a crate and lashed onto the endgate of the wagon.

For the first three days after leaving Steve Kemp's ranch, the small herd made record time. On the third day camp was pitched at the Weatherby ranch on Mineral Creek, three miles east of Alma. The Weatherbys were hospitable westerners, and soon Mrs. Weatherby was at their wagon, begging Mrs. Kemp to bring the children and come into the house.

After supper all of the Kemps gathered at the Weatherby home and spent a most enjoyable evening. Weatherby had just purchased an Edison phonograph, the first one in this section of the country. It was a curiosity to the Kemps. The machine played cylindrical records but had no horn. Sound was transmitted from the phonograph to the listener by cables similar to those used on a telephone switchboard. It was quite amusing to watch the expressions on a person's face while he was listening, for no one else could hear a sound.

From the Weatherby ranch the road, if it could be called such, followed Mineral Creek past the tomb of J. C. Cooney, one of the men who discovered the Cooney mine. The tomb was interesting, because it was a large boulder that had rolled from the mountainside into the creek bottom. It was about twenty feet high and twenty-five feet wide. Cooney was killed near this huge boulder, and his friends, who were mostly miners, drove a tunnel into the rock and placed his body in it. The entrance to the tunnel was sealed with cement and rock, and there was a plaque on the outside wall, which bore the following inscription:

J. C. COONEY

Killed by Victorio's Apaches, April, 29, 1880

Age: 40 years

The second night camp was pitched near the N-Bar Ranch, owned at this time by Bob Lewis, Ben Kemp's cowboy friend. Since the last time Kemp saw him, Lewis had married Maggie Higgins, daughter of Patrick Higgins, a Union soldier who was discharged from the army at Fort Tularosa in the 1870's.

Lewis insisted that the Kemps stay at the ranch house overnight, but since a roaring campfire had already been started, Mrs. Kemp decided to stay at camp. Lewis, who had been a friend of the Cox family for twenty years, jokingly remarked that they might be haunted by Abercome and Wilkerson, two men who were killed at the N-Bar Ranch a few years earlier, since they were camped within twenty feet of their graves. No one paid any attention to his remarks, except Benny, who watched the graves warily until he went to bed. He must have dreamed about spooks all night, because the next morning his father, whose bed he had shared, remarked that sleeping with the boy was like sleeping with a sack full of augers.

The last camp before reaching home was made in some large caves on Houghton Canyon, three miles northwest of the V + T Ciénaga ranch. The next morning everyone was in high spirits over the thought of nearing home.

From the mouth of Corduroy Canyon the route of travel followed the old North Star road. This road had been built by soldiers to haul in supplies when troops were stationed at Camp Vincent at the mouth of Taylor and Beaver Creeks in 1870. The road crossed Indian Creek, then followed the bed of a draw that headed out south onto what is now called Kemp Mesa. The small bunch of cattle being driven ahead of the wagon by Ben and Steve Kemp was about 150 yards in the lead. Progress was slow because there were several sharp, steep grades, and the two Spanish mules, Molly and Coalie, were hard pressed to pull the wagon up some of them. About a quarter-mile up the draw from Indian Creek the road was graded up out of the bed of the draw onto the west hillside. Coalie was on the upper side, and on hard pulls he would always fall into the collar with all his might. Ollie and Mrs. Kemp, with Mary Lilly, the baby, were riding on the wagon seat. The three older children, Benny, Julia, and Beulah, were behind the seat inside the wagon box, which was fitted with heavy bows and covered with a wagon sheet.

When the wagon had reached a point about forty yards up the grade, the singletree clevis on Coalie's side, which was worn from constant use, broke loose, and the mule fell forward, the singletree bumping him on the heels. When Coalie lunged, he threw Molly and the wagon over the side of the roadbed, and the wagon rolled down the hillside into the draw. When Ollie Kemp, who was driving, saw that the wagon was going over the grade, she jumped out on the upper hillside, but Mrs. Kemp and the children were carried with the wagon to the bottom of the draw, some forty feet below. When Ben and Steve Kemp heard Ollie's scream and the noise made by the overturning wagon, they looked back and saw what had happened. They immediately headed back down the road at a dead run, spurring their horses every jump.

Ben Kemp said later that when he reached the wagon, it was hard to tell which was squealing louder, the kids or the pigs. He was so scared that some of his family were seriously injured, he did not take time to raise the wagon sheet. Instead he grabbed his pocket-knife and slashed the canvas. Then he reached through the slashed opening and pulled the children out of the wagon, one at a time, examining each one for injuries.

Miraculously, no one was hurt. The heavy wagon bows had withstood the weight of the wagon and kept it from crushing its occupants. The left, front wheel of the wagon was broken into a dozen pieces, and a trip would have to be made to Taylor Creek for another. Luckily, the Moore place was only four miles away, so Mrs. Kemp, Ollie, and the children walked the remaining distance.

Providence seems to govern in cases of this kind. There were a number of times when everyone in the wagon would have been killed if the clevis had broken. In due time the wagon wheel was repaired, and the wagon was taken to Taylor Creek. After a short visit at the Moore ranch, Steve Kemp and his daughter, Ollie, returned to Blue Creek on horseback.

It was the first of October, and Ben Kemp decided it was time to start building the road to his homestead on Beaver Creek. The most likely route for such a road was down Indian Creek to where it entered Beaver Creek, then down Beaver Creek to the homestead site.

On the balmy afternoon of October 5, 1896, Kemp loaded his wagon with camp equipment, a crowbar, a miner's pick, and a long-handled shovel. After hitching Molly and Coalie to the wagon, he and his six-year-old son climbed aboard and headed for Indian Creek. They pitched camp about a quarter-mile below the old North Star road crossing on Indian Creek, where there was plenty of water and grass for the team.

The next day Kemp started removing rocks from the roadbed he had selected down Indian Creek. When enough boulders had been removed from the roadbed to make it look passable, Kemp hitched the team to the wagon and started down the canyon. When the wagon reached Beaver Creek, it became evident the road needed more improvement. The brake beam was missing from the wagon, and the mules had received such a beating from the wagon tongue that they were barely able to walk.

Beaver Creek was not as rough as Indian, but progress was slow, and it was after sundown when they reached an abandoned beaver-trapper's cabin at the headwater springs of the creek, some three miles below the mouth of Indian Creek.

A cold, southwest wind started blowing about mid-afternoon, and soon a fine mist began falling. A Towers slicker furnished the only protection against the cold wind, and by the time Kemp and his son reached the cabin, the boy's teeth were chattering like a pair of castanets.

While they were unhitching the team from the wagon, they heard a scream that seemed to echo up and down the canyon for miles. It came from the top of a high cliff on the south of the creek opposite the cabin. The scream started with a kind of moan, climbed to a shrill crescendo, then subsided back to the moan. It was the most weird and terrifying sound Benny had ever heard, and the hair on the back of his neck seemed to rise. He rushed to his father, who was tying the work team to a Gambel oak sapling, and asked in a frightened voice what had made the terrifying sound. "Oh," his father answered in a nonchalant voice, "that was just a mountain lion," and continued with his camp chores as though nothing had happened.

After caring for the team, they decided to start a campfire to warm their chilled bodies and cook supper. There was a fireplace at the back of the cabin, so Kemp took a chopping ax from the wagon and cut some short lengths of kindling from a pine log lying nearby. He gathered the wood into his arms, carried it into the cabin, and laid it on the hearth. Then he removed his slicker and hung it above the door.

The lion had screamed a second time while the wood-chopping was in progress, and although his father seemed to pay it no attention, Benny was badly scared and took a stand just inside the open door, where he could peep around the door at the high cliff across the creek. When Kemp had just touched a lighted match to some shavings, there was a rustling sound at the door, followed by a loud shriek from the boy. The scream startled the boy's father, making him scatter the kindling in every direction. He quickly turned around, and there was his son fighting fiercely to free himself from the slicker, which had fallen from the wall onto his head.

The next morning they continued their journey down the creek. When they had gone only a half mile downstream from the cabin, the team bogged down at a sandy creek crossing. The mules had to be unhitched and the wagon pulled out backward. After two day's travel from their camp on Indian Creek, they reached the bench of land where their home was later built. Although it had taken two days to travel only four miles, they felt that they were lucky to make it in that amount of time.

The weather had cleared by the time they reached the homestead site. Since the night air was cool, they built a roaring campfire, and after supper the boy entertained himself by throwing small twigs into the fire.

The scene around camp was wild but beautiful. The pure sparkling water in the creek murmured as it flowed past camp. The creek bottom was covered by a dense growth of black walnut, cottonwood, and Gambel oak, above which the stately crowns of yellow pine could occasionally be seen.

When the cloak of night settled on the deep canyon, it was almost pitch-dark. The night from the campfire was encircled by what seemed like a solid black wall. On the south side of the creek opposite camp, the canyon wall rose to a height of seven hundred feet. Four hundred feet of it was sheer cliff, with a rockslide running from its base to the creek bottom. Owls hidden in the small recesses in this cliff and others kept up a hooting conversation that echoed from wall to wall along the deep canyon.

Thousands of crickets snugly hidden under the malpais rocks that covered the steep mountainside were chirping a kind of accompaniment to the crackling campfire. Suddenly, from across the creek there came a loud yowl, followed by a deep, muffled roar that sounded like some kind of giant tomcat. The boy's interest in the fire suddenly ended, and he crept close to his father and asked in a frightened whisper if that was another lion. "No," said his father, "that's just an old bobcat."

After working on the road for three days, Ben Kemp took his son back to stay with the family at Taylor Creek. Then he returned to Beaver Creek and dismantled the beaver-trapper's cabin. He moved it to the homestead site and rebuilt it on a bench of ground, fifty feet above the creek bottom. After two weeks of back-breaking labor, the cabin was ready for the family to occupy.

The one-room cabin was nothing more than living quarters. It had a dirt roof, a dirt floor, and a smoky fireplace. There was a

131

small window at the back, and a door at the front. The space between the logs was chinked and daubed with mud. Through a crude structure, the cabin would provide warm protection from the cold.

Ben Kemp had an order for a load of freight for the V + T ranch. As soon as the family was settled, he hitched his work team to his wagons and headed for Magdalena. It was one hundred miles from Beaver Creek to town, and the round trip would take eight days. During this time Mrs. Kemp and the children would have to stay at Beaver Creek Canyon, which was frequently visited by lions, bears, and other wild animals of the forest.

The day after Ben Kemp left home, clouds began to drift across the sky, and by late afternoon the sky was overcast. When night fell, it was dark as pitch, and there was a high wind out of the southwest, which sounded like a hurricane as it roared through the pines on the canyon rim, a thousand feet above the lonely little cabin. When a mountain lion screamed several times at dusk, Mrs. Kemp called the children inside and closed the cabin door, bolting it from the inside. She built a fire in the fireplace, and everyone was safe, snug, and warm.

About midnight the wind settled, and a light but steady rain began to fall. The next morning it was still raining, and it continued to rain into the night. About ten o'clock the second night the dirt roof began to leak. It leaked during the rest of the night and all next day after the rain stopped. All of the bedding got wet. Since it was too cool to stay outside and too wet to stay inside, the family spent a miserable day and two nights.

When Ben Kemp returned from Magdalena, Mrs. Kemp told him in no uncertain terms that he could either put a different kind of roof on the cabin or take her and the children to her father's ranch on Taylor Creek, where they would at least have a little protection.

The next morning Kemp saddled a horse and rode to the Billy Keene ranch on Taylor Creek (now the Bob Ake place). He borrowed a froe and a cross-cut saw from Keene, then returned home. The next morning he felled a large, yellow-pine tree that grew at

132

the south foot of the bench of land, where the cabin stood. He sawed the tree into three-foot bolts and split them into halves. Then taking the froe, he split off enough shingles to cover the cabin. When he was finished, the cabin had a roof that would protect them from rain, and Mrs. Kemp was satisfied.

13.
Ranching on Beaver Creek

The Red River Land and Cattle Company owned a ranch called the DD-Bar, located on the East Fork, eight miles south of the Kemp homestead. The company had purchased this property from Dave Cantrell, one of the partners in the Petrie, Cantrell and Moore Cattle Company.

Cantrell and his partners had established the DD-Bar Ranch in 1882, but the partnership did not last long. A disagreement soon developed among the men and resulted in a gun fight. Moore was killed and Petrie relinquished his claim to the ranch. Cantrell sold the DD-Bar to the V + T, then made his home at Fairview, New Mexico, where he was a neighbor of Henry Cox and his family. His daughter attended school with the Cox children during the winter of 1886.

During the spring of 1897, the V + T hired a cowboy by the name of Charley LaBaum to stay at the DD-Bar Ranch. LaBaum, who held a deputy sheriff's appointment, carried a warrant in his pocket for the arrest of a man named Billy Wilson. Wilson had worked for the Hash Knife outfit near Holbrook, Arizona. He was a blond man with a sparse mustache, and he stood about five foot, five inches, and weighed about 125 pounds. He was shy and stuttered profoundly. No one would have suspected this jovial, bow-legged cowboy of being anything more than an ordinary cowpoke, but Wilson had plenty of nerve. He had held his ground among such men as the Grahams and Tewksburys during the Tonto Basin War.

After leaving the Hash Knife outfit, Wilson worked at several cow ranches in Arizona and New Mexico. During that time he was suspected of stealing a bunch of saddle horses, and a warrant was issued for his arrest. He was out of work, and when he heard that

134

Tom Henderson was hiring men for the summer roundup, Wilson headed for the V + T chuck wagon, which was camped at the Link Bar Link Ranch on Diamond Creek. En route to the chuck wagon he stayed overnight at the Billy Keene ranch on Taylor Creek.

The next morning Keene decided to accompany Wilson as far as the DD-Bar Ranch in order to look for some of his cattle that were watering on the East Fork. Neither he nor Wilson knew that LaBaum had a warrant for Wilson's arrest. When they rode up to the ranch house, LaBaum appeared at the kitchen door with a .45–70 Winchester rifle in his hand. Because he wasn't sure that the man with Keene was Wilson, he hesitated, and in so doing almost lost his life. Wilson recognized the deputy's intentions at a glance, so he drew his six-shooter and shot LaBaum before he could raise his rifle. The impact from the .45-caliber bullet knocked LaBaum back into the kitchen.

Keene was dumbfounded by what happened, and his first thought was to get away from the two combatants as quickly as possible. He reigned his horse around and headed for the nearest timber on the east side of the river, spurring his horse every jump. LaBaum, though seriously wounded, crawled back to the kitchen door and peeped out. The only man he could see was Keene, who was just topping out on an open ridge on the east side of the river. Using the door facing as a rest, LaBaum began to shoot at Keene. Luckily the distance was too great for accuracy, and Keene passed out of sight over the ridge without being hit. Wilson ran down the river and made a clean getaway without a shot being fired at him.

An hour after the shooting, Tommy Hill, a neighbor who lived three miles down the river below the DD-Bar Ranch, dropped by to pay LaBaum a visit and found him a very sick man with a bullet wound through the left side of his stomach. The nearest physician was Dr. Wiegmann, who ran the drugstore at Chloride, a small mining town on the east slope of the Black Range, some thirty-five miles away. Dr. Wiegmann was more than seventy years old, and Hill knew it would practically be impossible for the aged doctor to ride horseback over the rough mountainous country between Chloride and the DD-Bar Ranch. Clara Keene, Billy

135

Keene's wife, could always be depended on to help when anyone was sick or hurt. After Hill rendered what aid he could, he hurried to the Keene ranch and told Mrs. Keene that LaBaum was seriously wounded and unless he received proper care he would probably die.

Billy Keene objected to his wife going to the aid of a man who had just tried to kill him, but Mrs. Keene was a western ranch woman, and the thought of a seriously wounded person dying for the lack of proper care was more than her kind heart could bear. So she saddled her cow pony and rode to the DD-Bar Ranch where, with the help of ranch hands and neighbors, she properly dressed LaBaum's wound and helped nurse him back to health.

When LaBaum regained his strength and was able to ride again, he saddled his horse and left the ranch. His departure was somewhat a mystery, because he left his two dogs, Dan and Rover. Since he seemed to be rather fond of the dogs the neighbors thought he would soon return or send someone after them, but he was never heard of again.

It was possible that he might have been waylaid and killed by a notorious murderer and horse thief called the Apache Kid, who was making raids throughout the Mogollon Mountains at the time. In the early 1880's this renegade, a full-blood Apache Indian, was a trusted assistant of Al Sieber, the famous Indian scout, but on June 1, 1888, he was accused of trying to kill Sieber because he charged him with neglect of duty.

For this offense he was sent to the Ohio state prison to serve a term of ten years, but enterprising lawyers soon had him released and back on the San Carlos Reservation in Arizona. Soon after his return he was arrested again and tried. This time he was convicted and sentenced to a term of seven years in the penitentiary at Yuma, Arizona.

On the morning of November 1, 1889, Sheriff Glen Reynolds of Gila County, Arizona, and one of his deputies, a man named Hunkadory Holmes, left Globe with the Apache Kid and nine other Apache prisoners in a stagecoach headed for Casa Grande, where they would catch the train for Yuma.

At the end of the first day's travel the stage reached Riverside, a station on the Gila River, where the prisoners were kept under close guard during the night. The next morning the sheriff placed the Apache Kid and another Indian in the front seat, where they were handcuffed and shackled. The other eight he handcuffed in pairs, leaving them with one hand free.

A few miles from Riverside the road ascended a hill that was covered with a layer of sand nearly a foot deep. When the stage reached the foot of this hill, the stage driver, Gene Middleton, told Reynolds it was necessary that some of the prisoners walk to the top, because the team could not pull the coach through the sand with all of them aboard. The sheriff ordered the eight handcuffed Indians to get out of the stage.

The four-horse team then started their laborious climb up the hill, dragging the stage through the heavy sand, and was soon out of sight of the sheriff and his prisoners. Sheriff Reynolds lined his prisoners up and placed Deputy Holmes at the rear. Then he placed himself at the head of the group and started the march up the hill. This was a fatal mistake. The lead Indians stealthily diminished the distance between themselves and the sheriff while the two in the rear lagged back. When they got within reach of the officers, they gave a war whoop and fell upon them. In less than a minute the Apaches had overpowered and killed Reynolds and Holmes.

Then they took the keys from the dead sheriff's pocket, unlocked their handcuffs, and followed the stagecoach to the top of the hill, where Middleton was waiting for the sheriff and his prisoners to arrive. One of the Indians shot Middleton through the neck, and he fell from the stagecoach to the ground, where he lay sprawled in a puddle of blood.

The shackles and handcuffs were removed from the Apache Kid and his fellow prisoner in the stagecoach. When they all were free, the Indians started robbing the bodies of their victims. Among the items taken from the dead sheriff were his .45 six-shooters, a fine double-cased gold watch, and a money pouch containing $350.

After the blood-thirsty Apaches left the scene, the stage driver,

137

who was not dead, but seriously wounded, regained consciousness and made his way back to Riverside, where he reported what had happened.

Captain John L. Bullis was commanding officer at San Carlos Post. He was the Lieutenant Bullis who had chased Humpy Jackson at Fort McKavett in 1879. He was a capable and experienced officer, having served under such able men as General Ranald Slidell Mackenzie. When word of the killing at Riverside reached him, he made a determined effort to capture the murderers.

Every law-enforcement officer in southwestern New Mexico and southern Arizona was alerted. Within a year all of the Indians who participated in the murder of Sheriff Reynolds and his deputy were captured or killed, except the Apache Kid and an Indian called Ma-sai.

In May, 1890, Mexican *rurales*, under General Kosterlitsky, killed three Apache Indians along the northern border of the state of Sonora, Mexico. One of these Indians was carrying Sheriff Reynolds' watch and six-shooter, which the Apache Kid had supposedly stolen. Although this would indicate the *rurales* had killed him, they must have killed Ma-sai, because ranchers living in the rugged mountains of southwestern New Mexico and southern Arizona knew the Apache Kid had survived and at that time was the leader of a dozen renegade Apaches.

Three months after Kosterlitsky's *rurales* killed the three Apaches in northern Sonora, the Kid, with fourteen other Apaches, made a raid in the Black Range, where they waylaid and killed Oscar Pfotenhaur and Fred Baumbac, two prospectors, at their mining claims on the head of Chloride Creek. A few days later this same gang killed another miner in the Mogollon Mountains.

When Dave Cantrell heard about these wanton murders, he was enraged. Because he did not believe that the army would take action in time to apprehend the renegades, he called a meeting of his neighbors for the purpose of formulating a plan to stop the Apache raids. When Cantrell's neighbors assembled at his home, he suggested they send a wagon into Magdalena for a load of arms and ammunition. He insisted that with this supply of munitions

138

they could invade the Apache reservation and kill every Indian they found. When his neighbors refused to follow him on such a mission, Cantrell flew into a rage and called them cowards. At this point the meeting broke up, and the band of murdering Apaches were allowed to escape to the reservation.

Year after year the Apache Kid committed more crimes. No man could feel safe, knowing this murderous Indian was lurking in the wild section of country through which he had to ride. Death might greet a man any minute from behind some large boulder, a brushy mountainside, or the rim of a box canyon.

On February 27, 1893, the territory of Arizona enacted a law authorizing the governor to offer a reward of five thousand dollars for the capture, dead or alive, of the Apache outlaw and murderer, known and designated as the Kid.

By the middle 1890's, the Apache Kid had become a lone wolf, preying upon his own people as well as the white man. His own tribe hated and feared him. He would kidnap any squaw he fancied, carry her into captivity, and murder her when he tired of her company.

Mrs. Kemp had never relished staying at the isolated cabin on Beaver Creek when such characters as the Apache Kid were making raids through the country. When Tom Henderson offered Ben Kemp a job at the DD-Bar Ranch, she was ready to move. The family arrived at the ranch in the late spring of 1897, and on June 24 a fifth child was born. The baby was named Clara Lue after Mrs. Clara Keene and her aunt Lue Kemp.

Mrs. Keene had promised to be in attendance when the baby arrived. When word reached her, she saddled her horse and headed down the canyon at a run, her pony's feet kicking up a high spray of water at the creek crossings. By the time she reached the DD-Bar, she was soaking wet. Her hair had come down and was twisted around her face, giving her a disheveled and wild appearance. When she stepped through the ranch house door, she presented a picture Mrs. Kemp never forgot.

Because there was no well at the DD-Bar, drinking water had to be carried from a freshwater spring near the riverbank, about fifty yards north of the ranch house. Poison ivy grew near the trail to the spring and the vines looked similar to the wild grapes that grew along the riverbanks. Beulah and Mary, mistaking the poison ivy for a grapevine, sprinkled salt on some of the leaves and ate them. Soon they were deathly sick, and Mary fainted and fell off the steps to the dogtrot.

Mrs. Kemp was frantic and didn't know what to do. At this moment Bob Bullware and Pap Davison, two cowboys working at the Diamond Bar Ranch on Black Canyon, rode up to the house. When they learned what had happened, Bullware rode his saddle horse at a run to the mouth of Beaver Creek, where Ben Kemp was rounding up a bunch of cattle. Pap Davison stayed at the ranch house to help Mrs. Kemp with the children.

Since Mrs. Kemp had started the family wash that morning there was a tubful of hot water on the kitchen stove. At Davison's suggestion they placed Mary in the tub of hot water without removing her clothes. Then they put her in bed, covered with a heavy quilt.

By then Beulah had fainted, and she was lying in the dogtrot between the two cabins. She was given the same treatment as Mary, then the badly scared mother and Davison waited to see if the two children would survive. Within fifteen minutes they had regained consciousness, and in an hour they were out in the yard playing with the other children.

Dan and Rover, Charley LaBaum's two dogs, were still at the DD-Bar when the Kemp family arrived. During the interval between LaBaum's departure and the Kemp's arrival, the dogs had been making trips to the headquarters ranch, twelve miles north. Benny had to keep his dog Shep tied to keep him from following the LaBaum dogs. Although no one wanted to kill the dogs, something had to be done. There were many young calves on the range during the summer months, and sooner or later the two dogs would start killing them.

One morning in early June the dogs were missing, but the second morning, when Ben Kemp and his seven-year-old son walked into the yard at the DD-Bar ranch house, they noticed Rover sitting in

140

the river. The boy's father said, "Now I wonder what in hell is wrong with that dog." He had no more than spoken when the dog rose from his sitting position, waded a few steps up the river, and sat down again. Kemp uttered an exclamation of surprise, because he noticed all of the hair was singed off of the dog's south end.

A few days later he made a trip to the headquarters ranch and learned what had happened. The ranch hands told him they had tied cans to the dogs' tails and tried every other means they knew to get rid of the dogs, but had failed to keep them from coming back to the ranch. Finally someone thought of a sure, but inhumane, way of stopping them. He suggested that a Roman candle be tied to each dog's tail, with the shooting end towards the dog.

Since the Fourth of July was approaching, there were fireworks on sale in town, so someone bought a couple of Roman candles and brought them to the ranch. The two dogs were at the ranch when the candles arrived. They were caught, and a candle was lashed to Dan's tail with a grass string. He was headed toward the DD-Bar with the candle lit. When the first ball of fire seared him, he leaped forward with yelp, but before he had run fifty yards, the grass string burned in two, and the candle fell to the ground.

Rover was not as lucky. When the cowboys saw what had happened to Dan, they lashed the Roman candle to Rover's tail with bailing wire. When all was ready, he was headed south down the canyon towards DD-Bar, and the candle was lit. Like Dan, he leaped forward, and he was still yelping when he passed out of sight, because the candle was searing him with a ball of fire for every fifty yards he ran. As long as the two dogs stayed at the DD-Bar Ranch, never again did they go back to the headquarters ranch. One scorching was enough.

Occasionally there are people who, through jealousy or misunderstanding, begrudge others their success in their work. A man named Bennett, who was working for the company, was such a person. He was a troublemaker and did not value the truth. Soon he was claiming that Kemp was working for the company and mavericking from them at the same time. Finally he prevailed upon Sam Martin, who had worked for the company a number of years, to write a letter to Henry M. Porter, owner of the V+T, stating that Kemp was stealing from the company.

Porter, who considered Martin a reliable cowhand, ordered Henderson to fire Kemp. Since Henderson knew the accusations were false, he flatly refused. When Kemp learned that Porter had ordered him fired, he quit, and Henderson, knowing the injustice of the whole affair, resigned as wagon boss. Porter liked Henderson and offered him a job as general manager if he would continue to work, but Henderson was thoroughly disgusted and turned the job down.

Bill Lewis, brother of Bob Lewis, was present when Bennett dictated the letter Martin wrote to Porter. He confronted Bennett before Kemp and a bunch of cowboys at the DD-Bar Ranch a month later, and Bennett admitted that he had lied. He was fired, but the damage had already been done. Two dependable men with the company's interest at heart were gone. Bennett did not tarry long after he was fired. He saddled his horse, called LaBaum's two dogs, and left between suns. He was never heard from again.

After the Kemp family moved back to Beaver Creek, Tom Henderson's brother-in-law, Charley Gentry, and his family moved to the DD-Bar Ranch. Soon after they arrived, Gentry was thrown from his saddle horse and fatally injured. He lingered for more than a month before he died. All of the neighbors gathered to sit up with him and try to help, but there was nothing they could do. Total paralysis left him no way to convey a word or thought. Ben Kemp, who stayed with Gentry until he died, said only his eyes showed that he recognized anyone. When Mrs. Gentry entered the room, his eyes would light up and follow her movements until she passed out of his sight.

In an effort to save Gentry's life the ancient Dr. Wiegmann was brought across the Black Range on horseback. The thirty-five-mile ride almost killed the doctor. The morning after his arrival at the DD-Bar Ranch, someone asked him how he felt. "Tam!" said Dr. Wiegmann, tenderly feeling the seat of his trousers, "the whole ting iss sore."

Because Gentry's body had started to decay while he was still alive it was necessary that the body be buried immediately after he died. There was no lumber at the DD-Bar, so Bill Lewis, one of the V + T cowboys, volunteered to ride to the headquarters ranch and haul some back.

His saddle horse was in an alfalfa field across the river from the ranch house. When Lewis tried to walk the foot log across the river, he tripped and fell into the water. Furious with himself, he shouted, "You damned old clumsy fool, if you can't walk a foot log to get a saddle horse, you can walk to headquarters." And walk he did, wading the creek like a cow at the road crossings. When he reached the headquarters ranch, some twelve miles to the north, his feet were badly blistered, but he was still in a belligerent mood and gruffly told the sourdough to load a wagon with lumber. Then Lewis climbed into the wagon seat and without another word headed for the DD-Bar, arriving at sundown.

The men at the DD-Bar had been busy all day digging a grave on an open ridge directly across the river from the ranch house. There in the twilight of evening Gentry's grief-stricken family and friends laid him to rest.

Two months after the Kemp family returned to Beaver Creek, Ben Kemp purchased the old McDonald building on Hoyte Creek. It was a two-story log cabin with four rooms and a dogtrot.

While Kemp was moving the cabin to Beaver Creek, his half-sister and her husband, Will Long, arrived from Menard, Texas. The Longs liked the Gila country and decided to stay, so Kemp hired Will to help him rebuild the McDonald house on the bench of land where the original cabin stood.

Since shingles were needed to cover the cabin, they established camp at the west foot of Steer Mesa, where a stand of straight-grained pine trees grew. Using cross-cut saw, ax, froe, and draw-knife, Kemp and Long made fifteen thousand shingles. Then the shingles were hauled down Indian Creek to Beaver Creek and the homestead. Eventually the cabin was finished, and the Kemp family had roomier living quarters and a plank floor.

At shipping time in the fall of 1898, Ben Kemp and Bill Keene decided to put their herds together, and Gilford Chapman, Tim

Chapman, and Frank Davison helped them trail the herd into Magdalena. Mrs. Bill Keene, whom the Kemp children called "Auntie," was chuck-wagon cook, and Benny went along as assistant horse wrangler and chore boy.

When the herd reached Magdalena, Will Long was in town. He was enraged by a disagreement with Ben Kemp, threatening to kill him on sight. Carl Dunnigan, later a partner in the Munsen, Dunnigan, and Ryan hardware store at El Paso, owned a small store in Magdalena at that time. He was a personal friend of Ben Kemp and warned him to be on the alert for trouble.

On the second day in town Kemp, with his eight-year-old son and a justice of the peace, left the Dunnigan store and headed for the justice's office. Turning the corner of a small building, they came face to face with Long and Dunnigan, who were on their way to Dunnigan's store. Long sneered at Kemp and asked contemptuously if there was anything else he wanted.

"You bet there is," said Kemp as he lunged forward.

Long reached for his hip pocket but was too slow. Kemp had his six-shooter in his hand before Long could draw. There would have been a killing if Dunnigan and the justice of the peace had not flown into action. Dunnigan grabbed Long, and the justice grabbed Kemp as he yelled at the top of his voice, "Stop! Stop! I am an officer of the law, and I demand peace."

Long started backing away and disappeared around the corner of the building. The next morning he boarded the train for Texas, never to return.

As soon as the cattle had been shipped and supplies were bought, the chuck wagon and remuda started the return trip home. The first night camp was made on Nine Mile Hill, nine miles west of town. That night two horses were kept in for wrangling the next morning, and the rest of the remuda hobbled out to graze. When the wranglers went out to bring in the remuda the next morning, they discovered that someone had stolen all of the horses except the work teams.

The work teams were brought back to camp, and after a short discussion everyone agreed the best thing to do was to take the

144

chuck wagon to the A. L. Clements ranch at Cat Mountain and pitch camp until the stolen horses could be recovered. The horse thief had left a plain trail, which Ben Kemp and Billy Keene followed at a gallop. They had little patience with such a character and were fully resolved to kill him if he offered the least resistance.

It was late afternoon when the chuck wagon reached Cat Mountain, and Benny, though only a child, was badly worried. He realized his father was on a dangerous mission, one from which he might never return.

When a campground was selected, Gilford Chapman unhitched the team from the chuck wagon, but Mrs. Keene refused to climb down until she had arranged some playing cards on the wagon seat and examined them closely. After she had studied the cards for ten minutes, the worried expression left her face, and she climbed down from the wagon seat to announce that everything was going to be all right.

She said the horses had been found, there had been no fight, and Billy Keene and Ben Kemp would return with the entire remuda between sundown and dark. Gilford Chapman laughed and told her he had no faith in her cards, but everything happened just as she had predicted. Benny was mystified by Auntie's prophesy, and for a few years he dared not question her word. He considered her a kind of supernatural person who could even read his thoughts.

That night around the campfire Kemp and Keene told how they had run the stolen horses down. They said the horse thief, who had been watching his back trail, had discovered he was being followed. He was riding one of the stolen horses, so he roped his own horse out of the remuda and saddled it. When Kemp and Keene rode up to the remuda, there was no one around. The horse thief had abandoned them and ridden for his life. Since none of their horses were missing, they let him go and headed for Cat Mountain.

In May, 1899, a bunch of wild horses were grazing on the range along the Pelona Mountain divide and the open mesas north of North Water Spring. These horses had not been corralled in seven years although many men had tried to run them down.

John Graham and Ben Kemp knew that most of these horses were

145

mavericks and decided to try their hand at catching them. They asked Tim Chapman, Henry Graham, and Mike Sullivan to help them. Benny Kemp and his two cousins, Abe and Hosea Graham, aged nine and eleven, were taken along to ride day herd on the remuda.

Graham and Kemp, who were experienced frontiersmen, knew it would be impossible to catch the wild horses by running them. Their only alternative was to walk them down and then try to corral them. This method called for definite planning, hard riding, and disagreeable exposure to cool weather.

There was a large, round corral at North Water. It was constructed of heavy juniper posts set three feet into the ground, with strong pine poles built to a height of nine feet. Two wings ran seventy yards out from each side of the gate, creating an ideal setup for corralling wild cattle or horses.

The men pitched camp up the draw, out of sight of the spring and corrals. First of all, the remuda had to be trained to run into the corral. The horse wranglers were told that regardless of where the remuda was grazing each afternoon, when it was time to bring them in, they were to be brought back to the corral at a dead run. This was fun for the boys, who practiced cutting figure J's on every horse within reach of their saddle ropes.

The next part of the plan was to start walking the wild horses down. Since this job required someone who was a good trailer, Ben Kemp was selected. Kemp saddled his favorite horse and tied what provisions he could carry behind his saddle cantle. Then he rode into the open country west of the Luero Mountains.

Within an hour he sighted the wild horses on an open ridge about two miles away. There were about twenty head, including colts. Kemp was far enough away that the horses had not seen him. He headed his horse up a draw that ran parallel to the ridge where the horses were grazing. When he got within three hundred yards of the grazing horses, Kemp rode out of the draw onto the ridge. When the wild horses saw him, they sprang into action, making a half circle, then disappearing over the ridge in a cloud of dust. Two hours later Kemp came upon them, and again the horses ran off.

Kemp continued this throughout the day. When night fell he unsaddled his horse and staked him out. He ate a light meal, then spread his saddle blankets on the ground and bedded down for the night.

Early the next morning Kemp was again trailing the wild horses, and about noon he came upon them. They soon left him far behind, but he kept doggedly on their trail and jumped them several times during the day. By nightfall the wild horses had worked their way to the southern boundary of their regular range, the ridges between South Water and Boiler Peak. From there they turned east to the Mud Hole Springs, then to the points west of old Post Caliente on the Alamosa River. On the fourth day they swung west up Wahoo Canyon and back to the eastern edge of their regular range.

Kemp, who knew the nature of wild horses and their habits, had told Tim Chapman before leaving camp that they would probably leave their regular range when he started chasing them but would return to it in a few days if he could keep on their trail.

Because Chapman had neither seen nor heard anything of Kemp or the wild horses for five days, he started watching from high points north and east of North Water. On the afternoon of the sixth day Chapman saw the wild horses at a distance of about four miles. They were traveling at a walk and from all appearance were very leg-weary. Because of their weariness, Chapman had good reason to believe that his brother was not far behind. Sure enough, before he had ridden a mile towards the horses, he saw Kemp top out on a high ridge a quarter-mile behind the horses.

Before leaving camp, Chapman had roped out an extra saddle horse to provide a fresh mount for Kemp. He also brought a fresh supply of provisions which he knew Kemp would very much appreciate after six days of hard riding on scant rations. After the tired and leg-weary horse was exchanged for the fresh mount and Kemp had eaten his first square meal in four days, he and Chapman discussed the final moves in the capture of the wild horses. The horses were beginning to get weak, tender-footed, and leg-weary. It was spring and feed was short. Forced travel over rough country covered with malpais rocks had worn their feet down, making them no

147

match for the steel-shod, grain-fed horses that were kept continuously on their trail. The wild horses had become somewhat accustomed to seeing the lone rider, who could ride two or three hundred yards behind them and keep them headed in a general direction by riding out to the right or left. They would still run if he got too close, but only a short distance.

After the wild horses hit the east side of their regular range, they turned north over the open ridges near Paddy's Hole and followed the Continental Divide north to the south foothills of the Luero Mountains. From there they turned west towards Pelona Mountain. Since most of this country is open ridges, it was possible for the men at camp to keep in touch with the bunch and the man following them.

The horse wranglers, who had been having the time of their lives running the remuda into the corral every afternoon, were now given orders to start grazing their horses on the ridges north of the corral.

Three days later the wild horses showed up on a ridge about four miles north of North Water. The horse wranglers held the remuda at the foot of a steep ridge that ran northwest about a mile north of the corral. About thirty minutes later the wild horses dashed over the ridge and came within thirty yards of the remuda before they saw it. Before they knew what had happened, they were scattered among the remuda and started squealing and milling around. Within seconds the remuda headed for the corral at a dead run, with all the wranglers yelling and applying their ropes as whips.

When the running remuda reached the corral gate, the wild horses sat down on their haunches and tried to stop, but the momentum of the other horses around them slid them through the gate. When one fine stallion saw he was trapped, he killed himself by running straight across the enclosure and colliding head on against the pole corral. The impact broke his neck, and he died within seconds.

Graham and Kemp divided the unbranded horses of the wild bunch between them. They sheared the manes of the old mares that could not be corralled, and an operation was performed on one of

148

their front legs to keep them from running at high speeds. Then they were turned loose on the range again. Several hackamores, cinches, and ropes were made from the hair sheared from the manes.

Among the horses selected by John Graham was a year-old brown stocking-legged colt with a white blaze on its face. He gave the animal to Benny, who named him Baldy Socks. Years later Baldy Socks became one of the best all-around cow horses in southwestern New Mexico, a distinction that cost him his life.

A month after the wild horse work John Graham and George Havell, a neighboring rancher, made a trip into Magdalena after supplies. On their return trip, when they had reached a point about six miles east of Durfey's Well on the Plains of San Agustín, they saw two scrawny-looking animals run from the center of the road to an arroyo about fifty yards south. Wondering what they were, the men stopped their wagons and went to investigate. To their surprise they found two emaciated puppy dogs hiding in a hole they had dug in the arroyo bank for protection. The puppies were almost dead from thirst and starvation, and the ranchers, feeling sorry for the helpless creatures, caught them and put them in their wagons.

When they came to the fork of the road, west of the Point of Rocks, Havell turned south on the Fairview road to his ranch on Poverty Canyon, and John Graham continued on towards his home on Beaver Creek.

When Graham reached the Kemp ranch, he stopped his wagon and asked Benny if he would like to have a cute puppy. Benny was tickled pink, but when he got a good look at the starved animal, he almost backed out. The dog was all head and feet. His ribs stood out so prominently you could have counted them thirty steps away. Although Benny had a premonition the puppy would die, he picked him up and carried him to the house.

The puppy was dull gray with black stripes on his body and legs. When he regained his strength, he joined Shep in chasing stock out of the field. Benny called him Tige because of his courage in bringing in the cattle. Tige was a large dog when he was fully grown. He

149

measured about thirty-six inches at his withers and weighed one hundred pounds. It was learned years later that he was half Irish wolfhound and half greyhound.

Tige and his female companion had been imported from England by Montague Stevens, an Englishman who owned cattle in western New Mexico. The two puppies had been shipped by rail from New York to Magdalena, where they had been placed on a freight wagon that was consigned to Stevens at his SU Ranch, five miles west of Reserve.

Somewhere near the place Graham and Havell found the puppies the crate containing them had fallen from the top of the freight wagon and burst open. Since the freighter had not missed the crate until he reached Durfey's Well, twenty miles west of town, he had no idea where on the road he had lost them. When the two puppies found themselves free and alone on the open plain, they dug a hole in the bank of a nearby arroyo for protection. It was several years after Tige was dead that the Kemp family learned the name of his rightful owner.

Tige was an intelligent dog and soon learned never to chase rabbits or deer. He was obedient and easy to command, but brave and vicious in fights with wild animals. He was the only dog Ben Kemp owned which fought and killed a slightly wounded lion.

Tige's technique in holding wild cattle was the talk of the community. When cattle ran, he would chase them, and as soon as he could, he would circle in front of them. As a rule the cattle would gather into a compact bunch with their heads turned to the outside of the circle. After he had them bunched, Tige would run around and around them, and any animal that broke out would get badly bitten. Kemp could usually ride up and look the cattle over while Tige held them at bay. This saved many miles of hard and dangerous riding. Once in a while Tige would find a bunch of cattle he couldn't hold. When he did and if there was a maverick in the bunch, he would catch it.

On one such occasion Ben Kemp, Johnny Dines, Billy Keene, Johnny James, and Walter Hearn, who were riding down the divide between Taylor and Hoyte creeks, jumped a bunch of wild cattle.

This divide is exceedingly rough and brushy, and because of the brush they were unable to get a run at the herd. While they were trying to work the cattle into an open spot where they could get a look at them, the herd spooked and turned over the rim into Hoyte Creek. It was half a mile to the bottom of this canyon, over cliffs and rock-slides. The cowboys knew the futility of trying to over-take the cattle, so Johnny Dines, who had heard about Tige's feats, turned to Kemp and said, "Well, Ben, turn your dog loose."

Tige always followed about fifteen steps behind Ben Kemp's saddle horse. Kemp looked back at the dog and commanded, "Go get them, Tige."

Tige leaped over the rim and disappeared down the side of the canyon. Ten or fifteen minutes later the cowboys heard a cow bawl-ing at the bottom of the canyon, and Johnny Dines said with a tinge of sarcasm in his voice, "Well, I guess he has got a long ear."

No one answered him, but when they reached the creek bottom, Tige was holding an eighteen-month-old maverick by the ear. Ben Kemp built a small loop in his saddle rope, rode up to Tige, slipped the loop over the maverick's nose, and said, "Turn him loose, Tige."

Tige turned the maverick loose, and John Dines, who was watch-ing the performance, said, "That beats any damned thing I ever saw. You can pick my mount for that dog."

Dines raised horses and owned some of the best in the country, but his offer was turned down. He kept raising the ante until it reached a thousand dollars, but Kemp told him the dog was not for sale at any price.

The other Kemp dog, Shep, was a collie with black and tan mark-ings, a white breast, and a white streak running down the center of his forehead. He had been a gift to Benny from Rebecca Jackson before the Kemps left Texas. He was getting along in years, but he was a smart dog. The Kemp children had trained him to bring in the milk cows and calves from the steep mountainsides along Beaver Creek, thus saving them many hard and dangerous climbs. He was never taken out with Tige on cow work because he had a weakness for chasing rabbits and squirrels.

About the first of September, 1899, Ben Kemp decided to move

151

his family to Fairview so the children could attend school. Since two wagons were needed to haul the household equipment, Tim Chapman agreed to drive one of them, and Ben Kemp drove the other.

The first day travel was slow and disagreeable. The only way out of the deep canyon was to follow Beaver Creek to where it widened into the Corduroy Flats at the upper end of the Beaver box. From there the wagons turned south on the old North Star military road and followed it to the top of the ridge between Corduroy Canyon and Indian Creek. Then they drove east along the divide between the two canyons. There was no road, only cow trails, which were exceedingly rough. To make the trip even more disagreeable, a slushy snow began to fall.

Some large caves on Indian Creek, about two-and-one-half miles up Corduroy Canyon from the present road crossing, were a welcome sight to the tired and half-frozen family. A roaring campfire was built at the entrance of one cave, and soon everyone was warm and snug in its dry interior. Mrs. Kemp prepared a hot meal that everyone enjoyed as they listened to a waterfall cascading over the front of the cave, caused by rain and melting snow that fell from the mountainside above. It had taken a whole day to reach these caves, which were less than four direct miles from the ranch house at Beaver Creek.

The next day the wagons traveled to the head of Indian Creek, over into Boiler Canyon, then up this canyon to the Continental Divide. Camp was made on the other side of the divide, at some log cabins near the present location of the Charley Kline ranch, some three miles west of the seeping springs known as Mud Hole Springs.

Since the evening was cool, a fire was started in the fireplace of the largest cabin to keep the children warm. The adults entered the adjoining cabin and started cooking supper. While the four children, who were supposed to be taking care of Pearl, the baby, were having a romp, Mary opened the door and peeped out into the pathway between the two cabins. She turned to the other children and said, "Old Tige is sure dead this time." When the other children heard this, they rushed to the door and peeped out. Sure enough,

Tige was stretched out in a spasm. Something was terribly wrong with him, and the children began to wail and call their father and mother. When their parents came to the door and saw the dog, they knew that he had strychnine poisoning. They flew into action, using every means they could think of to save his life, but he died within a few minutes. They learned later that Charley Yaples, a rancher in that section of the country, had scattered poison over the range to kill coyotes that were killing his calves and Tige had eaten some of it.

After the family established residence in Fairview, Shep disappeared. They believed that he tried to go back to Beaver Creek and was either killed or died from eating poison. There was also a possibility that he made it back and, finding no one at the ranch, joined a wolf pack, because several animals that were half-dog and half-wolf were caught a few years later by trappers on Black Mountain near Beaver Creek. They bore markings that were similar in color and design to Shep's.

During the year that the Kemp family lived in Fairview, Black Jack Ketchum and his renegades were frequent visitors to town. On one occasion Big Ed and Mose Gibson, two of Black Jack's associates, rode into town and tied their horses to the hitching rail in front of the Meyers' saloon. They walked into the bar and bought a round of drinks. When the town's two merchants learned of their presence, they immediately locked their doors. It was probably a wise move, because the two renegades soon visited the Frank H. Winston store and, finding it locked, fired a shot through the door, trying to shoot the lock off. When they failed to shoot the door open, they walked down to Jake Blum's store and fired two shots through his door. Then they started back up the street, shooting at first one door and then the other.

The Kemp family lived in an adobe house on the south side of the street, about twenty yards west of the Meyers' bar. Mrs. Kemp, fearing that the outlaws would fire into the building, called all of the children into the kitchen at the back of the house, where they would be safe. Ben Kemp took a stand with his Winchester at a window facing the street and declared he would kill both of the out-

153

laws if they fired on his house. The outlaws shot through a window of the neighboring house, but did not fire on the Kemp dwelling.

As soon as the two outlaws had left the bar, Meyers locked the door and hid behind a large, box-iron stove that was used to keep the barroom warm. When Big Ed and Gibson returned to the bar and found it locked, they fired a couple of shots at the lock, trying to shoot the door open. When this failed, they unhitched their horses, mounted, and left town on a run, firing their six-shooters and yelling like Comanches as they rode.

It was a miracle that these outlaws were not killed. If Ben Kemp had been a cold-blooded killer, he could have shot both of them with the approval of the town's citizens.

Big Ed, whose legal name was Ben Kilpatrick, was killed by an express messenger near Sanderson, Texas, in 1912. Mose Gibson left the country and never came back.

The schoolhouse at Fairview was across the arroyo south of town, and the schoolteacher at that time was August Meyers, son of the owner of the bar. Mrs. Meyers, August's mother, ran a boarding house, and his sister Pauline owned and played a piano. The music fascinated Benny, who had never heard a piano before. His only acquaintance with music while the family lived at Beaver Creek had been the religious hymns his mother sang or the warbling of birds during the spring and summer.

During school one day in early March, 1900, there was an earthquake that caused the north wall of the adobe building to sway, first in and then out, leaving a four-inch crack between the side walls and the end wall. The children and teacher all scrambled out of the house without injury, but once they were outside, they were afraid to go back in. School was dismissed, and the schoolteacher reported the damage to Frank H. Winston and Thomas Schales, two of the school trustees. After they examined the schoolhouse, they said that it was too dangerous to use but that they thought it could be repaired by running two heavy, iron rods from one side wall to the other and clamping them into place. Winston owned a complete blacksmith shop, with dies, taps, and rod iron, but there was no single rod long enough to span the distance from one side

154

wall of the schoolhouse to the other. The only solution was to weld two of the rods together, but there was no one in town who could do it. While discussing the problem, Tom Schales mentioned Ben Kemp, who was doing some assessment work for him at the Edwards' camp in the north end of the Cuchillo Mountains.

"What?" said Winston. "You must be out of your mind, Tommy. That man's a cowboy and wouldn't know anything about welding."

Thomas Schales, who was an Englishman, said, "Woo, woo, woo, you can't tell about that man, and, don't you know, he might surprise you."

John Damron, who had been Kemp's partner in the water-well rig at Midland, Texas, in 1894, had moved to New Mexico and was living in Fairview. Schales asked him to go to the Edwards' camp and bring Kemp to town. When the two men returned to Fairview, Winston turned his blacksmith shop over to them, and within an hour they had the rods welded. The next morning holes were drilled through the side walls of the schoolhouse with a piece of hand steel. The rods were run through the walls and clamped back into place. Sixty years later this building was still standing with the rods in place.

In the last part of March, 1900, the Kemp family moved back to Beaver Creek. The silence of the deep canyon was broken by noise that only a healthy, footloose family can make. Years later Ben Kemp said that during this time there was a report that the Apache Kid was making a raid through the Black Range and upper breaks of the Gila. While riding the range adjacent to Beaver Creek, he would often wonder if everything was all right at the ranch house. On such occasions he would ride to the rim of the deep canyon and look down. If he could see lots of activity around the house and hear everything from a love song to bloody murder, he knew everything was just fine and would continue his ride.

During the summer of 1897, Kemp, who always kept a Winchester catalog, noticed a .30-caliber, model 1895 rifle listed. After checking on its range and striking power, he decided to buy one. Nearly every year there was a report that the Apache Kid was making a raid through the country. Kemp was convinced that if

155

the rifle equaled the catalog's claims, he could pick Indians off the high points near the cabin on Beaver Creek. Since there was no rifle of this kind in Magdalena, Carl Dunnigan ordered one from St. Louis, Missouri. The first ammunition sent out for the rifle was all solid jackets, and Ben Kemp put on an exhibition of shooting that left the V + T cowboys awed.

During the summer and autumn of 1900, Ben Kemp was chuck-wagon cook for the V + T. George Foster was wagon boss, and the cowhands included Ed and Jerry Kelly, Ab Alexander, Jack Bean, Walter Nephew, George Owsley, Billy Bodenhammer, and Bill Hutchington (alias Sourdough Bill). They were a jolly and carefree group of men, who were always rawhiding and playing pranks on one another. This was illustrated in a conversation about the .30–.40 rifle that belonged to Kemp.

One night while they were sitting around the campfire, the men were hotly debating about Kemp's rifle and its possibilities. Finally one of the cowboys said. "Mr. Kemp, what is the range of that rifle anyway?"

"Well, the Winchester people say it will shoot two miles with velocity," Kemp answered.

For five seconds after he answered the question, not a word was spoken. Then in a stage whisper one of the cowboys asked the man next to him, "What's that?"

"Why," said the other cowboy, "that's one of those little three-wheeled things that runs up and down the railroad track." There was quite an uproar of laughter, since a silly question had got a silly answer, with velocity and velocipede a bit mixed up.

After Tom Henderson quit the Red River Land and Cattle Company in 1897, Henry Porter decided he needed a general manager for the Gila division, so he hired a man by the name of Smart and sent him out to the Ciénaga headquarters. For some reason Smart was not satisfied with the setup and left within a year. Then Porter rehired Charley Woodley, his wagon boss in the early 1880's. Woodley claimed the outfit was run down and needed repairs, and when Porter failed to agree with him, he quit. Finally he hired Cole

Railston, a Diamond A cowboy from near Engle. Railston worked as general manager from 1900 until the company sold its interest to the Pollock brothers in 1909. The Pollock brothers kept him as their general manager until they sold the cattle and ranches.

Railston made a good general manager, but he had a tendency to fight with small ranchers, a trait that caused him trouble with his own ranch hands. Less than a year after he was hired as general manager, he drove out to the V + T camp at the Adobe Ranch and told his pack boss, Rufe Freeland, not to hold the small ranchers' cattle. This made his wagon boss, Happy Jack, angry, and the next morning as they rode through the outside gate at the ranch house to make the day's roundup, Happy Jack yelled at Freeland, who was about fifty yards away, "Rufe, hold the little men's cattle, and I'll take them to them." Railston jerked his horse to a halt, and then he and Happy Jack returned to the ranch house.

Ben Kemp was chuck-wagon cook at the time, and the wagon was camped in the ranch-house yard within fifteen feet of an open window to the room in which Railston and Happy Jack had their argument. The things that Happy Jack said to Railston were not complimentary, and he probably would have killed him if Railston hadn't backed down. When Happy Jack came out of the room, he was still raging mad, and as he passed the chuck wagon, he dropped his new Towers slicker to the ground, saying, "Here, Ben, this is yours. I'm off for Texas."

After Happy Jack's run-in with Railston, all the small ranchers were barred from working with the V + T wagon. So the small ranchers pooled and made their own cow work. This was to their advantage. The country over which they worked was rough and timbered, and there were many one- and two-year-old mavericks among the wild cattle that used this range. These mavericks were divided among the men who made up the pool. If they had been working with the V + T wagon, they could not have done this since the company would have claimed most of them. During the small ranchers' cow work every available man had to be used. Boys were used as day herders and horse wranglers, and soon these youngsters

157

had a little ditty they sang around the day herd. It was sung to the tune of "Riding Old Paint," and ran as follows:

Old Cole Railston came out from town,
He says I'm a wolf and my tail drags the ground,
He howled too loud and had to back down,
Instead of a wolf he sounds like a clown.

On one occasion during this time Ben Kemp and his nephew, Henry Graham, hunted mavericks in the Pot Hole country between Taylor Creek and Hoyte Creek. They were gone twelve days and brought back fifteen mavericks, one of them a three-year-old cow with a calf following.

One day during their camp at the Pot Holes, they were riding down the divide between Taylor and Indian creeks and found the tracks of a mother bear and two cubs. They thought it would be fun to rope them, but when they saw that the mother was a huge, brown bear, they decided to kill her and capture the cubs. Kemp was carrying his .38–.55 Winchester on his saddle, and without dismounting, he pulled it from the saddle scabbard, took quick aim, and fired. The heavy bullet hit the bear in the side but failed to knock her down. Giving a roar of pain, she cuffed the cubs until they climbed a tree. Then the infuriated animal charged Kemp and his horse. At times during the fight that followed the bear was close enough to reach for the horse's hind legs. Then Henry, who was sitting astride his horse seventy yards away, would yell, "Run, Uncle Ben! Run!" Since Kemp had only seven rounds of ammunition, he had to make every shot count, and he paid little attention to Henry. When he had fired his last shell, the bear was still on her feet, but blood was streaming from her mouth, and a few minutes later she staggered out of sight over a ridge.

Henry was riding a pet horse called Boady. This pony had been raised a dogie, because his mother had died when he was only two days old. He had never been known to buck. Ever since he was a young colt sucking a bottle, he had been used to people petting him. He was as gentle and unexcitable as a horse could be.

The cubs were still sitting in the pine tree that the mother bear

158

had made them climb, and Henry began trying to rope one of them. Finally he succeeded, but when the cub hit the ground, it charged Boady, hugged one of the horse's front legs, and began to bite. The docile, sleepy-headed pony suddenly came to life, and in cowboy language he went "high, wide, and handsome." Henry had to do some fancy riding to keep from being thrown. He hated to think what might happen if the mother bear returned and found him with one of her cubs roped. Boady finally kicked loose from the cub and quit bucking. Finally both of the cubs were caught, and their feet and mouths were tied, but no one could get within ten feet of Boady with one of them.

Kemp, who intended to make pets of the two cubs, decided to try to carry both of them on Gray Buck, his horse that was noted for bucking. After the cubs were rechecked to see that they were securely tied, Henry lifted them up, and they were stacked on the horn of Ben Kemp's saddle. Then Kemp and Henry headed for Beaver Creek. After riding a couple of miles, one of the bottom cub's front feet came untied, and he raked Gray Buck's front shoulder with his claws. Then and there the cow pony put on an exhibition of bucking seldom witnessed at a rodeo. The top cub was thrown from the saddle on the first jump, but the bottom one hugged the saddle horn with its free foot, and every time the horse jumped, the cub came up and hit Kemp in the face. After both cubs were thrown from the saddle and everyone was collected again, the cubs had to be killed, because it was impossible to get near either horse with them.

When the Kemp family moved to Beaver Creek in 1896, the mountains west of the creek were called the Little Range. Mrs. Kemp was responsible for the name being changed to Black Mountain, because she called them the Black Hills after a song she sang about the Black Hills of South Dakota. Later, Fred Winn of the United States Forest Service listed them on his maps as Black Mountain. Such names as Deer Canyon, Upper Gate Canyon, and Collins and Trap Corral canyons were all names given by the Kemp family.

Deer Canyon derived its name from a tussle Mary Kemp had

159

with a wounded deer that she shot on the north rim of the canyon. The deer, which had two broken legs, floundered down the steep side of the canyon with Mary in pursuit and fell into an eight-foot arroyo at the bottom. When the deer tried to scramble out of the arroyo, Mary grabbed it by a hind leg, and both of them fell back into the bottom. Then she finished the animal by cutting its throat with a butcher knife she had taken from the kitchen table that morning.

Trap Corral Canyon derived its name from a heavy log corral built to trap wild cattle in 1901 by Ab Alexander. Collins Canyon, Grandma Canyon, Shiney Hill, and Big Flats were names that have probably disappeared since the Kemp family left Beaver Creek in the year 1910.

The warm springs at the head of Beaver Creek were called the Big Springs by the Kemp family. The first water cress on the East Fork of the Gila River was planted in these springs. Mrs. Bill Keene brought cress from the Río Grande Valley in 1893 and planted it in a fish pond just north of their ranch cabin on Taylor Creek. In 1898, Ben Kemp took some of this cress and planted it in the warm springs at the head of Beaver Creek. The cress flourished, and by 1906 there was water cress from the headwaters on Beaver Creek to Cliff on the Gila River.

Cox Canyon, on the headwaters of Negrito Creek, and Cox Creek, a tributary entering Taylor Creek just above the present Wall Dam, were both named for Henry Cox, Mrs. Kemp's father. Collins Park was named after John Collins, who lived on the south side of the valley at the edge of a grove of oak timber. Kemp Mesa, between Taylor and Indian creeks, lies east of the old Kemp ranch house on Beaver Creek, and the west edge of the mesa was a part of the old Kemp horse pasture.

Such names as Corduroy Canyon, Railroad Canyon, Houghton Canyon, Indian Creek, and Taylor Creek were early names when the Kemp family moved into the Moore place on Taylor Creek in 1896. Corduroy Canyon derived its name from a corduroy roadbed that was laid along the canyon's floor by United States Cavalry in

160

1870 so that ox teams could pull loaded wagons over the marshy places along the bottom of the canyon without bogging down.

Railroad Canyon was named by the V + T cowboys, who noticed hundreds of wooden stakes left along the canyon by engineers of the Santa Fé Railway, who ran a survey from Magdalena to Silver City in 1885. Taylor Creek was named for James Taylor, who owned a ranch at the upper end of the main box on the creek. Taylor was killed on Thanksgiving night, 1909, in a gun fight with Ike Futch at a dance in Fairview.

Bicycle Flat, half a mile down the canyon south of the old V + T headquarters ranch, was named as the result of a wager between two cowboys named Ed Kelly and Sourdough Bill Hutchington, who were staying at the ranch in 1901. It was near Christmas time, and someone had sent them a collection of newspapers and magazines from Magdalena. Along with the reading material came a gallon jug of firewater. One afternoon the two cowboys came into the ranch early, and after turning their horses into the corral at the barn, they built a roaring fire in the fireplace at the bunkhouse. Although there was no snow on the ground, the day had been windy and cold. When they first arrived at the bunkhouse, they had both taken a drink out of the whisky jug, and after the room warmed up, they felt snug and cozy. Sourdough Bill started reading a copy of the *New York Times*, and when he read the sports' page, he found the returns on the latest bicycle races, giving the time and rate of speed. Sourdough had little knowledge of bicycles or how fast they could go, and the speed that the newspaper claimed they had traveled sounded unreasonable to him. Slamming the paper down on the floor, he yelled, "Hell, it's all a damned lie. It can't be done."

"What's biting you?" Ed asked.

Grabbing up the paper, Sourdough pointed his finger at the report and said, "Read that."

Ed Kelly, who had ridden a bicycle to school when he was a boy, read the article and said, "That's not impossible."

"The hell it ain't," Sourdough yelled.

"No," said Ed, "if you could pedal a bicycle fast enough, it could run as fast as a horse."

161

"Hell's fire," said Sourdough, "there never was and never will be one of them flimsy contraptions that can run that fast."

A year earlier the wagon boss, a man by the name of Jack Chandler, had quit and moved his family to Fairview. When the Chandlers first came to the headquarters ranch, Mrs. Chandler had brought a bicycle with her, but the roads were so rough that she could not use it. She had placed the wheel in the shed at the back of the ranch house and left it.

The argument about the speed of bicycles lasted the rest of the afternoon. When Ed recalled that Mrs. Chandler had left her bicycle out in the shed, he told Sourdough that the next day he would show him that it could run as fast as a horse. The next morning Ed examined the wheel and found it in fair condition. He pumped up the tires and circled it around the ranch-house yard a time or two. Sourdough, who was watching him, said, "I'll bet you five dollars that damn thing can't run as fast a horse." When Ed called his bet, Sourdough went out to the barn and saddled what he thought was the fastest horse in his mount. Ed rode the bicycle down the canyon around the point south of the ranch house to the level stretch of ground which was about a quarter-mile long. He stopped at the upper end of this level stretch and waited for Sourdough.

When Sourdough arrived, he threw Ed one end of his saddle rope and tied the other end fast to his saddle horn. Ed tied his end of the rope just below the handlebars on the bicycle, and they were ready to go. Sourdough started off slow to give Ed a chance for his money, but by the time he had covered a hundred yards, he was leaning forward in the saddle and quirting his horse, which was already scared and trying to put distance between itself and the odd-looking contraption that was being dragged along behind. Ed was managing to keep his balance fairly well, and it looked as though Sourdough was going to lose his bet, but when they reached a point about halfway across the flat, Sourdough ran over a boulder about a foot in diameter. When the front wheel of the bicycle hit the rock, it broke, driving the front frame back under the pedals. Ed hit the ground with terrific force and rolled fifty feet. Sourdough's frightened horse ran another hundred yards, dragging what was left of the bicycle, before Sourdough could circle him back to Ed, who had regained his feet and was groaning and rubbing the sore spots. Sourdough didn't seem the least bit concerned about the hard bumps that Ed had taken, but was still very interested in proving his point.

"Oh yes, you dim-witted numskull," he said, "I told you that damned thing couldn't run as fast as a horse." From that time on, the open stretch of ground around the point below headquarters (now the Slash Ranch) was called Bicycle Flat by the old-timers.

Many of the newer names, such as Wolf Hollow, Gillett Tanks, Bell Canyon, Green Fly, and Turkey Snout, were named by Dub Evans and his cowboys twenty-five years after the Kemp family first settled on Beaver Creek.

During the time that troops were stationed at Camp Vincent, someone was supposed to have discovered placer gold in Beaver Creek. It was reported that from three to five dollars a day could be panned out along the creek. Thirty years later one of the old soldiers, who had been stationed at the camp, led a party of six men up Beaver Creek in search of placer gold. They never found a trace, and it remains a mystery to this day why this man was so badly mistaken. The only mineral in the beds of both Taylor and Beaver creeks is a small amount of placer tin. The tin nuggets are heavy and can be panned, but their colors are mostly pink, red, or black, and have little or no resemblance to gold.

Soldiers from Camp Vincent must have spent quite a bit of their time prowling up and down Beaver Creek, because there was still plenty of evidence of their having been there when the Kemp family moved in twenty years later. While Kemp was clearing the bottom land just below his residence, he found a nickel-plated flute engraved with the name of the company and regiment of some of the troops stationed at Camp Vincent. The instrument was almost in as good condition as it was the day it was lost. Kemp, who valued it little as a souvenir, gave the flute to Benny, who left it lying on a doorstep where it was stepped on and ruined.

Undertakers Hill is the point at the mouth of Taylor and Beaver creeks. The road down this hill was built by the soldiers at Camp Vincent about 1870. It is a part of the old North Star route between Fort Wingate and Fort Bayard. The rock formation on this point is in layers, ranging all the way from an inch to several feet in thickness, which makes the roadbed look more like a flight of irregular steps than a road. The descent from the top of the hill into the creek was a hazardous undertaking, and from this the hill derived its name.

14.
The Capture of Black Jack Ketchum

From 1897 to 1900, Black Jack Ketchum and his renegades were frequent visitors to the Black Range and Mogollon Mountains. One of their holdouts was at what is known as Outlaw Park in the Black Range. This so-called park is actually a hidden canyon. At one time this canyon connected with Wahoo Canyon, which heads at the Continental Divide and runs east into the Alamosa River, a few miles north of old Post Caliente. Ages ago a landslide closed the mouth of the Outlaw Park Canyon so completely that anyone traveling up Wahoo Canyon would never suspect that a deep gorge had once entered it. Above the landslide the walls of the canyon consist of a series of cliffs that terminate at the bottom in tall, rock spires, with cracks between them so wide that a saddle horse can pass through them with ease. The floor of the canyon just above the landslide is almost level because of a dirt fill that has washed there from the surrounding mountainsides for untold centuries. The floor is about three hundred yards wide and covered with an excellent stand of grama grass. The canyon can be entered only at two points, and anyone who did not know the location of these hidden passages could not enter the canyon on horseback. The outlaws built a small cabin and a horse corral in the canyon. It was a wild place, well suited for wild men.

One day while Ben Kemp and two other small ranchers were riding with the V + T cowboys near the head of Wahoo Canyon, they topped out on a ridge and saw two men on horseback in the bottom of a draw. When the two men saw them, they quickly dismounted and pulled their Winchesters from their saddle scabbards. They laid their rifles across the seats of their saddles and drew a bead on the approaching cowboys.

Johnny Sauceer, one of the small ranchers, pulled off one of his gloves·and waved it at the men in the draw. They in turn motioned the cowboys to approach, but they remained concealed behind their saddle horses. When the cowboys rode up to the two men, they recognized them. They were Black Jack Ketchum and one of his followers, Big Ed Kilpatrick, the man who shot up the town of Fairview in 1900.

The outlaws were glad they had run into a bunch of cowboys instead of a sheriff's posse, and after asking a few questions, they joined the cowboys and rode back to the Adobe Ranch with them.

The chuck wagon was camped on the open prairie. It was autumn, and there was a light but cool wind out of the west. Everyone was wearing a coat or jumper to keep warm. The two outlaws wore heavy overcoats and stood around with their hands in their coat pockets, which showed the outline of heavy Colt's revolvers.

Ketchum and his pal were friendly enough and laughed and joked with the cowboys, but it was easy to see they were continuously on the alert. When the cook called chuck, the outlaws got their plates and filled them, but they were careful not to sit within arm's reach of anyone.

After supper the remuda was driven into a rope corral, and the men started roping out their night horses. Johnny Sauceer's mount was in the bunch. He raised his own cow ponies, and they were rated among the best in the country. He branded Flying X, and Black Jack, who had an eye for good horses, soon spotted one of Sauceer's. Pointing the horse out, he asked, "Who owns that Flying X horse?"

"I do," answered Sauceer, "but if you want him, take him."

"No," said Black Jack, "I'm not picking on little men. These big companies furnish me horses to ride." Then he turned to the V + T waddy who was roping out horses and said, "Young feller, just rope me out the two best horses the company owns in this remuda."

The V + T man did not hesitate. He roped what he thought were the two best company horses and turned them over to Black Jack and his partner. The two outlaws saddled the horses, mounted, and rode out of sight down Corduroy Draw.

166

Jack Chandler, who had been wagon boss for the V + T a few years earlier, was now working as outside man for Frank H. Winston, who owned the R-Bar-R. He was supposed to have a deputy sheriff's appointment, and after the outlaws left, someone said, "Jacky, them men were outlaws with a heavy reward on their heads. Why didn't you take them?"

"Hell's fire," answered Jack, "what you think I am, a damn fool? Them guys had me covered all the time. I'm not ready to commit suicide."

One of the horses the outlaws took was picked up later along the Mexican border, but the other one was never found.

Although Black Jack's gang did not steal from the small ranchers to any extent, they did ride their horses during some of their forays. This practice placed a few of the ranchers in an awkward spot. Such was the case when Big Ed and his partner found Ben Kemp's remuda grazing the range west of Beaver Creek. They rounded up Kemp's horses and roped out a fresh mount, turning their ridden-down ponies loose with Kemp's remuda.

A few minutes before noon two days later the two outlaws rode leisurely into Hillsboro, county seat of Sierra County, and tied their saddle horses to a hitching rack, where two other horses were hitched. They watched the courthouse until the sheriff went home for lunch. Then they casually walked into the town's bank, where one of them pointed his six-shooter at the cashier's head and told him to hand over all the money in the bank and be damned quick about it.

The cashier said later that the six-shooter barrel looked as big as a stovepipe to him, so he gave the bandit the money without argument. When the outlaw had the money in hand, he started towards the door of the bank building where his partner was standing guard, telling the cashier as he exited that if he as much as stuck his head out of the door while they were around, he would get it shot off.

The outlaws walked to the hitching rack, untied their horses, and rode leisurely down the road. As soon as they turned the first point out of sight of the town, they spurred their horses into a run and used every trick they knew to delay and confuse the posse which they knew would soon follow.

It was several minutes before the cashier thought it safe enough to slip out of the bank building and spread the alarm. When he did, a posse of eight men was quickly formed and started off in hot pursuit of the bank robbers. The trail of the outlaws led back into the rough country along the crest of the Black Range divide. There it was lost, and the posse was forced to return to Hillsboro empty-handed.

A ten-year-old boy noticed the outlaws' two horses while they were tied to the hitching rack, and when the sheriff returned from the chase, he gave him their description.

One of the horses was the brown-blazed, stocking-legged Baldy Socks. The only brand the pony bore was the Bush, which Ben Kemp used. With this information, the officers came to the conclusion it was Kemp and his half-brother, Tim Chapman, who robbed the bank. Word was sent to Charley Yaples, a deputy sheriff at Grafton, to locate Kemp and Chapman and find out if they were implicated in the robbery. Yaples, who knew both parties, had his doubts, but he saddled his horse and headed for Beaver Creek.

Kemp had not missed his two horses. He was riding the range east of Beaver Creek, between Taylor and Indian creeks, later known as Steer Mesa. One day when he reached a point just below the old Collins' cabin on Indian Creek, he dismounted and sat down beneath the drooping limbs of a pine tree to rest. When he had been there only a few minutes, he saw a man on horseback coming down the canyon towards him. Since the trail ran within fifteen yards of his shade tree, he just sat still and watched the rider approach. When the horse and rider had reached a point some fifty yards away, he could see that the man was Charley Yaples.

Kemp and his horse were partly hidden by the limbs of the tree, and Yaples did not see him. When Kemp realized that Yaples was going to ride by without seeing him, he called out, "Hello, Charley, what brings you over in this part of the country?"

Yaples was startled when he heard the voice of the man he was

Black Jack Ketchum. "Because his added weight had not been allowed for, he was given too much drop from the scaffold and was decapitated by the rope."

Rose Collection, Division of Manuscripts
University of Oklahoma Libraries

looking for coming almost from under his stirrups. He swung around with such violence that he scared his horse, which jumped and almost threw him. When he regained his balance, he reined his horse around and rode back to where Kemp was sitting. He dismounted and shook hands with Kemp, telling him what he had come for. This was the first Kemp had heard of the bank robbery, and he was worried as to what the outcome might be. He doubted that he would ever see his favorite saddle horse again. After talking a few minutes, Yaples was convinced Kemp knew nothing of the bank robbery, so he rode back to Grafton.

The next morning Kemp saddled his horse and rode out to the points west of Beaver Creek, where his saddle horses were grazing. To his surprise he found Baldy Socks and the other pony with the remuda, but he noticed that both horses were shod all around, whereas they had been unshod when he turned them out on the range. The horses also showed signs that they had been ridden unmercifully. Big Ed and his partner had returned to Beaver Creek after robbing the bank, rounded up Kemp's remuda, roped out their own horses, and left the country. The sheriff's office soon learned that it was Big Ed and his partner who robbed the bank and that the horses they were riding were stolen.

During the time that Black Jack and his gang were causing trouble, the express companies hired a man by the name of Scarborough to run them down. Scarborough was a tough man himself, having served a term in the penitentiary. When he was released from the penitentiary, the Wells Fargo Express Company helped him get a deputy U. S. marshal's appointment, with the understanding he would either kill or capture Black Jack and his gang.

One day while the Kemp family was returning from a visit to the Nat Straw place on the East Fork, Scarborough and another tough-looking character rode up alongside the wagon and motioned Ben Kemp to stop. When the wagon came to a halt, Scarborough said, "Mr. Kemp, I understand you let Tom Ketchum and his gang stop at your ranch."

"Scarborough," said Kemp, "I am a rancher, and it is an established custom in this country that when a man rides up to your house in late afternoon and asks to stay overnight, you ask him in. I never make it a point to ask a man who he is, what he has done, or where he is going. I treat everyone alike. If you or anyone else comes to my ranch, he will be welcome if he acts like a gentleman. Under the circumstances, what would you do?"

Scarborough thought this over a moment, then he raised his hat and scratched the top of his head, saying, "Well, I guess that is about all you could do." Then he and his companion rode up Taylor Creek towards the Keene ranch.

A few months later, some of Black Jack's gang waylaid Scarborough and another man near Hachita, New Mexico. Scarborough was shot through the thigh. The .30–.40-caliber bullet shattered the bone in his leg and killed his horse. He crawled into some rocks, and his companion went for help, but Scarborough bled to death before help reached him.

Later, Black Jack and two of his gang tried to rob a Santa Fé passenger train near Clayton, New Mexico. Just as they were about to succeed, a porter on the train eased open a door at Black Jack's back and shot him through the arm, shattering the bone. Ketchum knew he would soon need medical aid and told his two companions to go on to their favorite hideout in the Black Range and he would come to them later. The outlaws soon separated. Black Jack's arm became so painful he was forced to seek help immediately. He selected an isolated ranch and tried to ride to it, but was so weak from loss of blood that he fainted and fell off his horse a hundred yards short of the house.

When he regained consciousness, he crawled into the shade of a nearby tree and called to the people at the house to bring him a drink of water, but they had heard about the attempted train robbery and were afraid to go near him. Black Jack suffered untold agonies and decided he did not have long to live. He knew that gangrene had set in on his wounded arm and that he would die within the next few hours if he didn't get medical aid.

Two hours later the posse that was following Black Jack trailed him into the isolated ranch and saw him sitting with his back against the tree. The men, knowing they were facing a dangerous and

171

desperate criminal, were afraid to ride across the three hundred yards of open ground that separated them. They called to him, demanding that he come to them and surrender. Black Jack waved a white handkerchief with his good arm and told them he was too weak to walk and thought that he was dying. He begged them to come to him, but they suspected a trap. After a lengthy discussion two men volunteered to go to Black Jack, providing the rest of the posse would keep Ketchum covered with their rifles. Black Jack, thinking that he had only a short time to live, was glad to surrender.

After his capture, Ketchum was rushed to Clayton, where a surgeon had to amputate his arm above the elbow to save his life. Then he was placed in jail, and a close guard was kept on him. In a short time he was tried and convicted of murder and robbery, and the court sentenced him to be hanged.

It was several months before he was executed, and during this time he gained quite a bit of weight. Because his added weight had not been allowed for, he was given too much drop from the scaffold and was decapitated by the rope.

15.
A Mining Town and Its Citizens

About daylight on the morning of May 24, 1900, Benny was aroused from a sound sleep and hustled out to the back yard of the ranch house at Beaver Creek. Here he found Rusty, a flea-bitten gray horse, saddled and ready to go. Rusty had a red bandanna handkerchief tied around his neck and Benny's father told him to mount and pound saddle leather to get his Grandmother Chapman, who was living at the old Keene place on Taylor Creek at this time.

When Benny reached the yard gate at the Keene place, he saw his sixty-one-year-old grandmother come out of the house at a run, yelling for him to dismount. When she reached Rusty, she leaped into the saddle and hit him down the hind leg with a quirt. Rusty left with a bound, kicking water high in the air at the creek crossing west of the house.

Benny was mystified by all the excitement until his grandmother returned that evening and told him he had a brand new baby brother. He soon learned that the baby was named John Stephen Timothy after three of his uncles. He was the only member of the family with three given names. Years later all that was needed to start a fight with him was to call him John Stephen Timothy.

In 1901, Railston hired Ab Alexander as wagon boss. Several of the cowboys who had worked for George Foster while he was V + T wagon boss stayed on. Among them was a long, lanky, solemn cowpoke called Billy Bodenhammer. Everyone in the outfit liked Bodenhammer but rawhided him for being a bellyacher.

While talking over the things he had seen around cow camps, Bodenhammer said that in all his experience as a cowboy he had never seen the leggings put on anyone. This amused the other cowboys, who told him his experience was too short and he had too much lint in his hair to know about things like that.

One morning during the summer roundup the wagon was camped on Kennedy Canyon, and Bodenhammer, who was on horse wrangle, did not return to camp until after the other boys had eaten their breakfast. Ben Kemp, who was chuck-wagon cook, had cooked a tomato pie that morning, and the other cowboys had eaten all of it. When Bodenhammer found out what had happened, he began to bellyache, saying he liked those pies better than anything else and the dirty bums had eaten it all up and never left him a bite.

"Billy," said Kemp, "I would cook you another one, but you couldn't eat a whole can of tomatoes cooked into a pie."

"Oh yes I could," said Bodenhammer.

Jerry Kelly, another cowboy who was standing nearby, heard what Bodenhammer said. "Mr. Kemp," said Kelly, "if you cook him another pie and he fails to eat it, we will show him how they put the leggings on."

A number 3–size can of tomatoes with the proper amount of cold bread to make a pie filled a twelve-inch Dutch oven about three-quarters full. When the pie was done, Bodenhammer started eating as though he would finish it in no time, but after the third helping he began to slow down. Kemp, realizing that Bodenhammer could not eat all the pie, got a plate and tried to help out by eating some of the pie himself.

By this time several of the cowboys had selected favorable positions so they could catch Bodenhammer if he tried to run. When Bodenhammer realized that he and Kemp could not eat all the pie, he began to glance out from under the brim of his hat, trying to locate an opening for escape. Finally he thought he saw one. Throwing his plate to one side, he leaped forward, but before he had run twenty yards, he was overtaken and caught.

The cowboys dragged him to a fallen pine tree that lay a few yards from camp and placed him face down across the log. Two men held his feet while two others held his head and hands. Jerry Kelly picked up a heavy pair of Heisler chaps, tiptoed up to Bodenhammer, then swung the chaps down across Bodenhammer's buttocks with all his might. The noise made by the heavy chaps echoed down the canyon. It was immediately followed by a scream from Bodenhammer, who swore they were killing him.

After he had received ten licks with the chaps, Bodenhammer was released. When he regained his feet, he began tenderly feeling the seat of his Levis. All of the other cowboys started laughing, and one of them asked him if he had ever seen the leggings put on anyone.

"Hell no," he answered, "there was too many sons of bitches sitting on my head."

After the fall roundups Ben Kemp's mother and stepfather decided to move to Duncan, Arizona. Kemp went with them to help them with their cattle and look for a new range for his cattle. However, the Arizona range looked too dry and open to suit him, and he returned to Beaver Creek.

After Ab Alexander quit the V + T, he bought the N-Bar Ranch on the head draws of the South Prong of Negrito Creek. For a while he had a partner by the name of Buck Powell, but Powell was killed by a man named Allen in the Meyers' saloon at Fairview in 1902.

Nat Straw was a frequent visitor at the N-Bar Ranch. He was a true westerner, having lived on the frontier all his life. He had followed the cattle trails and worked as chuck-wagon cook for such men as Chisum, Goodnight, and Slaughter. People in the southwest corner of the state knew little of Nat Straw's life prior to the time he started working for the V + T in the early 1880's.

During one of Straw's visits at the N-Bar Ranch, Ab Alexander decided to make a cattle drive down the Middle Fork. He took Buck Powell, a hired hand named Shack Simmons, and Nat Straw with him. It was November, and several bands of Navajo Indians had come from their reservation to the headwaters of the Gila on a deer hunt.

When Alexander and his party reached a large sand bar on the Middle Fork, about a mile north of the Trotter place, they were suddenly surrounded by a bunch of Navaho bucks. The Indians advanced to within fifteen steps of the cowboys and dropped to their knees. Then they bowed forward until their heads almost

175

touched the sand and began a chant that the cowboys thought was some kind of ritual. All of the cowboys, except Nat Straw, were scared. There was no way to escape without riding some of the Indians down, which they had decided to do until Nat Straw said, "Just sit tight, boys. Everything is going to be all right."

He spoke to the Navahos in their native tongue. Then there was a long powwow, after which the Indians began to back away, bowing and raising their hands above their heads.

Alexander and the other two men were mystified and prevailed upon Nat Straw to explain the meaning of all this. Straw said in the mid-1870's he found it necessary to leave the part of Texas where he was working and find a place where he would be less well known. In his search for a suitable location he ventured into the northwest corner of New Mexico and found himself on the Navajo Indian Reservation. Since very few white man lived there at that time, he decided to stay.

A few years later he married a Navaho woman, who gave birth to four children during their marriage. Straw, who had a fair education, soon became one of the tribe's leading medicine men. He might have lived with the Indians the rest of his life, but during the time the Navahos were on the warpath, they had captured a white girl and kept her captive after Kit Carson put down the rebellion. Straw said the girl was about seventeen years old the first time he saw her and that he was the first white man she had met after her capture.

The girl wanted to return to her family and begged Straw to help her escape. At first he refused, because such an act would entail grave danger. Both of them would be killed if they were caught trying to leave the reservation. After the girl pleaded with him for a month, he began to formulate a plan of escape.

Straw knew the reservation like the palm of his hand, and as a medicine man he kept pretty well posted on what was going on among the Indians. When he saw their chance, he and the girl left at night and reached Albuquerque the next afternoon, covering a distance of 150 miles in a day and night.

After he had helped the girl escape, Straw was afraid to return to the reservation, so he ventured into the southern part of the territory and started working at cow ranches. Years passed and the Navahos forgave him for stealing the white girl, and because they remembered he was a wise and good counselor, they wanted him back. That was why they had surrounded him and the other cowboys. The Indians were trying to talk him into returning to the reservation with them, but he was still afraid and refused to go.

Nat Straw hunted and prospected for more than fifty years throughout the Mogollon and Black Range mountains. He killed more grizzly bears and trapped more mountain lions than any other hunter in this section. He caught the only jaguar ever heard of on the headwaters of the Gila River. The animal was trapped in the Taylor Creek box, and its pelt was kept on display at the V + T headquarters ranch. It was a curiosity to the ranchers and cowboys who had never seen one before. Nat was a personal friend of such men as Bear Moore, Bob Lewis, Captain Cooney, Dave Cantrell, Ben Kemp, Henry Cox, and other early ranchers living on the headwaters of the Gila. He was a man who liked to joke and tell yarns, and few people took him seriously. Like most of the early settlers, he was not interested in seeing his life history in print, and in 1941 he crossed the last divide without anyone ever knowing one-tenth of his vast and interesting experiences. He was laid to rest in the cemetery east of Silver City, which is located in the foothills of the mountain ranges he loved to roam. They were as much a part of his life as the air he breathed.

In 1902, Ben Kemp sold his cattle to a man by the name of Smith who owned the XSX Ranch near the present location of the Lyons Lodge on the East Fork of the Gila River. Smith sent one of his cowboys, George Ferguson, after the cattle. Since 150 cows and calves were a fair-sized bunch for one man to drive, Benny was sent along to keep the drags punched up. The cattle were driven down the East Fork, up Spring Canyon, then down Jordan Mesa to the point between the East and West forks of the Gila River.

After the cattle were delivered, Benny returned home to find his two uncles, Steve Kemp and Tim Chapman, his cousin Henry Graham, and a young man named Thompson at the ranch. Tim and

Henry were rawhiding Thompson, whom they had named Tonk-a-way.

Three days later a man riding a jaded horse rode into the ranch at sundown and asked if he could stay overnight. He was told to unsaddle his horse and get ready for supper, which would be ready in a few minutes. Ben Kemp, usually a close observer, noticed the man had a ring cut around the index finger of his right hand, and he told Thompson the man had probably come out of serious trouble, because the wound looked like one made by the trigger guard of a six-shooter.

Thompson had to share his camp bed with the stranger, because there was a scarcity of bedding. When they went to bed that night, the stranger said, "Now partner, if I come out of here kind of sudden-like, think nothing of it. I am subject to nightmares sometimes." Thompson, suspecting his bed partner was a desperate character, slept very little during the night.

The next morning, as soon as the stranger had eaten his breakfast, he saddled his horse and headed back down the creek in the direction from which he had come. Within an hour a posse of six men rode up to the ranch house and asked if anyone had seen a man suiting his description. They were told he had left the ranch house only an hour earlier and was headed down the creek. The posse was at a loss about why they had not met him.

The posse told the Kemps the man was a desperate criminal, who had beaten a man to death with a six-shooter at Kingston, New Mexico, three nights earlier. Then they headed down the creek at a gallop and trailed the outlaw to where he left the creek on the west side. They followed his trail across Black Mountain into the Middle Fork, where they lost it and were unable to pick it up again. The murderer drifted on into Colorado, where he was killed a few months later.

In August, 1902, Ben Kemp moved his family to Chloride, New Mexico, so the children could attend school. When the school term started, Mrs. Kemp was pleased to learn that Miss Maude Anderson of Hillsboro, New Mexico, was to be schoolteacher. Miss

178

Maude was a personal friend of Mrs. Kemp's family, having attended school with her two younger sisters, Sarah and Julia.

As soon as suitable living quarters were found for the family, Kemp got a job as miner at the Silver Monument Mine, some twelve miles up Chloride Creek from town, where he worked until the spring of 1903.

When Chloride's boom of 1894 ended, two saloon owners had closed their doors, leaving the bar fixtures intact. Kemp, who believed a good bar in town would be a paying concern, bought the fixtures of the best bar and went into business for himself. For a year there was a boom in the Chloride mining district, and his business flourished.

The Goodenough Mine was leased by a French–Canadian Company that hired a man named Woods as their superintendent. This company brought in an air-compressor and drills, the first in the Chloride mining district. Local hard-rock miners were astounded at the amount of footage these drills made. Because of such highfalutin equipment, a few people in the community concluded that the company was a fabulously wealthy concern, and a report was circulated that Woods received forty thousand dollars by mail on weekends to pay expenses.

About eight o'clock one evening preceding a payday at the mine, while Miss Maude, the schoolteacher was visiting the Woods's home, a masked bandit suddenly stepped through the parlor door and closed it behind him. He held a six-shooter in his right hand and a fifty-pound flour sack in the other.

Everyone was so taken by surprise that they just sat and stared. The bandit walked over to Woods and said, "I have come after that forty thousand dollars. Just hand it over and no one will be hurt."

Woods always paid by check, and he thought the man was trying to play some sort of prank. "My friend," he said, "you will certainly have to look somewhere else besides here to find that much money."

The bandit hit Woods alongside the head with his six-shooter, almost knocking him out of his chair. "Get that money," he said. "I'm not fooling."

179

Woods, realizing that this was an actual holdup, told his housekeeper to give the bandit all the money there was in the house. The housekeeper opened a trunk and dug out a ten-dollar bill, which she presented to the bandit.

"Hell," the man said, "I don't want that. Where is the payroll that came in on the stage tonight?"

"There was no payroll on the stage." Woods said. "I pay my men by check." Then he showed the bandit the check stubs. Satisfied that Woods was telling him the truth, the bandit started backing towards the door, and on reaching it, he stepped out into the dark night. Miss Maude had watched the bandit closely, and without being detected, she removed her rings and a small watch she was wearing and placed them in her mouth. Otherwise she sat perfectly still during the attempted robbery.

Miss Maude knew there were probably several men at the Kemp bar. After the bandit left, she ran up the street. When she reached the bar, she was out of breath and could hardly make herself understood. When the men finally understood what had happened, they grabbed what firearms they could find and ran back down the street.

Only a few minutes had elapsed since the bandit had left the Wood's residence. The men made a thorough search of the lower part of town but failed to come up with a clue about who the man was or where he had gone.

It was learned later that the bandit had foreseen what would happen. He ran up the bed of Chloride Creek at the west edge of town while the men at the bar ran down Main Street in the opposite direction. While they were looking for him in the lower end of town, he returned to his saddle horse that was tied to a walnut tree above town. Then he rode up Chloride Creek to a friend's house, where he removed the shoes from his horse's hoofs, bent them out of shape, and threw them away. Then he removed the clothes he was wearing, burned them in the cookstove, and went to bed.

Early the next morning he hitched four horses to a wagon and drove down the creek over the road he had traveled the night before, trying to obliterate his horse's tracks. He arrived in Chloride before sunup, went to Kemp's bar, and asked if Kemp needed some firewood hauled. Since Kemp was out of wood at the time, he told him he did. But he suspected there were other reasons for the man being in town that early, asking for work he ordinarily did not do.

The wood-hauler had not been gone from the bar more than thirty minutes when Bob Putnam, the deputy sheriff from Fairview, arrived with a posse of four men. When a thorough search through the lower end of town revealed no tracks, they came to the conclusion the bandit had gone up Chloride Creek.

Kemp and his son Benny knew this was a fact. Earlier that morning they had trailed the bandit up the dry creek bed west of town and found where he had kept his horse tied. Since Putnam was the type of man who asked few questions, the Kemps did not tell him what they had found.

Putnam and his posse headed up Chloride Creek and found a horse track here and there in the road. They thought these tracks belonged to the bandit, although they could not be sure. When the tracks could not be picked up above the Smith ranch, Putnam arrested Chancy Smith and Ed Bellah, who was working at the Silver Monument Mine and boarding with the Smith family. Because Putnam had no actual proof that these men were implicated in the attempted robbery, they were released.

There were two other bars in Chloride besides the Kemp bar. One of these, a combination bar and store, belonged to Charley Allen, who also had the mail contract between Chloride and Engle. Allen's halfway station for this fifty-three-mile run was at Cuchillo, where he kept a change of teams. There he met the northbound stage from Engle, driven by one of his employees at the post office in Calhoun's store. When the mail was made up, Allen would hitch a fresh team to his hack and return to Chloride. He made the fifty-four-mile round trip six days a week, rain or shine.

Allen's stage hack was a heavy buggy drawn by two wild Spanish mules. Allen was a small but agile man, and on mornings when he hitched the last trace, he would leap into the hack in one bound. This would always be none too soon, because the mules would start running before he settled into the seat.

The post office at Chloride was at the lower edge of town from

181

Allen's store and feed yard, and the postmaster, a Civil War veteran named Mark Thompson, would stand in front of the post office with the mail bags ready to go. As the stage flew by, he would try to throw the mail sacks into the bed behind the seat. If he failed, he would yell, "Hell, Charley, I missed." Then Allen would circle his mules on a wide plot of ground below town and come back up the street. If Thompson missed the hack going up the street, he would always manage to throw the bags into it as it came back down. By this time the mules would be winded and Allen would have them seesawed down to a trot.

Allen's bar was in the back end of his store, and only a canvas partition separated the two. Ladies who came into store to trade had to remain at the upper end of the counter away from the partition, or they would overhear conversations considered unfit for a lady's ears in that day and time. Even so, there were always a few women who seemed to be interested in articles on the shelves near the partition.

The wood stove that furnished heat for the building was located in the storeroom section. It was a large, cast-iron affair, set inside a box made by nailing two-by-four-inch scantlings to the floor. The box was about five feet wide, six feet long, and four inches deep. A three-inch layer of sawdust was spread inside the enclosure, making it an ideal place for throwing cigarette stubs, spitting tobacco juice, and catching shavings of gents who cared to whittle.

One day a man named Reed, for whom Reed's Peak in the Black Range was named, came to Chloride from his cabin on Sheep Creek with four burro-packloads of fine Irish potatoes, which he sold to Charley Allen. Feeling jubilant over the good price Allen paid him, Reed ambled through the partition into the bar, where he proceeded to imbibe more of Allen's bug juice than was good for him. When he left the bar, he wobbled back to the heating stove in the store, where it was cozy and warm. There he settled down in a chair for a good drunken snooze.

All might have gone well if it hadn't been for a young smart aleck named Charley Smith, who happened to have a vial of benzene in his pocket. When he saw Reed sitting by the stove, with his

182

hat removed and his long hair hanging down around his shoulders, he could not resist the temptation to pour some of the benzene on top of Reed's head. Shortly thereafter Reed stampeded and ran over the heating stove, turning it over.

Live embers from the overturned stove fell into the sawdust, setting it on fire, and the store would probably have burned to the ground if Allen hadn't kept a bucket of drinking water sitting on the counter nearby to cool the throats of men who drank his fire-water. Someone grabbed the bucket and splashed the water over the burning sawdust, putting out the fire.

Reed was fighting the top of his head with both hands and cursing at the top of his voice. When he got rid of the high-life and could talk, he offered fifty dollars to anyone who would name the person who had poured the benzene on his head, swearing he would kill the s.o.b. if it was the last thing he ever did.

Smith, knowing the old man meant every word he said, saddled his horse and left town. Since no one would tell Reed who had played the dirty trick on him, he packed his burros and went back to Reed's Peak, sore at the town of Chloride in general.

The other liquor establishment belonged to Dr. Wiegmann, who ran a drugstore in the front part of his building, a grocery store in the middle section, and a bar at the back. How the good doctor managed to take care of all three businesses was a puzzle to the citizens of Chloride, because he was an elderly and rather feeble man.

Among the doctor's steady customers was a miner by the name of Larry Hartshorn. Larry liked to ride into town, hitch his horse to a large oak tree that grew in the middle of the street in front of Dr. Wiegmann's establishment, and pass an hour or two visiting. He maintained that the Doc had an ideal setup. You could get your drinks, medicine, and groceries, all at the same time, without walking your legs off.

Hartshorn came into town one morning and tied his saddle pony to the oak tree. Then he went into the store section of Dr. Wiegmann's establishment and bought some groceries, which the doctor placed in a gunny sack so they could be carried on the saddle. After

183

buying the groceries, Larry sauntered back to the bar and drank four or five glasses of the Doc's Culebra Picar whiskey.

By the time he returned to the front door of the drugstore, he was feeling happy, but not steady. He wobbled out to his horse and tied the groceries behind the saddle. Then he unhitched the horse, mounted, and reined him around to ride up the street.

All might have gone well if Larry had tied the groceries down securely. When the pony turned, the sack of groceries swung around and thumped him in the flank. Then and there the cayuse decided to get rid of Larry and the groceries. With a loud "waunk!" he went high, wide, and handsome, throwing Larry up into the lower branches of the tree. When Larry came down, he hit the dusty street on his back, and a cloud of dust obscured him.

Dr. Wiegmann was watching Larry from the drugstore door. When he saw him among the branches of the tree one moment, then lost sight of him the next, the doctor became confused and yelled, "Vell, Larry, and did you coom down?"

Larry, rising from the dust to where he could see the doctor, said, "You damned, old, Dutch son of a bitch, did you think I was going to stay up there all day?"

Dr. Wiegmann's bar was partly responsible for some more excitement a short time later. Working at the Silver Monument Mine on Chloride Creek was a husky miner by the name of Edison. He was a sociable and likable fellow, neat and nice-looking when sober, but he went on periodical drunks that would last for weeks at a time. On one of these sprees, when he had been drunk for nearly a month, Hank Patrick, the justice of the peace, notified all the bars not to sell him any more whisky.

About two days later Edison ambled down the street to Dr. Wiegmann's drugstore. He stopped at the door and stood there a minute or two, as though in meditation, then he jerked his hat from his head, swung it around a time or two, threw it on the sidewalk, and jumped on it with both feet. After stomping the hat, he gave a war whoop and dived through the door into the drugstore.

Dr. Wiegmann said when Edison reached the center of the room, he stopped and gazed in horror at the medicine bottles that lined

184

the shelves. He yelled, "God-almighty, look at the cats," grabbed an iron poker from under the stove, and started swinging. Before Dr. Wiegmann realized what was happening, Edison had broken most of the bottles on the lower shelf.

Something had to be done to save the valuable drugs. At great risk of being killed, the doctor ran into Edison and caught him by the arm. Edison dropped the iron bar, and the doctor started running for the door, but Edison caught him just as he passed onto the sidewalk. When they reached the street, the doctor was kicking like a suspended tarantula and yelling at the top of his voice, "Somebody, come quick. This man is crazy."

Hank Patrick, the justice of the peace, and three other men were repairing the ceiling in the school building, about a block up the street from the drugstore. They ran to the doctor's assistance, and it took the combined strength of all four men to overcome Edison.

After the dust had settled and Edison was pinned down in the street, the men had to decide what they were going to do with him. There was no jail in Chloride, and they were afraid if Edison escaped, he would do someone serious harm. Someone suggested they chain him up, so Hank Patrick went to the blacksmith shop and brought back a long, logging chain and two padlocks. One end of the chain was locked around the oak tree that stood in the middle of the street and the other end around Edison's neck. Benny Kemp, Eddy Schmidt, and Alfredo Candelario, three boys who witnessed what had happened, were home by dark that night, and a yoke of oxen couldn't have dragged them outside.

A little after dark Ben Kemp, who was working at the Goodenough Mine, two miles up the creek from Chloride, rode into town. As soon as he learned what had happened, he went down to the drugstore where he found Edison still chained to the tree in the middle of the street. Kemp called on Hank Patrick and told him he would take care of Edison if he would turn him over to him. When Patrick finally agreed, Edison was unlocked and put to bed in a vacant house in the west edge of town, and Kemp stood guard over him until he was sober.

Another miner named Payne had a habit of getting drunk every payday. He would get dead drunk and lie in a corner of the Meyers' bar for hours at a time. One day some of the other miners noticed Payne lying in his favorite corner dead drunk and decided to have a little fun.

One of the miners, who owned a wagon and team, drove down to Jake Blum's store, where he loaded a large, dry-goods crate on the wagon. Then he drove back to Meyers' bar, and the other miners helped him place Payne in the crate. Then they headed for the Chloride graveyard, some two miles away. When they reached the graveyard, they unloaded the crate and placed it on some wooden crossbars over an unfinished grave.

After they drove the wagon and team over the ridge out of sight, the miners crept back and peeped over the brow of the ridge to see what would happen when Payne woke up. About two hours later they could hear him kicking around inside the crate, and a short time later he set up and gazed around at the tombstones. He shook his head, rubbed his eyes with the back of his hands, and looked again. Then, in a voice loud enough for the pranksters to hear, he said, "Resurrection day, by grab, and old Payne is the first mother's son on deck."

The joke was on the men who had hauled him to the graveyard. They returned to their wagon and left Payne sitting in the dry-goods box in the middle of the cemetery. The pranksters had been in Fairview less than an hour when Payne walked into the Meyers' bar and told the bartender he had just returned from the dead and was badly in need of a drink to revive his spirits. The pranksters paid for a round of drinks, and soon Payne was back in his corner, drunk as ever.

After the Kemp family moved to Chloride, Ben hired a man named Bob Neil to stay at the Beaver Creek ranch. One day Minnie Neil, Bob Neil's wife, rode from the ranch to Chloride to get the mail. The day after she arrived, a report reached Chloride that the Apache Kid was making a raid through the Black Range. Mrs. Neil had heard of the merciless crimes this outlaw had committed, and she was afraid to recross the Black Range. Although the report was

186

true, it was given little credence at the time, so Benny was selected to accompany her back to Beaver Creek.

They followed a road up Chloride Creek to the Silver Monument Mine. When they left the road to enter the You-Be-Damned Canyon, they had to follow narrow cow trails that wound their way along the edge of sheer cliffs, where, if a horse lost his footing, both horse and rider would be hurled hundreds of feet to the bottom of the canyon.

When they came to Monument Park, near the crest of the Black Range divide, the ground was more level and less rocky. In the soft earth along the trail they noticed many pony tracks and in several places what looked like moccasin tracks. Mrs. Neil was scared. She said Indians had traveled the trail, but Benny wasn't so sure. He maintained that the pony tracks belonged to stock horses that came to water and that the moccasin tracks were bear tracks. Regardless of which they were, no Indians were sighted, and the trip over the Continental Divide to Seventy-Four Mesa was made without further incident.

Five miles below the old Lowback place, at the mouth of Turkey Run on Hoyte Creek, the canyon narrows to a box. Before they reached the box, Benny began teasing Mrs. Neil about moccasins with four toes and the six-shooter she was wearing. It was a .45 Colt's she had borrowed from a friend at Fairview and looked like a small cannon on Mrs. Neil, who was a slender woman. Finally Mrs. Neil became annoyed with Benny, and, grasping the quirt that swung from her wrist, she charged the boy. Benny took off down the creek with her in pursuit, but after running him for a quarter-mile without getting within striking distance, Mrs. Neil gave up the chase.

By this time they were within a half-mile of the narrow box of the canyon. Benny kept riding without slowing down until he reached it. The creek bed that the trail followed was only twelve feet wide at the narrowest place in the box. At this point two enormous slabs of rock had fallen from the canyon wall above, forming an open A. The tunnel formed by the rocks was about sixty feet long, and it ran parallel with the trail. At the upper end of the tunnel there was an opening similar to a window, which opened directly onto the trail. Anyone traveling the trail would pass within six feet of a person hidden at the window and not see him.

When Benny reached the lower end of the tunnel, he dismounted and tied his horse to a small cottonwood tree at a bend in the trail, out of sight of the box. Then he crawled through the tunnel to the window. He didn't have long to wait. Soon he heard Mrs. Neil's pony entering the rocky creek bottom at the upper end of the box. Mrs. Neil still had the quirt swinging from her wrist and was idly tapping her pony as he traveled at a jog trot.

When she reached a point directly in front of the rock window, Benny gave what he thought was an Indian war whoop. Whether it sounded like one or not, it had the desired effect. Mrs. Neil reached for her six-shooter, but in her haste she grabbed too far back and missed the butt by a good four inches. As she brought her arm around in a complete circle, she hit her pony such a whack with the quirt that it almost knocked his hind legs from under him.

The yell and the whack from the quirt scared the pony, and he leaped fifteen feet on the first jump. When the pony turned the corner at the lower end of the tunnel, he bumped into Benny's horse, and Mrs. Neil screamed like a mountain lion, because she thought the Apaches had her. She didn't hesitate after running into the boy's horse, but took off down the creek as fast as her horse would run.

Benny, who figured he had better get out of the tunnel as fast as he could, hurried to his horse and leaped into the saddle. He was not a second too soon, because Mrs. Neil, after running down the creek a hundred yards, realized that it was the boy's horse she had run into, and when she glanced back over her shoulder, she saw him. Mrs. Neil reined her horse around and started back towards Benny, swearing she was going to beat him to death. About halfway between them was an enormous boulder that had rolled from the mountainside above ages ago. The trail ran to the right of this bounder, and the creek to the left.

Benny came down the trail at a run as though he were going to pass on the right side of the boulder, but when he was within a few yards of Mrs. Neil, who reached the boulder at the same time, he reined his horse to the left and passed down the creek bottom. Before Mrs. Neil could rein her horse around to follow him, Benny was fifty yards down the canyon, riding like the wind.

Mrs. Neil chased the boy for eight miles, and at one time she was almost within quirting distance, but Benny was riding the faster horse. When they rode into the ranch on Beaver Creek, Benny was a hundred yards in the lead. Bob Neil wanted to know if they didn't like each other's company. When Mrs. Neil told him what had happened, he laughed for an hour. Mrs. Neil never asked for Benny as an escort again.

The Apache Kid, after raiding through the Black Range, stayed overnight at the Fullerton ranch on the south edge of the Plains of San Agustín. He borrowed all the latest newspapers the Fullertons had and set up half the night reading them. As far as anyone knows, this was only time the Kid ever stayed overnight at a ranch occupied by white men after 1889, when he was implicated in the killing of Sheriff Glenn Reynolds at Riverside, Arizona.

From the Fullerton ranch the Kid went to Corner Mountain, and a short time later he stole a couple of saddle horses. One of them belonged to Emiel Kiehne, who lived at Frisco, New Mexico.

A short time later Ab Alexander and Kiehne picked up the Apache Kid's trail and followed it to the top of Main Elk Mountain, where they found him camped in a grassy saddle. Hoping to take him by surprise, they charged into his camp, but the wily Kid disappeared into the dense growth of fir and aspen that covered the north side of the mountain.

Kiehne and Alexander rounded up the stolen horses and drove them to the N-Bar Ranch, where, against Alexander's advice, they turned them loose to graze in a fenced-in ciénaga at the ranch. The next morning they found, to their consternation, that the Apache Kid had followed them on foot and stolen their horses again. This time he made a clean getaway. The horses were never recovered.

While Kemp lived in Chloride, he sold most of his saddle horses to a man named Humphreys, who resided at the James brothers ranch southwest of town. Humphreys would ride Baldy Socks to town occasionally and go on a spree, leaving his saddled horse standing on the street. Baldy Socks was trained to stand wherever the reins were dropped and would stand on the street in front of the bar for a day and night at a time. On several occasions Kemp, feeling sorry for the horse, unsaddled him, put him in the feed lot, and fed him at his own expense. Humphrey finally sold the pony to Charley Anderson of Hillsboro, which made the Kemps glad, because they knew Anderson loved horses and would take good care of him.

Among the horses Ben Kemp kept was a flea-bitten gray called Rusty. This pony was one of the last of the Seven H-L remuda. Rusty was one of those short-coupled horses that possessed great endurance. A good all-around cow pony, he was used as a cutting and roping horse. Ben Kemp rode Rusty at a rodeo at Chloride in 1903, winning second prize in calf-roping. Lee Nations won first prize but was challenged by Bob Ake, who claimed Nations caught his calf by the front feet. This resulted in a fisticuff that Ake was about to win, when Bob Putnam, the deputy sheriff, rushed in and broke it up. Ake and Nations then shook hands, had a drink at the bar, and parted on friendly terms. No complaints were filed and no arrests were made. The fight was treated as a part of the occasion's entertainment.

16.
Drilling Water Wells

Henry Cox, Mrs. Kemp's father, never fully recovered from the injury he received at the placer-gold mines near Hillsboro in 1895. He died at the Edwards camp, fifteen miles northeast of Fairview, on the morning of August 9, 1903, at the age of sixty-five. After his death Mrs. Cox and her youngest daughter moved to Chloride near the cemetery where her husband was buried. She lived there for three years. Her youngest daughter married a miner by the name of Walter Armour, who owned some mining claims on Chloride Creek. A short time after Julia married, Mrs. Cox died and was buried beside her husband.

When Ben Kemp realized the boom in Chloride was nearly over, he sold his bar to a man named Jake Herdin and moved his family back to Beaver Creek in April, 1904. How the family would survive on the ranch presented a problem. All of the cattle except a milch cow were gone. The saloon had sold for only one thousand dollars, and it was a foregone conclusion this small amount would not support a family of ten for long.

Jobs were scarce. The drought of 1903 had killed thousands of cattle. The V + T estimated their losses at over twenty-five thousand head. Cole Railston, the V + T general manager, was running the outfit on a shoestring, hiring only enough men to take care of the most essential jobs. When it was time to start the spring round-up, the wagon was short-handed, but Railston refused to hire more men. But when Walter Nephew, the horse wrangler, got sick and had to go to town for medical treatment, Railston hired Benny to take his place until he returned. The thirteen-year-old boy felt a heavy responsibility in taking care of the remuda.

To add to his worries, some of the horses in Nephew's mount were trained to buck. On the first day Benny was riding one that bucked down a steep hillside at the upper end of the V + T lake. A loose girth caused the boy's saddle to turn under the horse's belly. He was thrown to the ground, and his mount ran into the remuda that was grazing in the valley at the foot of the hill and scattered it in all directions.

At noon when the cowboys came back to the wagon to eat dinner and get a change of mounts, there were no horses. The boy was sure he would be fired, but the wagon boss just laughed and sent his men out to round up the remuda. The cowboys roped Benny's mount and removed the saddle, which was missing both stirrups and had a badly ripped seat. They helped Benny find his stirrups and repair his saddle. By mid-afternoon he had everything under control, with his saddle cinched down a little too tight.

While Ben Kemp was riding through the country in search of work, he stopped in at the old Y Ranch, then owned by Frank A. Hubbell, a sheepman who had purchased it a year or two earlier.

In 1892, the Y Cattle Company hired Nat Emmerick to dig a twenty-foot, square well to a depth of forty feet. The well was dug twenty-five yards in front of the ranch log cabin. It was lined with heavy lagging and equipped with three floor-landings, connected by flights of stairs, which led to the bottom of the well. The water flow, never a strong one, went dry in the drought of 1903.

In 1904, Hubbell hired a man named Tommy Garrett, owner of the first well rig in this section of the country, to drill a well at the Y Ranch. Garrett had drilled wells on the Jorando del Muerto, near Engle, New Mexico, and along the south edge of the Plains of San Augustín with the light Fort Worth rig he owned, but never had he encountered a boulder bed such as he hit sixty feet below the surface in the Y Canyon. When Ben Kemp arrived at Garrett's camp, drilling had come to a standstill, and he and his uncle, who was helping him, were thoroughly disgusted. Kemp sensed their plight and offered Garrett six hundred dollars for his rig, which Garrett accepted immediately.

After the deal was closed, Kemp returned home, jubilant over his purchase. This was the first well rig in western Socorro County. and he could foresee plenty of work ahead. Practically all of the

192

open range was poorly watered, and ranchers would need wells to expand their range. Even so, he soon learned that work was hard to find. The drought had crippled all the stockmen, and money was scarce.

Kemp's first contract was with the Red River Land and Cattle Company for a well to be drilled a half-mile north of the Bat Cave, on the south edge of the Plains of San Agustín. This well was put down in record time, because the earth formation was composed of silt, clay, and sand, which was washed down the surrounding mountainsides into the San Agustín basin.

The basin at one time was a lake fifteen miles wide and forty miles long. The water depth in this prehistoric lake had ranged from a few inches along its northern boundary to more than three hundred feet just offshore the southern edge. Although the lake was probably formed by melting ice during the glacial periods millions of years ago, the old terraces formed by lapping waves as the water dropped from one level to another can be easily traced along the hillside on the south of the plain.

The outlet to this lake was at the east end of the plain, where overflowing water cut a canal three hundred feet deep through a range of hills which divided the east and west halves of the Plains of San Agustín. The old wagon road from Magdalena to Reserve passed through this ancient spillway, which the Kemp children called the Headless Canyon.

The section of the plain nearest the Bat Cave was the lowest part of the lake, and as the water receded, countless millions of fish must have collected there and died. At a depth of fifty-five feet the drill bit cut through the overlying fill into a fifteen-foot strata of black mud, which contained so many fishbones that hundreds of them were carried to the surface by the bailer.

The Bat Cave is a shallow cave at the base of a high cliff that cuts the end of a ridge running northwest from the Continental Divide. This cave was the dwelling place of a prehistoric people. In the powdery, dry dirt at the back of the cave excavators found reed buckets, pieces of pottery, and hundreds of fishbones, which indicate this cave was occupied during the time the lake was in exist-

193

ence. The cave was named by early settlers, who noticed swarms of bats flying from its entrance at twilight on summer evenings. Ben Kemp and his son might have uncovered some valuable relics from this cave had they not been afraid of rattlesnakes.

The first morning at the Bat Cave camp, when Benny started to build a campfire, he noticed a two-foot rattler lying on the bed tarp alongside his father. Warning his father not move, the boy selected a solid limb from the firewood and hit the snake such a whack that he smashed its head flat. At the sound of the whack the elder Kemp jumped six feet out of bed, on the opposite side from where the snake was lying, without even ruffling the bed covers.

After the Bat Cave well was drilled, the well rig was moved back to the Y Ranch, where another well was started. The boulder bed was too much for the light machine, however, and the well had to be abandoned.

In the late summer of 1904 a tall, lanky individual named Frederick Winn arrived at the DD-Bar Ranch. He hailed from the eastern states and knew little of western ranch life. He asked the V + T pack boss if he could stay at the ranch until he could find some place to establish his headquarters. Winn had passed the forest ranger's examination and was assigned to the Elk Mountain district of the Gila Forest Reserve, later known as the Gila National Forest.

Winn was an educated man and a talented artist. While he was staying around the bunkhouse at the DD-Bar, he found time to draw some sketches of bucking broncos and gun-slinging bad men on the cowboys' tarps, which were the talk of the community.

Winn was almost deaf, and with his eastern accent and high-pitched voice, he furnished the cowhands lots of amusement. They liked to rawhide him about his job, telling him that counting all the saplings was too tedious for them, even at three times the salary he was drawing.

A forest ranger's salary at that time was seventy-five dollars per month, and out of this came all his expenses for equipment, clothes, board, and grain for his saddle horses. Moreover, he was unpopular with the ranchers, who had always run their cattle on an open range with no questions asked.

After Winn failed to find a suitable place to stay, he asked Ben Kemp if he could stay at the Beaver Creek ranch. Kemp agreed, and Winn moved into the twelve-by-fourteen-foot cabin called the smokehouse. This cabin had a clapboard roof, a dirt floor, a small window in the back, and a sagging door at the front. It was a far cry from all the luxuries enjoyed in modern ranger stations today. No rent was charged, but Winn agreed to pay fifteen dollars a month for his board and pasture for his saddle horses. Mrs. Kemp did his laundry at no extra charge.

Even at this low rate Winn found it difficult to meet his payments. Regulations required that he ride thirty miles each day except Sunday. This was practically impossible, but he tried. He kept two horses at Beaver Creek, two at the N-Bar Ranch, and two at Chloride. Reserve was the western boundary of his district and Chloride the east. It would be hard for anyone who has never ridden over this vast expanse of rough and broken country to realize the enormous task that he was undertaking.

During the time Fred Winn was stationed at the Kemp ranch on Beaver Creek, large bands of Indians from the Navajo and Zuni reservations came to the headwaters of the Gila River to hunt. They made drives and killed hundreds of deer. There would be piles of deer hair three and four feet high in their abandoned camps, because they scraped the hides clean of hair to make them easier to transport back to their reservations.

The Kemp family thought this was a wanton slaughter of game and tried to scare the Indians by telling them that the forest ranger at their house was a deputy game warden. The Indians paid little attention to the warning, and when Ben Kemp ran one down after chasing him half a mile up a mountainside, the Indian said, "Me got pass." He produced a note written on a piece of ordinary writing paper, which stated, "This is to testify that the bearer of this note is a good man." It was signed by Mrs. Nels Fields.

The Fields family lived north of Magdalena on Alamosa Creek, and Nels Fields, who was later state land commissioner, owned a cow ranch and hired Navaho Indians as cowboys. He spoke their language and was known throughout the southwest part of the state as Navajo Fields. The Indians trusted the Fields family implicitly, and the hunter probably thought his pass would take him anywhere.

Although hundreds of Indians came to the headwaters of the Gila every year to hunt, there was always an abundance of game. Turkeys came in flocks numbering from fifteen to fifty and drove the chickens away from their feed troughs within fifty yards of the main dwelling. On several occasions Beulah Kemp furnished the family with a turkey dinner by shooting a gobbler from a small window in the north side of the kitchen while she was preparing breakfast.

In a few years this hunters' paradise began to vanish. Wagon roads that were little more than cow trails changed to graded highways. Then thousands instead of hundreds came to hunt in the Gila Forest, and the game population dropped to an all-time low.

Fred Winn was transferred from the Gila to the old Datil National Forest at Magdalena, and there in the fall of 1907 he married a young lady schoolteacher. Everyone who knew them were their friends, and along with their good wishes came a few pranks. A little after dark on the evening they were married, nearly every bell in the Becker McTavish store was carried up to the new Winn residence. Even a three-hundred-pound church bell was carted to the house and placed in the front yard.

When all was ready, the pranksters discovered there was no one in the house. They searched downtown and found the newlyweds at the Bardale drugstore. Fred was escorted to the Hilton Bar where he ordered a round of drinks. Ordinarily this would have sufficed, but his mischievous friends blindfolded him and led him back to the drugstore, where they entrusted him to the care of their womenfolk. The women were to take him for a car ride to Nine Mile Hill west of Magdalena.

All of the conversation after Winn was blindfolded had been carried on in undertones, and since Winn was partly deaf, he had not heard a word. He still thought he was in custody of the men, and by the time the car reached Nine Mile Hill, he had called the women

196

every foul name he could think of. No one had spoken except Winn, and when they were ready to start back to town, the car was stopped and his blindfold removed. Winn could then see that he was the only man in the car. He was so ashamed of the language he had used he slumped down in the car seat and never uttered another word all the way back to town.

After a few years at Magdalena, Winn was transferred to Silver City to become supervisor of the Gila National Forest. He loved the great outdoors, and whenever he had a chance, he would leave the office, saddle his horse, pack his mule, and ride into the wildest part of the forest, where he would stay for weeks at a time.

In the spring of 1904, Cole Railston hired a cowboy, who gave his name as Jim Thompson, and made him line rider at the TUT Ranch on the west end of the Plains of San Agustín. Thompson came to the V + T chuck wagon on the afternoon of May 4, when it was camped about five miles west of the Bat Caves. The morning after his arrival he rode an outlawed horse called Flax that put on an exhibition of bucking that astonished the other cowboys and convinced Benny that all his mount could do was billygoat.

Three nights later near the Crawford ranch, on the south edge of the plains, Thompson's saddle horse stepped in a prairie-dog hole and fell while he was on graveyard guard around the cattle. This stampeded the herd, which ran towards the chuck wagon. When Thompson regained his feet, he managed to catch his half-addled pony and turn the cattle enough to miss the wagon by only a few yards. The cowboys, who had their beds spread on the ground, had to scramble to get on or under the chuck wagon. Cole Railston, who happened to be with the wagon at this time, maintained that Benny hid behind the coffeepot. The joke was not funny to Benny, because Railston's reason for coming to the wagon was to bring Walter Nephew back to take over the remuda.

Thompson worked with the wagon during the fall roundup and went with the herd into Magdalena at shipping time. The morning after arriving in town, he went to the Allen House for breakfast. There was only one vacant seat in the dining room when he entered. It was at a two-place table where a neatly dressed man was

197

sitting. Thompson was wearing his cowboy garb, which was worn and dusty. When he sat down at the table, the neatly dressed man gave him a contemptuous look, but Thompson paid no attention to him. He was hungry, and when his meal was served, he started eating with gusto. He reached across the table to carve a slice of butter from the rounded cone in the butter dish. As he did, the man on the opposite side of the table raised his head with an air of disgust and said, "Waiter! Bring me another dish of butter. This bum has contaminated this one."

Thompson rose slowly to his feet, reached across the table, and picked up the butter bowl with his left hand, then placed it in the palm of his right. He raised the bowl above his head and brought it down into the upturned face of the man, as he yelled, "Waiter! Bring me another dude. This one is damned well buttered."

For four or five seconds the so-called dude was busy clawing butter out of his eyes, and when he could see again, he tied into Thompson, and the battle was on. They turned over a table, broke a chair, and would probably have done a lot more damage if Milt Allen, the hotel proprietor, had not rushed in and stopped the fight. Each man paid Allen for his part of the damage and departed. For many months after that, mention of a buttered dude at the V + T cow camps was sure to cause a round of comments and laughter.

In the latter part of November, 1904, Thompson, while roping calves in a branding corral, got his hand mangled in the coils of a saddle rope and almost cut off two of his fingers. He was forced to go to Mogollon for medical aid, and when he returned to the V + T headquarters ranch, the wagon boss had hired another man in his place.

Since Thompson was broke after doctor bills were paid, he started riding from one ranch to another in search of work. He stopped in at the Kemp ranch on Beaver Creek and heard about the well rig. After discussing its possibilities with Kemp, he wanted to buy a half-interest. Benny had helped Kemp drill the first two wells, but the work was too heavy for the boy, so Kemp sold Thompson a half-interest in the rig, with thirty dollars as a down payment.

The winter of 1905 was the wettest in years, and travel almost

198

came to a standstill. The Glaze brothers, neighbors of the Kemps, lived on the head of Mule Canyon and were forced to make a trip into Magdalena after supplies. They mired their wagon and team a number of times and had to unload and reload their wagon so often that they wore the flour sacks full of holes.

A mile north of Indian Peak the road crossed a dry lake bed formed by an ancient lava flow, which there was no way of by-passing. Their wagon settled into the bed and their teams bogged down. They experienced some trouble in getting their teams to firm ground at the west side of the lake, which was about 150 yards wide.

They unloaded their wagon and packed their supplies to the west edge of the lake by foot. Among their supplies was a Manila cable that was three hundred feet long, but it was not long enough to span the distance from the firm ground at the west side of the lake to their wagon.

There was a stand of pine trees on the shores of the lake. On a rocky point that jutted out into the lake there was a large pine about eighty feet tall. Ollie Glaze took one end of the cable, climbed the tree, and tied the cable fast near the top. Then he tied the other end to the wagon tongue, allowing a few feet of slack.

Ollie took an ax and felled the tree away from the wagon. When the slack was taken up in the cable, the wagon leaped out of the mud hole like a frog, landing several feet closer to the west side of the lake. The distance between wagon and shore was then short enough for the cable to span. The team was hitched to the end of the cable and the wagon dragged to firm ground.

The well rig had stood idle all winter. Since it was the only source of income, finances had reached a low point. When the roads had dried out to some extent by April, Benny and Thompson started to Magdalena with six horses and two wagons, hoping to pick up a load of wool at some sheep ranch. There was an outlawed saddle horse in the span of their team. The horse, called Red Hide, had been broken to work and then balked. He was almost worthless.

When they came to the Point of Rocks, a camping ground on the south side of the Plains of San Agustín, they sighted a sheep camp near the road. Since they wanted to know if anyone in the vicinity

199

was shearing sheep, they stopped their team, climbed down from the wagon seat, and walked to the sheep camp.

They were both hungry as bears, and when the sheepherders invited them to dinner, they gladly accepted and ate heartily. Benny went back for a second helping of boiled meat and rice, and while delving into the pot, he pried two slabs of meat apart, and a handful of maggots fell out. His hunger vanished immediately, and he was ready to go back to the wagon.

When they returned to the wagons, Red Hide had cold shoulders and balked. Thompson climbed down from the wagon seat, and with a stick and a short piece of rope he made what he called a twister. He tied the rope around the horse's upper lip, twisted it tight with the stick, and said, "Now, Kid, you take the lines and start the team, and I will lead Red Hide until we get started."

When Benny spoke to the team, all of them tried to start except Red Hide. When Thompson pulled on the twister, he reared back and tripped the wheel horse, which fell on the wagon tongue and broke it in two. Now they were in a predicament—thirty miles from town with a broken wagon tongue and no way to repair it. For a few minutes all they could think of was killing the worthless horse, but that would do no good. So they examined the wagon tongue to see if there was any way they could fix it. Luckily, the tongue had splintered when it broke. If they could find enough baling wire, they could repair it so that it would hold until they could reach town.

Luck was with them. The Point of Rocks was a popular camping ground, and westbound freight wagons usually brought baled hay from town, because feed was short at this spot most of the year. In a short time they found enough wire to wrap the wagon tongue. The team was rehitched to the wagon, and a rope was tied from Red Hide's neck to the stretchers of the lead team. When he tried to rear back, he was violently jerked forward, and after floundering around for a hundred yards, he laid into the collar, and the trip on to Durfey's Well was made without further incident.

The next morning they reached Manuel Pino's sheep camp, a mile down the canyon below Durfey's Well. Pino was shearing sheep, and soon they had their wagons loaded to capacity. They wondered if they would be able to turn a wheel with the balky horse, but they had the advantage of a downhill start and managed to get under way. At half-past-three that afternoon they drew up alongside the loading platform of the Becker McTavish warehouse in Magdalena.

Thompson and Benny, who were tired, hungry, and dirty from working with the wool, were in a belligerent mood, and McFarland, the Becker McTavish warehouseman, sized them up with an air of disgust. Neither Thompson nor Benny had ever handled wool bags, and they were having quite a struggle trying to truck them onto the scales. After watching them a few minutes, McFarland, who was somewhat stout and portly, said, "Wait a minute. I'll show you damned Mexicans how to place wool on them scales."

Thompson, picking up one of the heavy weights that lay on top of the scales, said, "Yeah, you damned, old, pot-bellied son of a bitch, and I'll show you how to cave somebody's skull in two."

With a startled look, McFarland raised his hands above his head and started backing away, saying, "Wait a minute, wait a minute, my mistake. I thought both of you were Mexicans and couldn't understand English. Don't get sore." The wool was unloaded and weighed without further comment.

After Thompson and Benny bought supplies and loaded them into the wagon, they prepared to leave town. Thompson decided to ride the near-wheel mule, because it was easier to handle the team that way.

They left Magdalena about mid-afternoon, and when they came to the west edge of town, they met an automobile. This was the first car in Magdalena, and horses were afraid of it. To keep his team from bolting, Thompson drove to one side of the road and stopped. After the car had passed, he tried to start the team, but Red Hide balked. The lead team was slow to hit the collar, so Thompson called back to Benny, who was in the covered wagon, to hand him the four-horse whip, which he had just equipped with a brand new stock. When the whip was passed out to him, he made a wild slash at the lead team, and they hit the collar with a lunge, almost jerking Red Hide's head off.

This confusion caused the mule Thompson was riding to balk, and he hit the animal over the head with the new whip stock, breaking the stock in two. Thompson bellowed with rage and could have been heard a mile away. This was followed by a torrent of oaths seldom heard in any man's language. The team, already excited over the thrashing around, were frightened by this shouting and ran away, dragging the wagon down the slope into the road. Red Hide caused trouble all the way back to Beaver Creek. It was a trip the man and boy never forgot.

One day while they were talking about Thompson, Kemp said to Benny, "That man's name is no more Thompson than mine."

This proved to be a fact. Before long Thompson had gained confidence and told them his legal name was Albert Finch. It was learned later that he had gotten into an argument with a wagon boss in West Texas. The boss tried to draw a gun on him, but Finch beat him to the draw and would have killed him if another cowboy hadn't intervened and knocked Finch's six-shooter upward, causing the bullet to pass through the crown of the boss's hat, a fraction of an inch above his head.

Because Finch was sure the law would be after him for assault with a deadly weapon, he left Texas and came to Roswell, New Mexico, where he went to work for the Block Cattle Company. When he quit the Block's, he came to Magdalena and was hired by Cole Railston.

Albert Finch grew up along the Texas-Mexican border and spoke Spanish fluently. It was not long before this knowledge of Spanish paid off in securing work for the well rig. Many of the ranch owners were Spanish Americans, who spoke little or no English.

A few days after the trip into Magdalena with the balky horse, Finch saddled his cow pony and rode to the Plains of San Agustín. In less than a week he returned with word that he had found three wells to drill. Juan García, a sheepman, wanted a well drilled on the head of Railroad Canyon, and his brother, José García, wanted two wells drilled, one north of the Point of Rocks, and the other at Vega Blanca on the Plains of San Agustín.

The well rig was still at the Y Ranch, and before they could move it to the García place, they would have to build a stretch of road from the west foot of Coyote Peak to the crest of the Continental Divide. Although the distance was only eight hundred yards, the men would have to do some blasting and grading before the top-heavy well rig could be hauled over the road. It was a month before construction was finished.

After the road was completed, the camp equipment was moved to a small log cabin Juan García had built on Railroad Canyon, north of Indian Peak. Tents were pitched there, and the next morning Kemp and Finch drove the harnessed teams to the Y Ranch to haul the well rig to the new location. It took three days to make the trip, and Benny was left to hold down camp while they were gone.

On the second day after they left, Benny ran out of biscuits and was forced to cook some of his own. It was his first attempt at bread-making, and the results were not gratifying. He watched a bend in the canyon two miles below camp, and when the teams and wagons drove into sight the next day, he hurriedly buried his biscuits in a prairie-dog hole. That night when Ben Kemp went to cook supper, he said to Albert Finch, who was helping him, "I wonder what the hell that boy ate while we were gone."

Benny was graining the teams some twenty yards away and heard what his father said, but he never said a word. Years later he said that some of the round rocks lying around the García ranch might be some of his biscuits.

Juan García knew nothing about drilling wells, and 100 feet sounded like a mighty deep hole in the ground to him. When the well reached that depth, he was ready to abandon it, but Kemp kept drilling. At 102 feet the drill bit broke into an underground cavern or subterranean lake, which for thirty years furnished an abundance of water for thousands of sheep.

From the Railroad Canyon the rig was moved to the José García place, seven miles north of the Point of Rocks on the Plains of San Agustín. This location was in a stand of chamiso and rabbit brush interspersed with prairie-dog mounds, making it a likely place for rattlesnakes. No one spread his bedroll on the ground. Albert Finch slept in a wagon box, and Benny slept on top of some baled hay in the corner of the supply tent.

One dark night about a week after camp was established, Benny heard a rattler on the tarpaulin that covered his bed. Expecting to get a snake bite, he eased out of his bed and joined Finch in the wagon box.

The next morning while they were working on the turntable of a windmill tower at the back of the supply tent, a four-foot rattler crawled out of Benny's bed and headed for a chamiso bush. Finch, who had been rawhiding the boy for being afraid of mice, yelled, "Cripes and a girl named Kate." He jerked his six-shooter and shot the rattler's head off.

In less than thirty minutes after the snake was disposed of, Benny had his bed rolled out on a four-foot scaffold, where no rattler could reach it.

Benny sat around many campfires and listened to the men tell about long rides they had made. He had heard his father and Finch discuss the measures necessary to preserve a horse's strength on a long ride, and Benny wondered if he could make such a ride.

Finally his curiosity got the best of him, so he saddled Rusty and left camp one morning just as the sun was peeping over the Tres Montosas peaks, a few miles northeast of camp. That evening as the sun was setting over Black Mountain, he rode into the ranch-house yard at Beaver Creek. He had covered a distance of seventy miles, and both he and his mount were weary.

The first question his father asked him was where he had stayed the night before. Then wanted to know what was the matter. When he found out the ride was just a lark, his concern turned to anger, and he told Benny he ought to give him a good thrashing for riding a horse like that for no reason.

When work was completed at the Point of Rocks well, the rig was moved to Vega Blanca, located on the main road from Magdalena to Springerville, Arizona. During the summer of 1905 there were frequent visitors at camp. Among them were Mrs. Ada Morley, her son Ray Morley, and her daughter Mrs. Agnes Morley Cleaveland, all of Datil, New Mexico.

Mrs. Cleaveland was writing articles for the *Saturday Evening Post* at this time, and on her way from Datil to Magdalena she would occasionally stop at some shallow lakes near camp to water her work team. She drove a span of matched sorrels hitched to a sparkling new buckboard. Benny enjoyed her visits. She was always good humored, and usually brought him a collection of magazines to read. In later years Mrs. Cleaveland authored two books, *No Life for a Lady* and *Satan's Paradise*.

From the Vega Blanca Ranch the well rig was moved to Magdalena, where a contract was signed to drill a well for a man named Spackman, who owned a small grocery store. Spackman wanted the rig set up over an eighty-foot dug well. This entailed extra work, because casing had to be installed before drilling could start. Since there was no iron casing on hand, a twelve-by-twelve-inch box made of 1" x 12" x 18' lumber was used instead.

Spackman hired a nineteen-year-old Mexican boy to help install this homemade casing. After the boy nailed the last brace in place at the bottom of the well, he grabbed the drill cable and yelled for the hoist man to pull him up. The hoist on this model of Fort Worth machines was slow, and by the time he reached the top, he lost his grasp on the cable and fell eighty feet fack to the bottom of the well. Ben Kemp, who was operating the hoist, thought the boy had been killed, but soon he heard him calling for the rope to be sent down again. This time he made a loop at the end of the cable in which to place his foot, and was hoisted to the surface. The braces holding the casing in place had broken his fall, and except for a few scratches, he was unharmed. The next day after the accident the Mexican boy was married and proved his agility by doing the Spanish fandango.

After finishing the Spackman well, Kemp and Finch contracted to drill wells for Jesús and Boney Landavaso, two sheepmen with ranges east and west of the Luero Mountains. The first of these two wells was drilled on the Plains of San Agustín, seven miles south of the C-Bar-N. This well was finished in record time, and the rig was moved to the head of Railroad Canyon, where two wells were put down for Jesús Landavaso. The Kemp family moved out to the rig while these wells were being drilled. This was a welcome change after living three years on Beaver Creek. Since no water was found in these wells, Landavaso abandoned them.

In September, 1906, a contract was signed with Dave Farr, a sheepman who wanted a well drilled on Patterson Cutoff Canyon. The canyon derived its name from a former Union soldier, who used it in 1870 as a shorter route from his ranch at the west end of the Plains of San Agustín to Post Caliente on the Alamosa River, north of the present town of Monticello, New Mexico.

While Big Foot Wallace, a veteran of the Mexican War and famous Indian fighter, was visiting this post, he supposedly won a bet over the carrying range of his buffalo hunting rifle by shooting an Apache off a cliff half a mile down the canyon below the post.

In October, while work was in progress on this well, Ben Kemp had an attack of arthritis that confined him to bed. He and Benny were the only ones in camp. There was no doctor closer than Magdalena, some seventy miles away, and the boy could not leave his father to go to the nearest ranch, which was fifteen miles away. They had no medicine to alleviate the pain. The elder Kemp was suffering terribly, and Benny was badly worried over his condition.

To their surprise and relief, Jess McCarty, who had quit his pack boss job at the V + T, made a visit to camp in hopes of finding work. He was hired immediately, and with his help Ben Kemp was placed in a bed that was rolled out in a wagon box. Jess McCarty hitched a team to the wagon and drove to Beaver Creek, leaving Benny to take care of camp and the extra work horses.

After three days at the ranch a team of horses was hitched to a wagon, and Kemp was placed in a bed as before. Two of his daughters, Julia and Mary, drove the team and wagon down Beaver Creek to the East Fork of the Gila River, then down the river to the Middle Fork, and up the Middle Fork to the Gila hot springs. He stayed at the springs and took baths for twenty days. The baths helped, and in two months he was able to get around without the aid of a cane.

Jess McCarty returned to the well rig after taking Ben Kemp to Beaver Creek. Albert Finch, who had gone to Magdalena the day before Ben Kemp became so ill, returned to camp, and he and Jess, with Benny's help, continued to work on the well.

By April 10, the drill had cut its way to a depth of 225 feet, which was the end of their Manila cable. Since the men were also short on provisions, Albert Finch decided to take a wagon into Magdalena and bring back a load of supplies and enough steel cable to finish the well. He left camp on the morning of April 12, with the intention of returning on the evening of the twentieth. Benny, who was ill with neuralgia when he left, was unable to work, so the well rig stood idle, since Jess was kept busy doing the chores about camp.

On the evening of the eighteenth a strong wind began blowing out of the southwest, and dark clouds gathered over Pelona Mountain and the Continental Divide. When night fell, it was dark as pitch. Jess and Benny went to bed early and pulled the tarpaulin on their bed over their heads to cut out the howling wind. About eight o'clock the wind settled, and they were lulled to sleep by the soft patter of snow on the tent roof. About two o'clock the next morning they were awakened by a crash and discovered the tent pole had broken in two under the weight of snow. When they crawled from under the folds of canvas at daylight, they found that twenty-two inches of snow had fallen during the night.

The snowstorm presented a problem. Benny wanted to round up the work teams and head for Beaver Creek, but Jess wanted to wait for Albert, who he said would be in by nightfall. When darkness settled over the snow-mantled ridges, Albert had not arrived, and there was not a speck of grub in camp.

The next morning Benny picked up his rifle and waded through the snow until he found a rabbit. He and Jess had meat for breakfast, and only those who have been reduced to a diet of broiled rabbit without salt or bread can fully appreciate their plight.

By the third day a heavy thaw had left the ground so soft that travel by wagon seemed impossible. By this time the broiled rabbit

207

diet was too much for Benny, so he saddled Gray Eagle, one of the work horses, and headed for Beaver Creek. When he reached the top of the Continental Divide, Gray Eagle bogged down on the first prairie-dog mound he tried to cross. The melting snow had softened the earth so much it was boggy all the way across this rocky divide. By the time Benny reached Railroad Canyon, both he and his mount were caked with mud. From Railroad Canyon on to Beaver Creek the ground was more firm, and he rode into the ranch-house yard before dark.

Jess McCarty left camp at the same time Benny did, but he traveled down Patterson Cutoff Canyon, along the road that Albert would follow on his way back to camp. At a point six miles below camp he met Albert, who had been delayed in obtaining the steel cable and had made slow progress from Magdalena back to camp because of the muddy roads.

On May 1, Ben Kemp returned to the well rig. He was still handicapped from his recent illness but was able to direct work at the well. The drill bit had cut through three hundred feet of gray volcanic rock. At this depth the formation changed to a red conglomerate, and before the drill had penetrated ten feet into this formation, there was a strong flow of water.

While Kemp was working with miners at Chloride, he had learned that placer gold could be found in prehistoric riverbeds, and he suspected the conglomerate formation was one of these beds. There was no gold-panning pan in camp, but a large frying pan from which the grease had been burned served the purpose. The first pan of drillings showed a trailing of fine yellow grains, and Jess McCarty explained, "There's sure a lot of fine brass following that black sand."

Since brass is an alloy, everyone thought there might be gold. In an effort to determine this, a pound of the pannings was placed in a heavy iron laddle and brought to a melting temperature. Most of the sand disappeared, and when the rest was poured out, they discovered a yellow smear fused into the iron at the bottom of the ladle. Convinced more than ever that this was gold, Jess McCarty took an eight-ounce bottle of the pannings to Magdalena, where he entrusted it to Dick Barnes, a clerk in the ranch supply store, with the understanding he would send it to the school of mines at Socorro for an analysis. Barnes, who was inclined to drink too much at times, lost the bottle during a drinking spree. Before he reported its loss, the well rig had been moved to a new location, and no one knows to this day whether the yellow metal was gold or not. After three years the yellow blotch that was fused into the bottom of the melting ladle showed as plain as it did on the day it was removed from the forge, and the Kemp family believes to this day it was gold.

From the Patterson Cutoff the well rig was moved to the Bat Cave, where another well was put down for the Red River Land and Cattle Company. After finishing another well for the company near the TUT Ranch on the west end of the plain, the rig was moved to the Fullerton ranch on the south edge of the Plains of San Agustín.

While work was in progress on this well, one of Will Fullerton's sheepherders found an old Spanish saber in a cave along the rim rock south of the Bat Cave. Evidently the saber had been owned by one of Coronado's men during his expedition to Zuni in 1620. It was in excellent condition, and inscriptions such as those used in the latter part of the sixteenth century were plainly visible on the blade, plate, and scabbard. This was remarkable, considering that it had probably been leaning against the dry inner wall of the cave for more than 275 years. The sheepherder, who didn't realize its value, sold the sword to Fullerton for eight dollars.

While the Glaze brothers were in Magdalena during January, 1907, they met a boy about eighteen years old, who gave his name as Johnny Campbell. He said he wanted to live on a western cow ranch, and Ollie Glaze, who wanted someone his age for company, invited him out to their ranch on Mule Canyon.

Campbell, whose home was in St. Louis, Missouri, had a high-school education, and when Ben Kemp learned this, he wanted to hire him as schoolteacher at Beaver Creek. After Campbell visited the Kemp ranch, he decided to take the job. The wild-looking box canyon below the Kemp ranch house fascinated him. Every morning a fresh set of animal tracks could be found along the trail that

209

ran through the thickets of oak, cottonwood, and box elder that grew along the floor of the semi-box canyon.

After Johnny Campbell started teaching, he would stroll down the creek before and after school hours, examining tracks of lions, bears, bobcats, and other inhabitants of the forest which had traveled along the trail the night before.

The Kemp children were amused. They suspected Johnny had read too many western novels. The new teacher was due for his share of pranks from this mischievous bunch.

On one occasion the Kemp girls were trapping raccoon along the creek. They were having little success, and when Johnny noticed this, he told them they couldn't catch a coon if it was tied to a tree. Every morning when they went to run their trap line, they found Johnny's tracks on the trail. They suspected he was responsible for the raccoons staying away, so they decided to put a stop to it.

Among their traps was a number-4 wolf trap, and one of the girls said, "He thinks he is so smart, let's set a trap and catch him." They set the number-4 trap in the trail at a bend in the creek, three hundred yards below the ranch house, and concealed it with dirt and tree leaves. A two-foot iron pin was driven into the ground. The chain to the trap was tied to the pin with heavy wire and twisted with a pair of pliers.

The next afternoon when school was out, Johnny ambled down the trail and was caught in the trap. He tried to open the trap with his hands, but the springs were too strong. Then he tried to pull the iron pin up, but it would not budge. He realized he would have to remain in the trap until help arrived. He visualized what would happen to him if a grizzly bear found him caught like this. He began to yell, and someone at the house heard him. Benny went down to investigate and found Johnny caught in the trap. He helped him remove the trap from his foot, and they returned to the house. Since Johnny was not in a talking mood, no one asked him any questions.

Johnny Campbell never stayed to finish his school. In a short time he returned to the Glaze ranch, and from there he returned to St. Louis. The Kemp family never heard of him again.

From the Fullerton ranch the well rig was moved to the mouth of Nester Draw, where a well was drilled for Juan Sanchez y Vijil. When this well was completed, Ben Kemp bought Albert Finch's interest in the rig, and Finch bought a partnership in another well rig.

Since it was near the middle of November by this time, Ben Kemp and his son Benny decided to return to Beaver Creek for a few days. On their arrival they found the family in a state of excitement.

A large grizzly bear had visited the cow corral two nights earlier and stampeded the milk cows. Since the corral was less than fifty yards from the house, the family had heard the cows run, but it was the next morning before they discovered the cause. The bear's tracks showed plainly in the soft earth around the corral.

There had been a good mast that year, and the bear was lapping acorns in a stand of oak trees on the east side of the creek, about four hundred yards up the canyon from the house. Kemp took Benny's .30–.40 carbine, and, warning his family to keep quiet, he walked up the canyon, where he hid and waited for the bear.

The family gathered at the edge of the bench on which the house stood and listened. Just before dark they heard a shot which was followed by a yell that echoed and re-echoed up and down the canyon. They were afraid to go see what had happened and afraid not to. Their anxiety was relieved thirty minutes later when Ben Kemp returned to the house and said he had shot and wounded the bear.

Kemp and his son Benny took their dog Joe and returned to the scene of the shooting. It was easy to find the spot, because the huge bear had twisted a three-inch oak sapling in two when he was shot. The dog trailed the bear up Grandma Canyon. They found drops of blood and pieces of shoulder bone, but darkness forced them to abandon the trail.

Ten days later one of the V + T cowboys ran a bunch of cattle over the north rim of Kemp Mesa and found the carcass of the bear. It had traveled three miles after receiving the mortal wound. This was the last grizzly bear that Ben Kemp killed.

17.
The Apache Kid's Last Horse Wrangle

Since no one had been to the post office at Chloride in more than two months, Ben Kemp and Benny decided to go get the mail and at the same time pick up Kemp's .30–.40 rifle, which he had loaned to Billy Keene, who was living in Chloride at this time. Keene had borrowed the rifle several months earlier with the intention of accompanying some men from the Swift Packing Company of Chicago on a hunting trip into the Black Range. He had used the rifle on several other occasions and was particularly pleased with its accuracy.

When the Kemps reached Chloride, they rode directly to the Keene residence, which at this time was on the east side of the street near the post office. Billy Keene was in the front yard when they rode up and went with them to help water and feed their horses.

When they returned and entered the yard gate at the front of the Keene residence, the boy and his father noticed a day's washing hanging on the clothesline. A large iron pot used for heating water had a roaring fire burning around it. Billy Keene, who was in the lead, said to the elder Kemp, "Ben, come over here. I want to show you something."

They walked to the pot and Keene raised a piece of corrugated iron roofing that was covering it. As he did, the wildly boiling water carried a human head to the surface. The head did a half turn and disappeared back into the bottom of the pot. It was a hideous looking thing. The eye sockets were empty, and long, black hair entwined the dark, shrunken face.

Benny, who was following a step behind his father, almost fell over backwards in horror, and the elder Kemp said sharply to Keene, "What the hell do you think you are doing?"

Bill Keene, with his wife and adopted son. "It was the Apache Kid whom Billy Keene's posse had killed."

Keene laughed at their consternation and began to explain. He said that about the first of September two horses were stolen from Charley Anderson, who lived on the South Prong a few miles west of Chloride. One of the horses was the blaze-faced, stocking-legged Baldy Socks that Ben Kemp had caught at North Water in 1899.

The day after the horses were stolen, Jim Hiler, Anderson's brother-in-law, and Johnny James, a neighboring rancher, rode up to the Anderson ranch house. Anderson told them what had happened, and they promised to help him track the horse thieves down.

The three men picked up the trail of the stolen horses, which led northwest. They sent a messenger to Chloride with word that the horse thieves were headed north up the Continental Divide. But on reaching the Continental Divide, the trail crossed over to the James brothers' cabin on the head of Diamond Creek.

They found the cabin ransacked. What the horse thieves could not take with them, they had tried to destroy. Flour, feathers, and pieces of cloth covered the yard in front of the cabin, where they had ripped open sacks and pillow cases and emptied their contents on the ground. A search of the horse pasture revealed that two horses were missing. One of them was Eddy James's favorite cow pony, Comanche. As they had anticipated, the horse thieves turned north from the James ranch towards the crest of the Black Range.

After the messenger reached Chloride, he was delayed in finding anyone interested enough to follow Anderson's party. Finally he found enough volunteers in Chloride and Fairview to form a posse of six men. These men were Bill Keene, Mike Sullivan, Charley Yaples, Walter Hearn, Harry James, and Bert Slinkard. The posse selected Billy Keene as their leader.

At half-past two on the afternoon of September 4, 1907, the posse left Chloride and headed north towards the head of Wild Horse Canyon. They intended to cut across the Continental Divide north of the Mud Holes, where they thought they would apprehend the horse thieves. By sundown they had reached the Walter McClure ranch on the head of Wild Horse Canyon. They asked

214

McClure, who rode his range regularly, if he had seen or heard anything of Anderson's party, and McClure told them he had not. This was disconcerting news. Since it was late and there was no advantage in riding after dark, the posse decided to stay overnight at McClure's ranch and get a new start the next day.

Before daylight the next morning they were ready to travel. Keene divided his men into two parties. He sent Charles Yaples, Walter Hearn, and Bert Slinkard to the Sebe Sorrels ranch on Pole Canyon, with instructions that if they heard anything of Anderson's party or the horse thieves, one of them was to meet him at the head of Wahoo Canyon at daylight the next morning.

Taking Mike Sullivan and Harry James with him, Keene headed west towards the Mud Holes, keeping a close watch for any sign of the horse thieves. Then he swung north to the Adobe Ranch, but no one there had seen or heard anything of them. Keene and his two men then cut east towards the Continental Divide. They watched closely for horse tracks, but except for range horses, none were found.

By daylight the next morning they were on the head of Wahoo Canyon, and somewhat to their surprise, they found Sebe Sorrels waiting for them. He told them that a trail, presumably that of the stolen horses, had been found north of Wild Horse Canyon. It led towards old Post Ojo Caliente on the Alamosa Canyon. If the trail was that of the horse thieves, they were probably trying to reach the rough and rugged San Mateo Mountains.

Keene rejoined the rest of his party at the Sebe Sorrels' ranch. They all agreed that if the horse thieves crossed Alamosa Canyon, they would work their way back towards the San Mateo divide. If they did this, the best chance of catching them was to reach the divide before they did and head them off. When the posse was ready to ride again, Sebe Sorrels insisted on joining them, and was promptly accepted.

After they left the Sebe Sorrels ranch on Pole Canyon, the posse crossed the Alamosa River and hit West Red Canyon a few miles below the Welty ranch. They continued up the canyon, expecting to cut the San Mateo divide north of Milligan Peak.

The man who found the tracks of the stolen horses believed that Charley Anderson and his party were still following the trail, and this proved to be true. Anderson, Johnny James, and Hiler trailed the stolen horses north from the James ranch to a point a few miles south of the Mud Holes. There the trail turned northeast, crossed Poverty Creek below the mouth of Straight Gulch, and followed the Wild Horse–Poverty Creek divide to a point a few miles east of the Atkins ranch. Keene and his posse had crossed the trail earlier where they least expected to find it, and therefore missed it.

At Ojo Caliente, Johnny James's horse went lame, forcing him to drop out of the chase. Anderson and Hiler continued to follow the trail, which led back into the western foothills of the San Mateo Mountains. Several miles northwest of Ojo Caliente they found the stolen horses grazing in a small glade at the bottom of a canyon. All of the horses were hobbled. Anderson, seeing no one around, dismounted and started to unhobble Baldy Socks. Just as he leaned forward to untie the hobbles, the report of a high-powered rifle rent the still mountain air, and a bullet zipped through both sides of Anderson's unbuttoned vest, missing his body by a hair's breadth. Anderson leaped back into his saddle, then he and Hiler beat a hasty retreat back down the canyon towards Ojo Caliente. Although they had seen no one, they did not doubt that both of them would have been killed if they had not left as they did.

After Keene and his posse left the Welty ranch, they continued up West Red Canyon to a point just below the mouth of Water Canyon. There they met Mrs. Hutchison and her children, who lived on the east slope of the San Mateo Mountains. She was on her way to the Welty ranch to visit her aunt, Mrs. Lou Welty. Keene knew that she had passed through the saddle on the main divide at the head of the canyon, and he asked her if she had seen anyone or noticed the tracks of any horses. When she told them she had not, the posse was convinced that they were too far north, so they turned southeast up Water Canyon. Several hours later they topped out on the main divide north of Blue Mountain. They found no sign of horse tracks, so they turned south down the main divide.

It was almost dark when they reached the south slope of Blue Mountain. From a vantage point on this high peak, which sits astride the San Mateo divide, they could see the reflection of two large campfires on a mountainside near what they thought was the head of San Mateo Canyon. Since it seemed unlikely that the horse thieves would build such fires, Billy Keene and his men decided they were signal fires built by Anderson and his party. It was hazardous to try to travel the crest of the San Mateo divide on a dark night, but there was reason to believe that the fires were an urgent message for help. So the posse decided to try to reach them at any cost. Picking their way along the rough divide was exceedingly slow and partly guesswork. In the darkness they lost their way and made a wrong turn which terminated in a rimmed rock mesa from which there was no way to descend. They were forced to return to the main divide, which took most of the night. When they reached the divide, they stopped to get a little rest and wait until there was enough light to travel.

At the first sign of day someone discovered horse tracks leading down the main divide in the direction of the campfires they had seen the evening before. Everyone quickly mounted, and the posse began following the trail as fast as possible along the rough divide. In less than thirty minutes the posse reached a deep saddle in the divide. A short distance down this saddle they ran onto a bunch of hobbled horses. Billy Keene immediately recognized Baldy Socks, and Harry James spotted his horse, Comanche. Since none of the horses that Charley Anderson and his party were riding were in the bunch, Keene and his men were almost sure the campfires they had seen the evening before were those of the horse thieves. Why they had two large fires was a mystery to the posse. As soon as the posse reached the stolen horses, Mike Sullivan saw a wisp of smoke rise from the bottom of the canyon below them. Everyone then realized that they were within three hundred yards of a camp. They had little time to plan a course of action, because they knew the people in camp would be coming after their horses within the next few minutes. They decided that Harry James and Walter Hearn would take the posse's horses out of sight over the

217

brow of the mountain on the north side of the saddle and stand guard over them while the rest of the posse hid among the stolen horses to see who came after them.

As soon as James and Hearn left with the horses, Yaples and Slinkard concealed themselves behind a large fir log that lay on the mountainside. Keene, Sorrels, and Sullivan had not yet taken cover when Mike discovered two Indians coming up the mountainside. Fortunately, there was a stand of pine grass on the mountainside which curved back towards the crest; otherwise the Indians would have seen them. Keene told Sullivan and Sorrels to hide and not to shoot until he did. Then he dropped into a shallow depression made by an uprooted pine. Mike Sullivan sprawled behind a small tree, and Sebe Sorrels hid behind a rock not much larger than his hat. This scanty protection left them practically in the open, and it does not seem possible that the Indians failed to see them.

The lead Indian, who was the larger of the two, was carrying a .30–.40-caliber Winchester cradled in his left arm. The smaller Indian who was also armed, was trailing the lead Indian by thirty yards. They were approaching the white men from the east just as the sun was rising over the distant San Andrea Mountains, throwing a ghostly shadow over the Jornada del Muerto. The white men knew if the Indians discovered them, they would have to fight to the finish and some of them would probably be killed. Keene decided to take no chances. He drew a bead on the lead Indian and let him advance to within fifteen yards of him. As he pulled the trigger, Sullivan and Sorrels also fired. The lead Indian sprang six feet into the air. The terrific impact from the soft-nosed bullets knocked him backward, causing his rifle to be flung thirty feet down the mountainside from his lifeless body.

At the report of the rifles the second Indian flew into action. Before the posse could bring their sights to bear on him, he was leaping down the mountainside and dodging through the pine timber in a desperate effort to save his life. A fusillade of rifle shots followed his retreat, but none of them brought him down, and, running like a deer, he passed out of sight into an aspen thicket on the north side of the mountain.

Bert Slinkard and Charley Yaples had taken no part in the shooting, and as soon as it was over, they crawled out of their hiding place from behind the fir log. The men who were guarding the posse's saddle horses were told to bring them down. When they arrived, they all examined the body of the dead Indian. Billy Keene said that directly over the heart there were three bullet holes that could have been covered with the palm of one hand.

Since they didn't know how many Indians there were, the men approached the camp with caution, but they soon found that the camp and all its equipment had been abandoned. Examination of the tracks in camp revealed that there were two children and at least one more adult besides the two encountered on the mountainside.

After a quick survey of camp part of the posse returned to the scene of the shooting and took up the trail of the Indian who had run around the north side of the mountain. When they reached the aspen thicket that the Indian had entered, the posse turned back. Billy Keene believed that the Indian had received a mortal wound, because on the rocks and ground there were blood splatters like those made by a buck deer shot through the heart.

When everyone was sure that there were no more Indians around to ambush them, they returned to the camp and started searching through the equipment. Among the items they found was a gold-filled Elgin watch and a ball of cloth string that had a five-dollar bill wound into its center. They also found several Indian bracelets made of Mexican silver and two or three rings. After the posse selected what they wanted to keep, they threw what was left of the camp equipment into the fire and burned it.

Then they rounded up the saddle horses and headed for Chloride, leaving the body of the dead Indian where he fell. Although they killed an Indian horse thief, they were not sure that the government would approve of their actions. So before they left, they all made a solemn promise never to tell the actual facts of the shooting. When Keene's party arrived back at Chloride, they learned of the Indian's attempt to kill Charley Anderson and realized that they had killed a dangerous and desperate character.

219

In the late afternoon of the day Keene's posse killed the Indian horse thief, Ralph Turner, a V + T cowboy who was riding line from the Monica Tanks at the north foot of the San Mateo Mountains forty miles north of where the killing occurred, returned to camp after a hard day's ride. He was weary, so he turned his horse in the corral without unsaddling him and went to the one-room log cabin that was his living quarters to rest a while before doing the chores and cooking his supper.

He lay down on his bunk and started reading a newspaper someone had brought him. He was alone at the camp, and except for an occasional chirp of a bird, the silence was so profound that a person could have heard a pin drop. Turner had been reading only a few minutes when he had a premonition that something was wrong. He peeped over the top of his newspaper at the open door of the cabin and found himself looking into the piercing eyes of a desperate-looking Indian. Turner was so dumbfounded he didn't speak at first. He wasn't sure whether his visitor was a man or a woman since Indians dressed and looked alike to him. It was evident that the Indian was badly in need of food because she kept pointing at some scraps of cold food that lay on the small table in the center of the room and then to her mouth. When Turner regained his speech, he began asking the Indian in Spanish what tribe she belonged to, but she refused to talk. The Indian kept shaking her head and pointing at the food on the table. Finally Turner nodded his head in consent, picked up his paper and pretended to read. The paper had a small hole near the center, and Turner managed to watch his uninvited guest through the hole without being detected. The Indian, though apparently famished, ate very sparingly. Thinking that Turner wasn't watching, she concealed food in the bosom of her shirt. Suddenly the Indian disappeared. Turner rushed to the door of the cabin, but could not see anyone. He went to the corral, mounted his saddle horse, and circled the ranch house looking for tracks, but he could find none.

A. L. Clements had three men working at his ranch on Estaline Canyon, three miles east of the Monica Tanks. Turner had no desire to stay at his lonely ranch cabin after this mysterious visit, so he rode over to Clements' and told them what had happened. Two of Clements' men, Henry Graham and Miles Dyer, wanted to return to Monica Tanks immediately, but Jack Bess, Clements' foreman, thought it best to wait until morning.

By daylight the next morning the four men were at Monica Tanks, and Henry Graham, who was an expert trailer, picked up the Indian's tracks and followed them a short distance to a piñon tree that had a drooping limb on which two papooses had been tied. The limb swayed down to within fifteen inches of the ground and the children had been well hidden. The reason for the Indian stowing food in the shirt was then apparent, and the men were sure that it was a woman. What a lone squaw on foot with two small children would be doing a hundred miles from the nearest reservation at this time was more than the cowboys could comprehend. Since they thought it indicated some kind of trouble, they decided to track her down and find out what it was. The trail was taken up in earnest and followed south from the Monica Tanks to the top of the San Mateo Mountains, then along the crest of the main divide. Later the trail dropped off of the east side of the mountain into the deep canyons and high ridges south of Rosedale. Most of the tracking had to be done on foot, but Graham kept steadily on the trail hour after hour. The men were sure that they would overtake the Indians, but when night fell, they were still on their trail. They had traveled almost forty miles along the canyons and ridges that day. How the Indian had managed to outdistance them and keep out of their sight was more than the cowboys could understand. Darkness forced the cowboys to abandon the trail and return to the AL Ranch.

The night after the cowboys quit the trail, an Indian woman was seen taking scraps of food out of a swill barrel behind the Harvey House in San Marcial, a small railroad town on the Río Grande, fifty miles south of the Monica Tanks cabin. Since this was out of the ordinary, the incident was reported to an officer of the law, who watched the swill barrel and captured the woman when she returned for more food scraps.

When she was questioned, the woman told the officers that she was the wife of the Apache Kid and that white men had killed her husband at the head of San Mateo Canyon in the San Mateo Mountains and had chased her with her two babies for two days. She said that she was glad that the Apache Kid was dead, because he was a bad Indian who had committed many murders and stolen many horses. She said that he was cruel to her and that he beat her and kept her chained in camp. She claimed that he kidnapped any squaw that he fancied, and when he tired of her company, he would murder her and leave her body in the hidden recesses of the mountain ranges over which he roamed. How many of these hapless Indian women he murdered will never be known.

The woman and her babies were placed under guard in a small, one-room, adobe building that had only one door and one window. Sometime during the night the woman, by leaving her two babies, managed to escape to a farm near town, where she stole a horse. She fashioned a bit from a piece of barbed wire, placed it in the horse's mouth, and twisted it around his lower jaw. Then she rode the horse bareback eighty miles across the Jornada del Muerto to the Mescalero Indian Agency, where she reported to the agent in charge and told him what had happened. The agent notified the authorities at San Marcial and had her two children sent to the Mescalero Indian Reservation where they or their descendants are probably living today.

A short time before the Indian horse thief was killed, a rancher named Saunders, who lived near Kingston, was waylaid and murdered while searching for some goats he owned. Prior to his death Saunders and a hermit named Red Mills had a misunderstanding, and circumstantial evidence pointed an accusing finger at Mills. Although Mills denied any knowledge of the killing, it looked as though he would be found guilty when the case came to trial. After Mills was placed in jail, sheriff's officers investigating the case discovered that Saunders had owned a gold-filled Elgin watch, which was missing when his body was found. On inquiry it was learned that a short time before he was murdered, Saunders had sent his watch to a jeweler to have it repaired. The jeweler who repaired it

The Apache Kid "became a lone wolf, preying upon his own people as well as the white man."

had written down the serial number and inscribed one of his own in the back of the case.

The Indian horse thief had been in the vicinity of Kingston at the time Saunders was killed, and the Elgin watch that was found in his camp was sent to the sheriff's office at Hillsboro. When the serial numbers were checked with those of the jeweler, they were found to be identical. Since there was no longer any doubt that the Indian had killed Saunders, Red Mills was released.

By the time the watch was checked, a report came from the Mescalero Indian Agency that it was the Apache Kid whom Billy Keene's posse had killed. Keene and all of the men who were with him were relieved to hear this, but for some reason they never collected the nine-thousand-dollar reward that was offered for capture of the Kid dead or alive.

When the men from the Swift Packing Company came down to hunt, they soon learned what had happened and prevailed upon Billy Keene to bring them the Apache Kid's head for a souvenir. Keene rode the thirty miles back to the head of San Mateo Canyon, where the posse had left the body lying on the ground, and severed the head from the carcass with a hand axe. He placed it in a gunny sack, which he tied on his saddle, and rode back to Chloride. He was in the process of cleaning the skull for what he called "posterity's sake" when the two Kemps rode into town.

This was exciting news to the boy and his father. They thought it was quite a coincidence that the .30–.40 rifle that Kemp had bought nine years earlier to defend his home against the marauding Apache was instrumental in writing the final chapter of the Kid's wild and evil career.

18.
Alamosa Country

After drilling the Nester Draw well, a contract was signed with Mrs. Agnes Morley Cleaveland to drill a well at her ranch five miles north of the Datil post office. It was about the middle of December by the time the rig reached her ranch, but it had been an open fall, and outside of being a little cool the weather was excellent.

The creek crossing two miles north of the Baldwin store was narrow and boggy. When Kemp came to it, he whipped his team into a gallop and hit the creek, knocking mud high into the air, and the momentum carried the heavily loaded wagon across. When they reached the ranch, Mrs. Cleaveland wanted to know how they ever made the crossing at the mud hole, and Ben Kemp replied, "Oh, we made it all right but we sure tore it up like a sow's bed."

Work on the well at Mrs. Cleaveland's ranch took most of the winter. Instead of setting up camp, the Kemps stayed at the ranch house and paid Mrs. Cleaveland board.

During the winter firewood for the cookstove ran low, and Mrs. Cleaveland sent Benny over to Johnny Payne's ranch to borrow a wagon reach, since the one on her wagon was broken. Benny had no idea what a wagon reach was and was ashamed to ask. When he arrived at Payne's ranch, he found Johnny gone and was forced to go to the house and ask Mrs. Payne to loan Mrs. Cleaveland the wagon reach. Mrs. Payne, who was busy cooking, said, "Certainly, be glad to. It's down on the running gear of the wagon at the corral. Just go down and take it off."

Benny went down to the corral and looked over the running gear of the wagon, but he couldn't figure out what part of it was the reach. So he returned to the house and said, "I can't find it." Mrs. Payne went back to the corral with him and pointed out what

225

Benny had always heard called the coupling pole. His face was pretty red, but he learned a new word that he never forgot.

Mrs. Payne was a New Yorker, as was her neighbor, Mrs. Ray Morley. Mrs. Morley paid the Paynes a visit the day after they had butchered a beef. Mrs. Payne was cooking a cowboy dish called "son-of-a-gun," and Mrs. Morley raised the lid on the pot and said, "Sally, what in the world are you cooking?"

"Oh," said Mrs. Payne, who had learned a few of the western ways, "that's the entrails. Johnny always makes me eat them and the hide first."

Mrs. Morley, who was staring at the pot with a horrified expression, was almost convinced that Mrs. Payne was telling the truth. She exclaimed in a shrill voice, "Well! Ray couldn't force me to eat anything like that." Everyone had a good laugh at her expense, and she learned later that the hide was not a part of the dish.

The following spring Kemp signed another contract with Will Fullerton for a well eight miles east of Datil. This 367-foot well was the deepest ever drilled with the light rig. The rock formation, which was of volcanic origin, was filled with countless small, clear crystals. Ants carried millions of these to the surface and deposited them on their mounds. The crystals reflected the bright sunlight, and the Kemp children called them "sheepherder diamonds."

While this well was being drilled, Mrs. Ada Morley paid the Kemps a visit. She was on a return trip from Magdalena to Datil by way of North Plain. She arrived in camp about noon and was invited to lunch, which was served by Beulah and Mary, who were cooking for the drill crew at that time. Mrs. Morley was good-humored and tried to strike up a conversation with the girls. When she learned Beulah's name she made the mistake of singing a verse of "Beulah Land, Sweet Beulah Land." Although she stayed in camp for more than an hour, she failed to get a word out of Beulah.

Two more wells were drilled at the Datil post office, one for Fred Baldwin, who was combination merchant and postmaster, and the other for a sheepman named Gutierrez. Because of a money panic at this time, work was scarce, so Ben Kemp decided to go to Beaver Creek for the rest of the winter.

226

They hitched the teams to two wagons and drove to Magdalena, where the wheels on Benny's wagon were replaced with new wheels with four-inch tires. These new wheels saved his life a few days later.

Benny's wagon, which was drawn by four mules, was loaded with three hundred feet of green lumber, six sacks of cement, and other building materials estimated to weigh three thousand pounds. The two wagons loaded with supplies left Magdalena on the morning of December 20, 1908. Benny was elated over getting to go home. He had been at the drill camp for the past nine months.

The two wagons, with Benny's leading, reached the west edge of Kemp Mesa at four o'clock on Christmas Eve. Since the road leading down the rim of the canyon to the ranch house was crooked, rough, and steep, the lead team on Benny's wagon was unhitched to make it easier to maneuver on the short turns.

The last stretch of steep road led straight to the house, and at the top of this stretch there were a few feet of comparatively level ground. When Benny's team reached this spot, they balked, and he had trouble getting them started. When they did start, it was with a bound. Benny, who was walking alongside the wagon, tried to stop them by pulling on the reins, but they had cold-jawed and were headed down the steep grade straight towards Mrs. Kemp and the children, who were coming up the road to meet him.

There was a tree growing so close to the road that Benny could not pass between it and the wagon without being crushed. He was forced to run on the upper side, wrapping the reins around the tree. This caused the reins to part, letting the team loose.

In a final effort to stop the team, Benny grabbed a small pole used as a brake lever. He ran alongside the wagon and began putting pressure on this makeshift brake. The hind wheels were dead-locked, but the wagon had gained so much momentum the team was still traveling at a gallop. Benny might have been able to stop the wagon if the brake had held, but the small lever on the brake bar broke, tripping Benny and causing him to slide feet first under the wagon between the front and rear wheels, and the right rear wheel passed over his chest.

227

The unbraked wagon then forced the team into a run. They headed straight for the house and Mrs. Kemp. She and some of the children would have been killed, but the mule on the upper side of the road grade outran the one on the lower side, causing the wagon to leave the road and high-center on a rock wall at the lower edge of the road bed, where it finally stopped.

Benny was picked up and carried to the house, apparently dead. His father was convinced he would not survive, but his mother would not give up. After she had administered medicine and attended him for half an hour, he regained consciousness. The next day he was better, but could barely breath. It was more than three months before he was able to resume work.

A few months later Ben Kemp had an accident on the same road and was nearly killed. Juniper wood for the cookstove had to be hauled from the top of Kemp Mesa into the creek bottom. About a quarter mile below the rim of the mesa the road ran parallel to a small ravine called Grandma Canyon. At this point the grade was exceedingly steep and rocky. When the wagon started down this grade, it gained momentum and began bouncing over the rocks. The mule on the upper side of the grade became frightened and started to run, causing the wagon to leave the road. The wagon fell twenty feet to the bottom of the canyon and landed on top of Kemp. Large boulders were scattered around the bottom of the canyon, and Kemp fell between two of them. The boulders held the wagon and wood off his body. Kemp was stunned for a few minutes, but he miraculously escaped serious injury. As soon as he could, he crawled out from under the wood and found the team tangled in the harness and quite a bit more bruised up than he was.

While he was in Magdalena, Ben Kemp met Johnny Payne, who owned a ranch at Red Lake north of Alamosa. He needed a well because the lake at his ranch had dried up. Early in March, 1908, Kemp moved his rig to Payne's ranch, which was about forty miles north of Magdalena.

When this well was finished, Kemp signed a contract with José Armijo to drill a well about eight miles northeast of Red Lake. As soon as the rig was moved to this new location, Kemp was forced to return to Beaver Creek because of illness. He left Jess McCarty and Henry Graham at the rig. Since Henry was leaving in a few days for Reserve, Benny, who had been attending school at Beaver Creek, was sent to the rig to help Jess.

When Benny arrived, he found Henry Graham in camp. Jess McCarty, who was left in charge, had gone to Magdalena after a load of supplies. Two days later their supplies ran out, and Benny and Henry were forced to eat broiled rabbit without salt, which was no more appetizing than the first time the boy had tried it.

Since there was nothing to do, time passed slowly for the two boys. There were a few wolf traps in camp, so they set one and caught a coyote. The coyote's foot was not injured by the trap, and they tied his mouth and feet so he could not bite or scratch. They heated a branding iron and ran the Bush brand on the coyote's left shoulder. Then they ear-marked him, strapped a small bell around his neck, and turned him loose. As the coyote ran off, the bell swung around and around his neck.

Five years later Tom Payne, Johnny Payne's brother, who was also a rancher in the Alamosa country, was trying to locate some of his saddle horses, one of which wore a bell. When he rode out to the mesa where his horses usually grazed, Payne could hear the bell, but could see no horses. He was even more puzzled because there were no tracks. After he had heard the bell for about the third time, Tom became worried. He couldn't figure out whether someone was playing a trick on him or he was losing his mind. Then one morning he rode around a large rock at the foot of the mesa, and a coyote wearing a bell jumped up and started running across the prairie. Tom wondered if it was someone's pet, but undoubtedly it was the same coyote the two pranksters had turned loose.

From the Armijo well the rig was moved about six miles north, where a well was started for Don Manuel, a sheepman who lived on the Alamosa River. The rig had not been there long when Nels Fields paid them a visit. He owned a cow ranch about eight miles southeast of the drilling location. He said that he was reminded of a time when a cow outfit he was working with camped at the exact spot of the well rig's location.

It was in July and the summer rains had started. The day before camping there, the cowboys had made a circle towards the head of Alamosa Creek, and one of their horses had thrown a shoe. The man who owned the horse roped him out of the remuda next morning and started to reset the shoe. While he was digging caked mud out of the horse's hoof, he found a gold nugget about the size of a large pea embedded alongside the frog of the horse's foot.

Nels said the cow work was forgotten, and an intensive search took place. The remuda was trailed where they grazed during the night, and all of the ground was closely examined. The search continued for five days. The cowboy's saddle horse was backtracked over the ground they had covered the day before, but no sign of anything resembling gold was found.

On December 17, Ben Kemp and his son hitched three spans of horses to a wagon and drove to Magdalena. They arrived in town during a snowstorm, and the next morning the temperature dropped to thirty-two degrees below zero, the coldest temperature on record. They were forced to remain in town until the morning of the twenty-second, when they continued their trip home.

After they arrived at Beaver Creek, they stayed over a day and then took the family to Chloride. On December 28, 1908, Julia, the oldest Kemp girl, was married to Jess McCarty. The newlyweds returned to Beaver Creek with the family, and during the following February they moved to the well rig, where Julia cooked for the drill crew.

On March 14, 1909, one of the heaviest snowstorms in years hit the Alamosa country. When the snow quit falling, it was thirty inches deep, and travel almost came to a standstill. On the afternoon of the fifteenth, Lawrence Parsons and his family, who had a ranch eight miles north of the well rig, arrived in camp. His team had given out from pulling their buckboard through the deep snow, and they were forced to stay overnight.

The next morning Kemp loaned Parsons a span of mules to help pull the buckboard the remaining eight miles to his ranch. It took five hours to cover the eight miles, and would probably have taken longer if Benny and another boy had not ridden ahead to break trail. Benny was practically snow-blind when he reached the Parsons ranch, and he was so badly burned from the glare of the bright sun on the snow that he could barely get around. He was in misery for several days.

Work on the Don Manuel well continued until the middle of April. When the well reached a depth of 314 feet, the contract was completed. When Kemp asked for his money, however, Manuel flatly refused to pay him, because there was no water. The contract was turned over to a lawyer named Fitch in Socorro. When the lawyer explained to Manuel what could happen to him if he failed to meet his agreement, he quickly changed his mind and paid Kemp in full.

The next move was to the Nels Fields ranch, where they drilled a 125-foot well that furnished plenty of water. When the Fields well was finished, there was no more work in the Alamosa country. So Jess McCarty quit and went to work for Frank H. Winston, who owned the R-Bar-R Ranch on Cuchillo Negro Creek below Grafton.

The next well contracted was on the Plains of San Agustín, north of the C-Bar-N Ranch. Ben Kemp and his son were the only ones left to move the rig the eighty miles to the new location. When they reached the crossing on Alamosa Creek, they found that it was powdery, dry quicksand. Twenty feet from the north bank the wagon wheels sank to a depth of eighteen inches. It was impossible for the teams to pull the five thousand pound rig to the south bank of the creek, and no extra teams were available. Kemp and his son wondered if they would ever be able to reach the south bank of the creek with their heavy equipment.

They carried a pick and shovel to the south bank of the creek and dug two trenches eight feet long, eighteen inches wide, and three feet deep. Then they wrapped a heavy logging chain around two posts, which were eight feet long and eight inches in diameter. The posts were placed in the bottom of the two trenches. The two

231

ends of the chain were pulled through a small trench that ran at a right angle to the two main trenches and midway to the bottom. The three trenches were filled with dirt and packed tight. The "dead men" were now ready for their strain.

In the equipment used for loading the rig onto a wagon was a double and triple block and tackle threaded with three hundred feet of new, one-inch cable. The blocks were carried to where the dead men were buried, and the triple block tied hard and fast to the chain. The blocks were pulled full length of their span, and the double block tied to the two-inch drill cable that was lashed to the tongue of the wagon on which the well rig was loaded.

A team was hitched to the fall rope, and the span of the block and tackle closed. This had to be repeated several times before the heavy rig was pulled onto firm ground on the south side of the creek. It required eight hours of grueling work to move the rig and its equipment a distance of eighty yards.

When Kemp and his son had moved all of the equipment to the south side of Alamosa Creek, they hitched the teams to the wagons and started for Abbe Springs, about eight miles southwest of the crossing. It was sundown when they reached the springs, and both of the Kemps were dog-tired and hungry. Half a mile east of the springs a man named Chavez owned a cow ranch, and since they were short on provisions, they walked over to the ranch house with the intention of buying some eggs. When they arrived, the Mexican family was not friendly, but finally agreed to sell their hungry-looking visitors two dozen eggs. Kemp and Benny returned to camp, where they cooked and ate the entire batch.

They rolled their bedrolls out on the ground and retired early, but got little rest. The small black ants commonly found around piñon and cedar trees were out, and hundreds of them crawled into their beds and over their faces during the night.

The next morning about eight hundred quail came into Abbe Springs to water. The hills surrounding the springs were a natural habitat for quail, and the springs were the only watering place for miles.

In due time the rig reached the new location, and a well with plenty of water was soon completed for a young sheepman named Chavez, who resided at Los Lunas.

While drilling the Chavez well, the two Kemps visited another rig that was drilling a well about five miles east of their camp. This rig was using a Stickney gasoline engine for power, the first of its kind they had seen. After watching it operate a while, Ben Kemp decided it had horse power beat six ways for Sunday. Benny was jubilant over the decision to purchase an engine, because it had been his job to follow the team around the circle of the horse-power sweep and keep the horses at a steady gait. How many hundreds of miles he had walked in performing this duty, he did not know, but many days he had walked from sunup until dark.

While working in the vicinity of the C-Bar-N Ranch, the Kemps met Tom Tucker, who is mentioned in *Arizona's Dark and Bloody Ground*, Earle R. Forrest's book about the Tonto Basin War. It was the first time Ben Kemp had seen Tucker since 1884, when Kemp led a squad of Texas Rangers into Deming, New Mexico, and Tucker mistook them for some of Curley Bill's men.

From the Plains of San Agustín the rig was moved to the Benton Satathite ranch on the Alamosa, north of old Post Ojo Caliente. On November 20, Ben Kemp made a trip to Beaver Creek, and when he returned two weeks later, he found the Alamosa community in a state of excitement.

On Thanksgiving Day, Benny had accompanied the Satathite, Welty, and Tucker families to a dance being given at Fairview on Thanksgiving night. He knew most of the people living around the small mining town, because he had attended school at Chloride a few years earlier. Since Jess McCarty, his brother-in-law, and a friend named Dave Sorrels, were running the old Meyers' bar, Benny anticipated having a gay and enjoyable time.

The dance started at 8:00 P.M. and seemed to offer a good night of dancing. The only disturbance was a disagreement between Al Hagan, Sam Satathite's brother-in-law and Benton Satathite. But no one paid any attention to the argument, since it was not serious.

At 8:45, Benny walked down to the bar, which was on the same side of the street as the dance hall, to visit with Jess McCarty.

While he was there, he noticed Jim Taylor and Ike Futch, two of his friends, in conversation near the center of the barroom. He walked over to them, shook hands, and told them they were missing a lot of good dancing. Then he returned to the dance hall, which was about thirty yards up the street from the bar. When he reached the hall, a lively two-step was in progress, so he joined in and danced the set out. While he was dancing, he noticed Tom Tucker, one of the boys who had come to the dance with him, watching the dance through the plate-glass window at the front of the hall. Thinking that Tom would like to dance if he knew any of the local girls, Benny walked out onto the boardwalk at the front of the hall, with the intention of bringing Tom into the dance hall and introducing him to some of his girl schoolmates.

The dance had been in progress for an hour and fifteen minutes. The moon had risen over the Cuchillo Mountains to the east, and the streets of the little town were bathed in moonlight. Benny looked down towards the bar and saw a group of men standing in the middle of the street. Just as he started to speak to Tom Tucker, there was a quick movement among the men, followed by the report of a heavy caliber revolver, which was followed immediately by the sharp crack of a lighter caliber weapon.

The crowd in the center of the street scattered and ran in all directions, leaving two men who were shooting at each other as fast as they could pull the triggers of their weapons. This had happened so quickly Benny didn't realize for a few seconds what was taking place. Then he noticed a long, lanky individual who was running down the street in the line of fire. Bullets were whizzing around the man, and he was straining every nerve in his body trying to put distance between himself and the two combatants.

On the corner directly across the street from the Frank H. Winston store was a vacant house from which the windows and flooring had been removed, leaving only the sills to which the floor had been nailed. When the man reached this building, he dived through a window onto the sills inside.

On his way from the bar to the dance hall was a bowlegged cowboy called Billy Dodd. He was a small man who walked with the

234

peculiar gait of men who have spent years in the saddle. When the shooting started, Dodd neither increased nor slackened his speed, but kept casually on his way. When he had reached a point near the west end of the boardwalk, which joined the dance hall and the Reilly Hotel, a bullet from the heavy caliber revolver hit the ground within six inches of his feet, knocking gravel in all directions. Dodd jumped like a cow stung by a heel fly and made a beeline for the front door of the hotel. Someone was standing in the door, watching the fight, but this did not hamper Dodd. Running at full speed, he collided with the man, knocking him back into the hotel.

A cowboy working for Patrick McAughan, who lived near Grafton, rode into town to attend the dance. He had reached a point directly in front of the dance hall when the shooting started. When a bullet whizzed past his head, he forgot the dance, reined his horse around, and ran back up the street in the direction from which he had come. After he had covered a hundred yards, the rapping of his quirt could still be heard above the pounding of his horse's hoofs. Tom Tucker nodded his head in the direction the man had disappeared and said, "That guy is in a hell of a hurry, ain't he?"

Benny never answered him, because he saw one of the two men in the gun fight fall to the ground. At the same instant a bullet whizzed by his head. The man who was left standing stepped forward and snapped his empty revolver at his enemy. Then he started stumbling backwards as though he had lost his balance, and when he had completed a small quarter circle, he dropped to the ground.

Benny, thinking the gun fight resulted from a drunken quarrel, turned to Tom Tucker and said, "Tom, we had better get inside the dance hall. If anyone finds out we saw this, they will keep us in Hillsboro for the next ten years."

When Tucker did not answer, Benny started for the door but failed to make it. Mrs. Futch and Jim Taylor's son, a boy about fourteen, tried to enter the door at the same time he did. They were running full speed and collided with Benny, sending him sprawling. By the time he had regained his feet, Mrs. Futch had

235

forced her way through the crowded door and was running down the middle of the dance hall, screaming, "Ike is killed, Ike is killed."

A waltz had just started, but when Mrs. Futch started screaming, the musicians stopped playing, and people began to ask questions. Bert Slinkard, who was dancing with Mrs. Taylor, yelled, "Go on with the dance. That was only a bunch of firecrackers you heard."

Evidently Mrs. Taylor knew it was not firecrackers, because she started for the door at a run. By this time Benny was back trying to enter the hall, and when Mrs. Taylor broke through the jammed door, she collided with him, knocking him back onto the sidewalk. Benny decided there was no use trying to get into the hall. He saw Johnny James in the crowd at the door and asked him what had happened. James told him that Ike Futch and Jim Taylor had shot it out and killed each other. This did not seem possible to Benny, who had talked to both of them less than thirty minutes earlier. In his estimation they were levelheaded, and to his knowledge they had been friends a few months earlier.

There had been fourteen shots fired in less than ten seconds. The shooting had taken place directly in front of the old Meyers' bar, where Jess McCarty was working. Benny feared that a stray bullet might have passed through the plate glass at the front of the building, and he walked down to the bar to investigate. He found Jess safe, but on his way to the bar he noticed there were three people lying in the street instead of two and wondered who the third one could be, since James had told him that Futch and Taylor were the only ones killed. He learned later that the third person was Mrs. Taylor. She had fainted when she had arrived at the scene of the fight and found her husband dead.

There was quite a crowd in the barroom, including a long, lanky individual named Barry Cox, who was telling his friends he was leaving for Hillsboro as soon as he could saddle his horse.

"Why not wait until morning, Barry?" Dave Sorrels asked.

"No," said Cox, "another one might start. I'm leaving." And he rode on to Hillsboro that night.

The bodies of the two men were carried to the dance hall and laid out on the floor, where their wounds were examined. Futch had two gunshot wounds, either of which would have been fatal. A soft-nosed, .38–.40-caliber pistol, evidently the first shot fired by Taylor, passed through his body just above the hips. The second bullet, the one that knocked him down, grazed his right arm below the elbow and entered his body near the right armpit, coming out against the skin on his left shoulder.

Taylor had two wounds in his right chest, one just above and one just below the nipple. Both of these bullets passed clear through his body, missing the backbone by a half-inch. Either one of these bullets would have knocked him down if they had been heavy caliber, but the .25-caliber bullets from Futch's automatic pistol passed through his body leaving him to die on his feet. There is little doubt that the short, choppy steps as he stumbled backwards were his final death struggle, because he never moved again after falling to the ground. The fight killed everyone's desire for dancing, and most of them left the dance hall with a feeling that two men had met their deaths because of a meaningless misunderstanding.

When Benton Satathite and his party returned to the Alamosa, they found that the four hound dogs he had left at the ranch had killed all of his wife's chickens and their pet antelope. So in more ways than one, their Thanksgiving had been anything but pleasant.

A short time after Ben Kemp arrived back at the well rig, he received word that the gasoline engine he had ordered was in Magdalena. He made a trip into town after the engine and hired a man named Ed Owens to install and operate it. When Owens arrived at the rig, he found the drive pulley on the engine was too large, and nearly a month passed before a replacement could be obtained.

By this time it was getting near Christmas, so Kemp decided to send a four-horse wagon into Magdalena after a load of supplies and return to Beaver Creek for the rest of the winter.

A few days before the wagon was ready to start, Benny was stricken with a severe case of tonsillitis. Since he needed the care of a physician, he had to make a trip into town. He hitched a span of Spanish mules to a buckboard, climbed into the seat, and drove

237

the sixty-five miles into Magdalena in a little less than nine hours.

Two of the Kemp girls were visiting "Grandma" Matilda Sata-thite at her ranch on Big Pigeon Canyon. Ben Kemp had to have the team and buckboard that Benny had driven to town so that he could go get the girls. Kemp and Ed Owens hitched six horses to a wagon and drove to Magdalena, where they found Benny much improved from his recent illness and ready to start home.

Ben Kemp left Magdalena for the Satathite ranch on the morning of December 20. He told Owens and Benny to meet him at the forks of the Magdalena—Patterson Cutoff road, three miles down canyon below Paddy's Hole, about sundown on the afternoon of December 22.

The day he left town, a blizzard hit Magdalena and the surrounding country, and temperatures dropped to thirty below zero. Benny and Ed Owens were dismayed, but this did not alter their preparations for the trip to Beaver Creek.

As directed, the freight wagon left Magdalena on the morning of December 21, 1909. Owens and Benny hoped to reach Durfey's Well, twenty miles west of town, but there were about six inches of snow on the ground, which slowed down travel. Icicles nearly a foot long formed on the team's noses, and it was necessary to stop them occasionally and break the ice that formed in the hair of their tails to keep it from beating their hocks raw. Frost in the air was so dense it gave the appearance of snow. Fence wires looked like two-inch bristling cables, and the squeal of the wagon wheels cutting through the snow could be heard for a quarter-mile.

Benny and Owens were dressed like outdoorsmen on the Canadian border, but the cold wind chilled them, and they were forced to walk to keep warm. Walking was awkward because they were unaccustomed to such heavy garb.

When dusk began to settle, they were five miles short of the protective grove of oak trees below Durfey's Well. They were afraid that their teams would freeze to death if they camped on the open plain, but this was a risk they had to take. The teams had reached the end of their endurance for the day.

They positioned their wagon broadside to the wind, unhitched

238

the six weary work animals, and blanketed them. Then they tied them on the leeward side of the wagon to protect them from the icy wind, fed them plenty of hay and grain, and hoped the horses would still be alive the next morning.

After they cared for the teams, Owens and Benny threw their bedrolls together and went to bed. Although they did not sleep warm, the next morning they were delighted to see that all of their work horses had survived. The morning was clear but very cold. They had to be careful when touching the hame buckles and trace chains, because without gloves their hands stuck fast to the frosty metal.

Better time was made from Durfey's Well to the agreed meeting place at the fork of the Patterson Cutoff road. There was plenty of piñon timber at this point, and soon after camp was pitched, a roaring campfire was going. In a few minutes Ben Kemp and his two daughters arrived in camp.

They had been fighting the cold all day and had kept from freezing by heating malpais rocks in campfires, then wrapping them in burlap sacks and placing them on the floor of the buckboard.

The next camp was at Indian Peaks. Although the snow was deeper there, the cold was less severe, because there was plenty of tall pine timber. On the fourth day between sundown and dark the freight wagon reached the upper end of the Beaver Creek box. Since it was impossible to guide the wagon down the deep box canyon after dark, the teams were unhitched and driven to the home ranch. The next morning they were driven back to the wagon and hitched up, and the remainder of the trip was completed by noon. After four days of snow and frigid weather, the comfort of the warm log cabin was truly appreciated.

On December 26, Benton Satathite and Al Hagan rode into the ranch on Beaver Creek. They were on their way to Naco, Mexico, and wanted Benny to go with them as far as Sheldon, Arizona, and bring their saddle horses back. Benny's father did not approve of this trip, but finally agreed to let him go.

Benton and his two companions left Beaver Creek on the morning of December 27 and traveled down the Gila gorge to Cliff, then across the high country west of Cliff to Bitter Creek. At sunup on New Year's Day, 1910, they reached Bob Gillespie's home on the east side of the Gila River from Sheldon, which was a flag station on the A. T. & S. F. Railway. Gillespie, who was an uncle of Benton, was a veteran of the Tonto Basin War. He was wounded in the fight with the Tewksburys at Middleton's cabin in Tonto Basin about August 11, 1887.

When he was ready to start back home, Benny talked John Damron and Boss Kemp, two of his cousins who were living near Duncan, Arizona, into returning to Beaver Creek with him. They traveled through the upper Gila gorge on their way back. The entire trip was made without a camp bed. Trying to sleep on saddle blankets in zero-degree weather was a hazardous undertaking, and they suffered severely from the cold.

Benny and his two cousins reached Beaver Creek on the afternoon of January 12, 1910. Ben Kemp, who had been wondering where he could find enough men to run the well rig on a twenty-four-hour basis, hired Boss and John, and preparations were made for returning to the Alamosa.

After the cold spell in December the weather cleared off, and every evening Halley's Comet decorated the sky—a sight that would not be witnessed again for seventy-five years.

About the twentieth of February, Kemp took his crew to the Benton Satathite ranch, and work began on the well. They had been there only a few days when Benton and Al Hagan returned.

When the Satathite well was completed, the rig was moved to the Jack Tucker ranch, four miles to the north up the canyon. Trouble was encountered on this well when the drill bit hung on a bent place in the well casing and the tower of the rig was pulled down. The Manila cable was cut at the ground level, and the drill tools fell two hundred feet back to the bottom. It took several days to build a new tower and retrieve the drill stem from the well.

The next location was eight miles southwest of Nester Draw, where another well was drilled for Juan Sanchez y Vijil. While this well was being drilled, Ben Kemp made a trip to Magdalena and met his old friend and neighbor, Jeff Hill, who was living in town

240

at this time. Hill told him that a sheepman named David García, who owned ranches near Atarque, a small village north of Quemado, New Mexico, wanted fifteen wells drilled. On the strength of this information, Kemp hired two extra men and sent them to the well rig with written instructions for Benny to take charge and move the rig to Quemado as soon as the Vijil well was completed.

The Vijil well was finished by the first of April, and the rig was moved to Quemado. When Benny notified David García, he discovered that García did not want a single well drilled. He was then confronted by a bad situation. It was necessary that the rig be kept working to pay expenses. Although there was plenty of unwatered range, a survey of the surrounding country failed to find anyone in need of wells.

Although it had been a policy never to sign a contract for a well less than a hundred feet deep, Benny was forced to take any work available. He drilled a shallow well for Anastasio Baca at New Quemado. It was the first of its kind in that section of Socorro County.

When the Baca well proved a success, Ramon García, a sheepman living in West Quemado, wanted a well drilled three miles northwest of Rito Gap. Benny miraculously escaped serious injury while work was in progress on this well.

Water for the rig had to be hauled from Quemado. Since there was no wagon tank, fifty-gallon oil drums had to be used. The eight-mile stretch of road between Quemado and camp was fairly smooth except for gullies and the pass through Rito Gap, which was sideling and rocky.

On one of his trips to Quemado, Benny was accompanied by Al Claxton and Arthur Mansfield, the two new men in the crew. They bought a few supplies, including two dozen fresh eggs without cartons. Al Claxton decided to carry them in his hat to keep them from breaking. He selected a place between the water barrels at the backend of the wagon box and sat down.

It was dusk by the time they reached Rito Gap on their return to camp. Benny, who was driving the four-horse team, could not see the roadbed plainly. To keep from running off the road, he

241

guided the wagon too close to the upper side, and the left front wheel hit a rock. One of the water barrels, which weighed over four hundred pounds, tilted and hit Benny, knocking him out of the wagon. He passed over the brake lever as he fell, and the foot bracket on the lever caught in the cuff of his trousers leg and swung him head down alongside the front wagon wheel on the right.

He dropped the lines as he fell, and the unguided team ran down the mountainside. Benny dangled alongside the front wheel for fifty yards before the cuff on his trousers leg tore out, causing him to fall head first into a pile of malpais rock.

Arthur Mansfield, who was standing on the opposite side of the wagon box from Benny, crawled over the dashboard onto the wagon tongue and gathered up the lines. By this time the runaway team had reached the foot of the mountain, and Mansfield managed to circle and stop them. A few minutes later Benny reached the wagon. He was badly bruised, but not seriously injured.

While Al Claxton was trying to keep his balance among the rocking barrels as the wagon bounced down the mountainside, he dropped his hat and broke every one of the eggs. This was a real calamity to the three men, who had been eagerly anticipating fresh eggs for breakfast.

When work was finished on the Rito Gap well, Ed Owens, Al Claxton, and Arthur Mansfield had to be discharged, because no other wells could be contracted. They were personal friends as well as good workers, and it was a blue day when they had to leave. After the three men left, the rig sat idle for nearly a month, and time passed slowly for the men left in camp.

A former county surveyor named Jerry Otto was living in a cave a mile west of camp. During the early 1880's, Otto helped the United States Land Office run the first survey over the Black Range and the headwaters of the Gila River. He was now a cranky and lonely old man in his late seventies. Benny spent most of his time at the cave visiting with Otto and trying to learn a few things about a surveyor's transit. Within a few days they were good friends, because Otto had found someone still interested enough to listen to his vast and interesting experiences.

242

19.
Mesa Redondo

When Ben Kemp arrived at camp and discovered there was no work, he decided to drill a well at a choice location, equip it with a windmill, and sell it to the highest bidder. He saddled Rusty and left camp to make a survey of the surrounding country. He selected a spot on the west side of a valley, about three miles wide and nine miles long, which extends from some low hills south of the location to the salt lake seven miles to the north. A good stand of grama grass interspersed with clumps of chamiso brush covers the valley floor.

A low mesa skirts the east edge of the valley, and at the south and upper end of the mesa an extinct volcano raises its crown above the skyline. The peak, which is called Sierra Pomo, glows from a dull to a bright brick red in the setting sun. Nestled at the foot of this cone-shaped peak is an ancient, pitch-black lava flow that is twisted into every conceivable shape. One obscure cow trail led through this tangled mass, but most of it was impassable.

West of the location is a plateau called the Mesa Redondo which is elevated four hundred feet. The mesa, which is three miles wide and six miles long, is surrounded by sandstone rimrock ranging from a low bench at the west end to a cliff a hundred feet high at the east, where the well was later located. Millions of years ago this sandstone mesa had been the soft sandy bottom of rivers or lakes, and the tracks of dinosaurs are plainly visible in the sandstone along the mesa's rim.

Seven miles to the north is a large extinct volcano crater, one and a quarter miles in diameter. Three hundred feet below the rim of this crater is a shallow salt lake, which covers two-thirds of the crater bottom. The water in this lake is only about two feet deep, except for two holes near its southern edge where salt water rises from an unknown depth.

Near the center of the main crater are two volcanic cones. One of these cones, evidently formed by the last eruption, is hollow and at one time was an enormous blast furnace that hurled billions of tons of cinders high into the air. Two hundred feet down from the rim inside this cone is a round, bottomless lake, two hundred feet in diameter.

When cinders from the last eruption rained back to earth, they formed sloping banks into the main crater. Wagon roads were easily graded through this loose material down to the crater's floor, and a small village, including a store, post office, and school, was built on the lake's north shore.

Evaporation causes a crust of salt to form on the shallow bottom of the lake and on any other object the salt water touches. There are several soft-water springs, which form pools along the south and east sides. These pools drain into the salt lake. Sometimes wild ducks alight in these pools and swim out into the salt water. When they do, enough salt to keep them from flying soon collects on their wings. Unless they return to the fresh water where the salt will dissolve, they soon die or are caught by bobcats or coyotes.

Indians from the Zuñi and Navaho reservation have obtained salt from this lake for centuries. Some of them went through a sort of ritual when they came to the lake. Their gift tokens to their salt gods were short sticks tied with colored feathers and turquoise beads which were thrown into the small lake inside the volcanic cone. Anyone caught gathering the beads were despised by the Indians, who considered them robbers of the salt god.

The Indian method of removing salt from the lake was simple. He pitched his camp near shore, stripped down to a G-string, picked up a sack, waded out into the shallow water of the lake, and sat down. Then he dug up the crusted salt with a sharpened stick and scooped it into the sack with his hands. When the sack was full, he lifted it up and waded back to shore.

The old Zuñi salt trail leads north from the lake to their village on the Zuñi River. Although it has not been used for the past eighty years, it is still traceable.

In the prehistoric past, many people inhabited the country around the salt lake. Ruins of large villages have been found. What became of these people is a mystery that may never be solved. Thousands of hieroglyphics decorate the face of sand-rock cliffs, but modern archaeologists have not been able to decipher them.

The Kemp family found many fine pieces of pottery buried beneath these ruins, as well as many beads and arrowheads. Near Sierra Pomo they found a corn rick. Corn and cob were burned into a charred mass, showing that although covered with dirt, they had been exposed to terrific heat.

From all indications these people worshiped the sun. Almost all of their burials were on the east side of their dwellings, and the graves were covered with ashes.

On June 18, 1910, the well rig was moved from the García well to the Mesa Redondo location, where a well that produced twelve gallons of water per minute was brought in at a depth of 125 feet. The water, which was found in sand, was almost pure, having practically no minerals.

A twelve-foot Eclipse windmill with pump and equipment was placed over the well, and it was offered for sale at eight hundred dollars. Because of the choice location it was a bargain at this price, but there were no buyers. Within a short time there was imminent danger of losing the well and its equipment. To prevent this from happening, Boss Kemp filed a homestead on the land where the well was located.

A contract was signed to drill a well at Red Hill, nine miles west of the Mesa Redondo, for Henry Goesling, a sheepman who owned ranches near the Arizona border. Since Boss Kemp was needed at the well rig, a man named Bud West was hired to take care of the Mesa Redondo ranch while he was away.

In October, 1910, Ben Kemp and Boss drove the teams and wagons to Beaver Creek to move the family to the Mesa Redondo. When they got there, Boss saddled his horse and rode to Duncan, Arizona, never to return. It took several days to prepare to move. After Boss left, there was no one except Mrs. Kemp and the children to help load and drive the wagons. The family owned twenty-five milk cows, and Beulah was assigned the task of trailing these through. Since they had only one pony and five burros as saddle animals, travel was slow, and the cattle reached the Mesa Redondo in better shape than when they left Beaver Creek.

During this time John Damron and Benny had managed to build a house at the Mesa Redondo. Although it was not a magnificent structure, it provided protection against the frigid weather during the winter months.

When six months had passed and Boss failed to return, the Kemps became concerned over losing the homestead. Finally Boss relinquished his claim, and Benny, who had just come of age, filed a homestead on the land, and the place was secure.

The well rig stood during most of 1911. Ben Kemp decided to put his teams and wagons to use hauling freight for ranches in western Socorro County, a venture that almost cost him his life. He contracted to haul five thousand pounds of salt from the salt lakes north of the Mesa Redondo to the W. J. Jones ranch on Legget Canyon, eight miles west of Reserve.

Kemp's daughters, Mary and Pearl, and a neighbor, Polk Mc-Daniels, who lived in Luna Valley and was also hauling salt to Reserve, decided to go with him. Their route from the Mesa Redondo to Reserve was over roads that were little more than rough, rocky cow trails. There were several steep hills where the trail wagon had to be dropped, the lead wagon pulled to the top, and then a trip made back to the foot of the hill after the trail wagon.

Kemp was in the lead with his two wagons when they reached the foot of what is known as Gallo Hill, which has a steep mountainside nearly half a mile to the top. He uncoupled his trail wagon, and the eight-horse team pulled the lead wagon to the top without much trouble. Then he unhitched two spans of his team, drove them back to the foot of the mountain, and hitched them to the trail wagon, which was loaded with two thousand pounds of salt.

When the trail wagon reached the level ground at the rear end of the lead wagon, it was halted. The lead span of mules was removed, leaving the wheel team hitched to the trail chain. Kemp squatted down between the lead and trail wagons and raised the

246

The Beaver Creek Homestead

The Mesa Redondo Ranch

247

trail wagon tongue. He told Mary to drive the team while he guided the stirrup of the tongue over the horn on the rear axle of the lead wagon.

Two thousand pounds of dead weight was heavy for one team, and the horses laid into the collar hard, jerking the wagon forward. The stirrup was within four inches of the horn when the right front wheel of the trail wagon hit a rock. This jerked the trail tongue to one side, causing the stirrup to miss the horn.

The trail wagon closed in on the rear end of the lead wagon, catching Kemp's head between the two. Why his head was not crushed like an eggshell will always remain a mystery. When the team was stopped, he dropped to the ground, and his two daughters were frantic. Their screams soon brought Polk McDaniels up the mountainside, and, not knowing what else to do, he dashed a canteen full of cold water over Kemp's head. This checked the bleeding from his ears, mouth, and nose, but within a few minutes the pupils of his eyes turned in towards the bridge of his nose.

McDaniels thought he was dying, so he saddled a horse from his work team and left on a run for Henry Graham's ranch on Apache Creek, some twelve miles south of where the accident occurred, to tell Benny, who was helping Graham build a log cabin. Since there was no way to get a doctor, Benny immediately saddled his cow pony and made the best time he could to Gallo Hill.

When he arrived, he found his father alive but in serious condition. By this time his eyes were so badly crossed he saw a double image of any object he tried to look at. His head was swollen to almost twice its natural size. Benny was badly frightened, but his father assured him that he would be all right. Since he could not see to drive the team, it became Benny's responsibility to see that the wagons reached Reserve.

Driving an eight-horse team and two wagons over a narrow, crooked road that wound its way through and over high, rocky mountains was not child's play. After three days that seemed like three weeks to Benny, the wagons reached the Jones ranch on the Legget Canyon, and the salt was delivered.

When Billy Jones learned the extent of Ben Kemp's injury, he insisted that he go to Mogollon and see a doctor. Jones said that Montague Stevens, who owned a sawmill on Legget Canyon, had an order for three thousand feet of lumber to be delivered to a man named Cunningham at Glenwood, New Mexico. Since freight on the lumber would pay for a trip to Mogollon, Ben Kemp decided to take the job.

Mary and Pearl were left with the Henry Graham family, and the wagons were driven to Montague Stevens' sawmill, where they were loaded with three thousand feet of lumber. From Stevens' sawmill they bounced their way down Saliz Canyon to the Kelly ranch on the San Francisco River. From there they swung west to Gut Ache Mesa, then down Spurgeon Mesa to where the road fell off a rimrock into the river again. This was a terrible road, if it could be called such. It was rough, narrow, rocky, and sideling and had high hills and deep canyons.

On the fourth day after leaving Stevens' sawmill, the wagons reached Alma. There Ben Kemp talked with Billy Jones's brother, Louis, who was one of the members of the Jones family who had come to Milligan Plaza with him in 1885. Louis Jones told him he would borrow two saddle horses and go with him to see the doctor at Mogollon. Kemp hired a man named Ford to help Benny drive the teams on to the Cunningham ranch on White Water Creek, and he and Jones mounted their horses and rode to Mogollon.

The doctor, on examining Kemp's eyes, told him that when his head was caught between the two wagons, blood vessels behind his eyeballs ruptured and clotted. The pressure from these clots caused his eyes to cross, throwing his vision out of line. He said that in time the clots would dissolve and his vision would be normal again. He was right, but it required three years.

During the summer of 1910 a man named Carter moved his small herd of cattle into the east foothills of Texano Mesa and established camp at one of the dry lakes that filled with water during the rainy season. Carter was a small man, standing about five feet, five inches, and weighing about 125 pounds. He had the bow-legs typical of men who have spent most of their lives in a saddle.

The winter following Carter's arrival at Texano Mesa was dry,

249

and by late spring there was no water in the shallow lakes around his camp, so he was forced to move his cattle to a new location. When Carter learned that Ben Kemp had a good well of water and plenty of range, he arranged to bring his cattle to the Mesa Redondo. He brought his family with him, but they did not stay long. Carter wanted a ranch of his own, and within three months he filed a homestead on a tract of land on Carrizozo Draw north of the salt lakes.

Soon after he moved into the Salt Lake community, Carter claimed to have seen a neighboring rancher riding a stolen horse. Ben Kemp paid little attention to the report until one day when a crony of the accused man walked into the Mesa Redondo carrying a blood-splattered riding bridle. Kemp suspected foul play and backtracked the man to an arroyo where he found a dead horse with a bullet through its brain. To his surprise the dead animal was Baldy Socks, the horse that had been caught with the wild bunch at North Water in 1899. So ended the life of a good cow horse, whose faithful service had been the envy of other than honest men.

During the summer of 1911 a drifter by the name of Fowler appeared in the Salt Lake community. Fowler claimed he was born in the No Man's Land of Oklahoma and boasted he had been a member of several outlaw bands. Regardless of whether this was true, his body bore many scars from knife and gunshot wounds, showing that he had taken part in several vicious fights. He was a jovial man and a good worker. He would give you the shirt off his back, but steal it back at the first opportunity.

During the summer months rainfall had been heavy and grama grass on the open draws north of Sierra Pomo was knee high. Fowler borrowed a mowing machine and hay rake from the owner of the ranch where he was staying and cut several tons of hay which he offered for sale. Since Ben Kemp needed hay for his work teams during the winter months, he offered Fowler twenty dollars a ton in the stack. Fowler, who was glad to get out of hauling the hay, promptly accepted the offer.

Within a day or two Benny and John Damron began hauling the

250

hay to the Mesa Redondo. During this time Fowler decided to make a trip to Magdalena. Several days passed, and Fowler failed to return to the hay camp. Finally Ben Kemp received a letter in which Fowler stated that he was in the county jail at Socorro and demanded that the money for the hay be paid to him in person at the jail.

Benny was sent to Socorro with the money, and Fowler told him what had delayed his return. He said that after he left the hay camp, he drove to the ranch where he was staying and butchered a beef. He placed the beef in a wagon and drove to Quemado, where he intended to sell it to Nicasio Baca, a local merchant.

All might have gone well if Shep Casey, the district cattle inspector, had not been in town. He demanded that Fowler show him the hide of the beef. Fowler did not have the hide. He told Casey he had left it at the ranch where he was staying. Casey told him that was no excuse, and he would have to place him under arrest for selling beef illegally.

They were sitting side by side on a bench in Baca's store while the argument over the hide was going on. When Casey told Fowler he would have to place him under arrest, Fowler, who was a young and powerful man, placed a half nelson on Casey and pommelled him unmercifully with his fists.

When Fowler released him, Casey ran out of the store but soon returned with a .401-caliber automatic rifle. Fowler suspected Casey would return with a gun and was watching for him through the window in the store door. When Casey appeared at the door, Fowler fired his six-shooter through the wood panel below the glass. The heavy .45-caliber bullet passed through the door, hit the magazine on Casey's rifle, and ricocheted downward, striking him in the groin. Casey staggered back out of sight from the door, and Fowler thought he had killed him. Wishing to make sure, he opened the door and peeped out. This was an almost fatal mistake.

Casey, who was only slightly wounded, was standing against the wall of the store building. When Fowler peeped out, he fired point-blank at Fowler's head. The heavy-caliber bullet passed so close to Fowler's head it partly addled him. When he regained his sense

251

of direction, he started running towards the back of the store. Casey would probably have killed him before he reached the door, but the bullet from Fowler's six-shooter had bent the magazine of his rifle and rendered it useless except for the one shot Casey had fired at Fowler's head.

Fowler, not knowing that Casey's rifle was out of commission, ran out the back door and quickly climbed into his wagon. He drove back to the ranch where he was staying and obtained a hide for the beef he was trying to sell.

He armed himself with a .25–.35-caliber Winchester rifle, tied a saddled, half-bronc pony to his off-work horse's hame, and returned to Quemado. It was late afternoon by the time he arrived back in town, and Casey had left for the Nation's cattle ranch at Sierra Prieta, several miles to the north. So Fowler, who was in a mean and dangerous mood, started towards Magdalena.

About eight miles east of Quemado he met an automobile driven by Charley Chadwick of Albuquerque. There were two other men in the car with Chadwick, and the car was driven to one side of the road to let Fowler pass. The bronc Fowler was leading was scared by the automobile. He jumped over the work horse's back and landed astride the wagon tongue. Fowler had quite a tussle pulling the team to a halt. Then he trained his rifle on the three men in the car and said, "You sons of bitches, get out of that car and straighten this team and bronc back like they were or I will kill every damned one of you."

Chadwick and his two friends did not doubt his word. They lost no time in unhitching the team from the wagon, removing the bronc from the wagon tongue, and rehitching them again. During this time Fowler sat on the wagon seat in stony silence, with the cocked rifle trained on them. When the team and bronc were ready to go, Chadwick handed him the lines. As Fowler drove up the road, he watched the three men closely until they climbed into their car and drove away.

When Fowler reached Magdalena, he camped for three days at a wagon yard owned by a widow named Hubbard. On the day he left town Mrs. Hubbard discovered someone had stolen a set of harness, some mining tools, and other equipment she had stored in a small shed adjoining the wagon yard.

Meanwhile Charley Chadwick and his friends returned to Magdalena, where they filed a complaint against Fowler for threatening them with a deadly weapon. A warrant issued for his arrest was placed in the hands of a deputy sheriff, who found out that Fowler had left town early that morning. The deputy and his assistant followed Fowler's trail towards Datil.

Fowler was making good time and had almost reached Datil before the officers overtook him. Because he thought he had made a clean get-away, he was taken by surprise, and the officers had the drop on him before he knew what was happening. The officers disarmed him and drove his team and wagon to the Baldwin ranger station, where they left them in charge of Forest Ranger Gauge. Fowler was taken back to Magdalena, given a preliminary hearing, bound over to the action of the district court, and placed in the Socorro County jail. Because he was unable to make bail, he had not been able to return to the hay camp.

During the spring session of district court in 1912, Carter was shot down on main street in Magdalena by the man he claimed to have seen riding the stolen horse, Baldy Socks. Ben Kemp and his nephew John Damron were at the Becker McTavish wagon yard at the time, preparing their wagons to haul a load of freight to the Nation's ranch at Sierra Prieta.

When they arrived at the scene of the shooting, Carter, who was fatally wounded, was being escorted to a hotel. The town's citizens had gathered into a large crowd that turned into a violent mob when they learned Carter was unarmed. A quick-thinking deputy sheriff saved the man who shot Carter from being lynched by placing him in a car and rushing him to the Socorro County jail.

The town's doctors did their best to save Carter's life, but he died early the next morning, and the county lost an honest and upright citizen.

Bud West, the man Ben Kemp had hired to stay at the Mesa Redondo on completion of the well, filed a homestead on a tract of land a mile northeast of Kemp's ranch house. There was no well

253

on his land, and he was staying at the Mesa Redondo until he could get one drilled.

A little before noon one day two territorial rangers arrived at the Mesa Redondo ranch house and asked Mrs. Kemp if she knew where they could find West. She told them he had ridden out on the range but would probably be back to the ranch by noon.

About an hour later West was seen approaching the ranch from the east side of the valley. The rangers warned everyone to stay inside the house. Then they mounted their horses and rode down to the cow corrals about a hundred yards south of the house. When West saw them, he must have thought they were some of the neighboring cowmen, because he rode up to within fifty yards of the corrals.

One of the rangers, a man West knew, stepped into view from behind his saddle horse with a rifle in his hands and said, "Lisia, throw up your hands." West started to rein his horse around, but the ranger brought his rifle to bear on him and said, "If you run I'll kill you surer than hell." When West realized there was no possible way to escape, he rode up to them and surrendered. He was taken back to Chaves County, and two of his brothers came to live on his homestead.

During the late spring a stray cow, followed by a large, un-branded calf, started watering at the Mesa Redondo watering corral. Ben Kemp and his son kept a watch on them to see if some odd iron would be run on the calf.

On a previous occasion Ben Kemp had used field glasses to watch three men while they altered the brand on a stray yearling. He reported the act to the cattle inspector at St. Johns, Arizona, but the animal was not picked up. After a year the altered brand was barred out, and one of the men placed his recorded brand on the animal.

One afternoon about a month after the stray cow and calf had started watering at the Mesa Redondo, Henry Graham arrived at the ranch, driving a cow and calf. He was enraged by an incident that had occurred at the LN roundup a few hours earlier.

Graham told the Kemps he had purchased two cows from a farmer at Luna Valley, a small settlement forty miles southwest of the Mesa Redondo. The cows had strayed or been driven onto the LN range. A Luna Valley rancher, who was hauling salt from the salt lakes, had seen one of the cows grazing near the road at Penasco Spring, a few miles south of the LN reservoir. He notified Graham, who rode to the LN roundup wagon where he found his cow and her calf being held in the holdup. When he tried to cut them out, his right of ownership was questioned by a rancher living on Penasco Draw.

During the heated argument that followed, Graham tried to pull the rancher off of his horse but failed. The rancher reined his horse around with such force that Graham's grasp on the man's chaps was broken. The rancher left on a run while Graham stood in the dust kicked up by his horse's feet and yelled for him to come back so he could "wup hell out of him." Since the rancher did not come back, Graham cut his cow and calf out of the holdup and drove them to the Mesa Redondo.

When Graham described the other cow he was looking for, the Kemps knew it was the stray cow and calf they had been watching. The morning after Graham arrived at the ranch, Ben Kemp and his son saddled their horses and rode out with him to the valleys north and east of the Sierra Pomo crater.

Since both the cow and her calf had been to the watering corral the day before, they expected to find them in a short time. To their dismay, they rode until noon without finding them. Positive they were somewhere near, the men continued their search. Late that afternoon they found the calf, but the cow was missing, and the calf was freshly branded with West's brand.

Kemp and Graham suspected that the cow had been slaughtered, and by daylight the next morning they were in their saddles, headed for the lava beds around the Sierra Pomo crater. After searching for several hours, they found the cow's carcass. She had been driven to a secluded spot in the lava flow, where she was roped and her throat was cut. Her stomach had been ripped open so that her remains would be quickly disposed of by coyotes and other carnivorous animals.

255

Graham was thoroughly angered by then and lost no time riding to the West ranch. He told the West brothers they could have their choice of either paying him fifty dollars for his cow or being prosecuted to the full extent of the law. The West brothers realized they were in serious trouble, and one of them hurried to the Penasco ranch, where he borrowed the money, a tarnished fifty-dollar gold piece, with which they paid Graham.

Because Kemp doubted that such men would stop short of anything, he wrote Governor McDonald at Santa Fé a letter in which he described the situation, and asked for a territorial ranger's commission.

The governor answered Kemp's letter, stating that he was aware of the situation confronting him and fully sympathized, but was unable to send him a commission because the ranger force was being disbanded. He advised Kemp to take his letter to Sheriff Emiel James at Socorro as a recommendation for a deputy sheriff's appointment. This was done, and James appointed Kemp deputy for the duration of his term as sheriff of Socorro County.

During the spring of 1912 three men robbed the store at Mogollon, New Mexico, and killed the proprietor. Two of the men were identified as John Gates and a Mexican by the name of Gregorio Narrango. The third man was a Mexican miner, who was well known for his drunken rampages.

When Sheriff Emiel James at Socorro heard about the robbery and murder, he immediately went to Mogollon. He learned that Narrango was still in town and soon had him under arrest. After he asked him a few questions, James was on the trail of the Mexican miner, who was trying to reach the Mexican border and had stopped at a ranch a few miles away in an effort to obtain a fresh horse.

When James came within sixty yards of the house where the Mexican miner was staying, the outlaw stepped into the yard with a rifle in his hands. James jerked his rifle from the saddle scabbard and quickly dismounted. He called on the miner to surrender, but the outlaw raised his rifle and fired at the sheriff. James dropped to a squatting position, firing at the same time. His frightened saddle horse suddenly jerked the bridle reins he was trying to hold and spoiled his aim. He quickly tried to lever another shell into his rifle, but it jammed. James turned the bridle reins loose and grabbed for his six-shooter, but found the holster empty. The revolver had fallen to the ground behind him when he squatted down.

James was in a tight spot. He knew if he couldn't dislodge the jammed shell in his rifle within a few seconds he would be killed. He pulled out his pocketknife and hastily opened it. Then he pried the shell loose by running the blade under it. By this time the Mexican miner had fired three shots and missed, which didn't seem possible at this short distance. After the jammed shell had been removed, James levered another one into his rifle and shot the outlaw through the head, killing him instantly. Sheriff James was a small, soft-spoken man, who gave the impression he would not harm a fly, but after this fight no one ever doubted his nerve again.

After the robbery in Mogollon, John Gates parted company with his two companions and headed for Mexico. Before he could reach the border, he was captured and imprisoned in the Luna County jail at Deming.

Late one afternoon during the latter part of July, 1912, two young men rode up to the Mesa Redondo ranch house and asked if they could stay overnight. Although the ranch was poorly equipped to accommodate visitors at the time, Ben Kemp asked them to dismount and unsaddle their horses. They were pleasant and jovial men, but failed to introduce themselves.

The previous night they had stayed at Leo Oswald's ranch, some fifteen miles to the north, and he had directed them to the Mesa Redondo. The two men sat up until nearly midnight visiting with the Kemp family. When they were ready to retire, Benny and John Damron invited them to share one of their camp beds, which was rolled out on the dirt floor in a tent about fifty yards south of the ranch house.

The next morning the two men saddled their horses. When they were ready to leave, the older one said, "Well, we have got to be riding." Then they reined their horses around and headed up the road towards Johnson Basin. The Kemps were puzzled about who their visitors were. A few days later they met Oswald at the Salt Lake post office and questioned him. He told them that the men were John Greer and a friend.

A short time after these two men stayed overnight at the Mesa Redondo, they rode into Deming, leading a saddled horse. A political rally had drawn a large portion of the town's population downtown. The two men rode through town at a regular saddle gait, and no one paid them any attention. They went to the Luna County Courthouse on the outskirts of town, where they caught the jailer off guard and forced him to unlock John Gates's cell. After Gates stepped out, they locked the jailer in the cell and bade him farewell. Then the three men walked out of the jail, mounted their horses, and left town at a brisk trot.

By the time the jailbreak was discovered, John Gates and his two companions were several miles away. No one had the least idea what direction they had taken on leaving town, but it was natural to suspect that they would try to reach the Mexican border.

Gates had been a member of Francisco Madero's band of guerrillas during the Mexican revolution of 1910. He had fired the first shot in the battle of Juarez when Madero's forces captured the city in 1911. A short time later in a battle at Casas Grandes, Madero's forces were defeated. During the fight John Greer, who was also a member of Madero's guerrillas, was shot through the head and body. He was seriously wounded and would have been killed if John Gates had not placed him across his saddle and ridden out of the fight with him.

On the morning of August 10, 1912, a man named Sully, who was general manager of the Kennecott Chino Mines Division at Santa Rita, New Mexico, was driving from Santa Rita to Hurley. When he and his three companions reached a point near the Portwood ranch south of the Bayard station, they were quickly surrounded by three masked bandits on horseback, who shot a hole through the windshield of their car and ordered them to halt.

When the car was stopped, the outlaws advanced and demanded the forty-thousand-dollar Chino Mines payroll that Sully usually took to Hurley on that day of the month. Because of a change in schedule for bringing the payroll out, Sully did not have it with him. After the bandits searched his car, they broke the spark plugs to render it useless. They then robbed Sully and his party of what valuables they had and rode back into the rough and broken country on the west slope of Kneeling Nun Mountain.

Sully made the best time he could to Hurley and sent word to Portwood, the constable at Santa Rita, telling him to round up a posse and run the outlaws down. Portwood had trouble finding anyone to go with him. Finally a man named Moses and a former cowboy named Jackson, who were working at the mine, agreed to go with him.

The three men left the Santa Fé Railway station at Santa Rita on horseback and worked their way up the rough and rocky west side of Kneeling Nun Mountain to a point near the summit. When they failed to see any sign of the outlaws, they dismounted, tied their horses to a bush, and climbed up a large rock, where they could get a better view of the surrounding country. While they were scanning the mountainside below them, they heard a sharp command, "Drop them guns." They looked back up the mountainside and saw the three outlaws with their rifles trained on them. Moses and Jackson dropped their rifles, but Portwood, who had left his rifle on his saddle, fell off the rock on which he was standing and started running towards his saddle horse. John Greer began shooting at Portwood with a .45 Colt's automatic pistol. Portwood had run only a few steps on the rough mountainside when he tripped and fell. Realizing that it would be foolish to resist any longer, he gave up.

While one of the outlaws held a rifle trained on Portwood and his party, the other two walked up to them and searched them for side arms. They broke their rifles over a rock to make them useless. One of the outlaws told Moses it was poor policy to hunt for outlaws when riding a white horse and wearing a white shirt.

The outlaws discussed what they would do with the three officers. One of them suggested they take their boots to slow them down in walking back to the mine, but the other two members of the gang argued against it. During the argument John Greer pointed to a fine pair of boots one of the possemen was wearing and said to one of his pals, "Your boots are getting kind of old. Why don't you take them?"

"Hell, I couldn't wear them," said the outlaw. "They are four times my size."

Portwood and his party were lucky that the outlaws did not take their boots, because it would have been impossible for them to walk back to Santa Rita barefoot. After the outlaws berated the officers a while, they took what rations they had, gathered up the reins of their saddle horses, and left.

The Grant County sheriff was then called. He and a posse of six men took up the outlaws' trail from where they had held up Portwood's party and followed it to the top of Kneeling Nun Mountain. When they found one of the horses that Portwood's party was riding, the sheriff had hopes of soon running the outlaws down. But a few miles farther on he lost their trail and was unable to pick it up again.

By this time Greer and his party must have realized that every law enforcement officer along the Mexican border had been alerted to keep a sharp lookout for them. The Luna County sheriff reasoned that they would head into the rough and broken country along the Black Range divide. He and a deputy named Hall and a state ranger named Smothers headed north along the Continental Divide.

John Greer and his party had enough provisions to last them several days. As the Luna County sheriff had anticipated, they followed the Black Range divide north to a point near the Adobe Ranch. By this time their rations were running low, and they decided to take the risk of visiting the ranch to replenish their supplies.

The Adobe Ranch sat on an open prairie, about two miles north of Adobe Mountain, on the east side of a draw. The gate to the horse pasture fence was about fifty yards east of the house. The sheds and horse corrals at this time were about the same distance

260

to the southeast. Anyone approaching the house could be seen for some distance.

A friend of the Kemps, who lived a few miles north of the Salt Lake post office, made a trip to Capitan, New Mexico, a short time after John Greer and his party visited the Adobe Ranch. He had attended school at Capitan a few years earlier and knew John Greer personally. While visiting friends, he met one of the men who was in John Greer's party, and this man gave him an account of what happened.

This man claimed that when they rode into the Adobe ranchhouse yard, they thought they were in luck, because the house was unlocked and there was no one around. All the cowboys working at the ranch were out riding on the range. They had been there only a few minutes, however, when one of them saw three men on horseback approaching the ranch across the open prairie. The three outlaws first thought these men were cowboys returning to the ranch, but since they were not sure, they decided it was best to get away from the ranch house. So they mounted their horses and rode out to meet them.

When the three men on the prairie saw Greer and his party coming towards them, they dismounted and stood on the opposite side of their saddle horses. This often happens on the open range, where men, weary from sitting in the saddle, will take advantage of a short wait to dismount and stretch their legs. Nevertheless Greer and his party were suspicious and kept a close watch. When they came within 150 yards of the three men, John Greer said, "Boys, I think I saw a rifle glint across the seat of one of them saddles." He reined his horse to the left. A high-powered rifle was immediately discharged, and Greer fell to the ground with a bullet through his neck and died within seconds. The three men on horseback were the Luna County sheriff and his posse.

When John Greer's two companions saw him fall from his horse, they jerked their rifles from the saddle scabbards, jumped from their horses, and lay flat on the ground. By this time a hail of lead was flying in their direction. The officers were shooting as fast as they could pump shells into their rifles.

Both of the outlaws' horses stampeded, and one of them dragged its rider out of the fight while he was trying to hold it by a rope tied around its neck.

The lone member of the outlaw gang was now in a tight spot. He lay flat on the ground in an open prairie, which furnished nothing more than broomweed or an occasional anthill for protection.

The officers were also in the open. Their horses had jerked loose from them when the shooting started. Smothers lay prone behind a broomweed and the sheriff sought protection behind an anthill but Hall stood upright in the open. He would fire a shot, jump to one side, and fire again. Hall was an expert with a rifle, and his bullets were coming uncomfortably close to the lone outlaw, who realized he would be killed if he didn't stop Hall soon. He readied his .30–.40 Winchester and fired the second after Hall had jumped and landed. The .30-caliber, soft-nosed bullet passed through Hall's heart, and he dropped to the ground dead.

The bandit now turned his attention to Ranger Smothers, who was firing through a broomweed, which was only a screen and furnished no protection. His first shot missed Smothers, but his second shot hit him between the eyes, killing him instantly.

The sheriff was in a tight spot. His two companions were dead and every time he moved, the outlaw shot some more of the ant-hill away. Although the ants were stinging him, he had to lie still and let them sting or get killed. After what seemed like an eternity, the bandit got to his feet and walked over to Greer's body. When he found Greer dead the bandit returned to the Adobe ranch house, where he took some food. Then he started walking in the direction in which the saddle horses and his partner had disappeared.

His partner, who was watching from the foothills north of Corduroy Canyon, saw him and brought his saddle horse to him. Both of them headed for the Sacramento Mountains, which one of the outlaws knew like the palm of his hand. They reached there safely and were in hiding when Kemp's neighbor visited Capitan, north of the mountains.

John Gates soon tired of living like a wolf in the mountain hideouts and went to El Paso, where his wife lived. Officers, who were keeping her under surveillance, soon had him in custody. He was returned to Socorro, where he was later tried and convicted for the murder of Hall and Smothers. He was sentenced to be hanged and was one of the last men to be so executed in Socorro County.

During the spring session of district court in 1912, Fowler was tried and found guilty on a charge of grand larceny. He was sentenced to three years in the penitentiary at Santa Fé. He was released after a year, and returned to the Salt Lake community. He did not resume friendly relations with his former partner, whom he claimed sold his wagon and team while he was in the penitentiary and never sent him a cent. He was furious over this and threatened revenge.

A month after Fowler's return he came to the Mesa Redondo and begged Ben Kemp for work. He claimed he had learned the error of his ways and wanted a chance to make good. Kemp, who believed anyone should be given a chance to live a better life, hired him to help John Damron and Benny with the well rig. For the first thirty days no one could have asked for a better hand, and the Kemps began to think he had changed for the better. But after a month with the rig his old urge hit him, and he started stealing from the Bitterman Sheep Company, the outfit Kemp was drilling wells for. Fowler was promptly fired from his job, but did not leave the community.

By the spring of 1914, the West brothers were ready to leave the Salt Lake community. Fowler, who had managed to stay in the neighborhood, bargained with them for the West homestead. West relinquished his rights, and Fowler filed a homestead on the land. With Fowler as their nearest neighbor, the Kemps were never sure of what might happen next. His ranch was a rendezvous for renegades who drifted into the community.

A short time after Fowler gained possession of the West ranch, Sheriff Jim Cash of Greenlee County, Arizona, arrived at the Mesa Redondo. He was following a man who had robbed the Clifton bank. He had lost his trail a few miles to the south and came to

263

Kemp's ranch to ask for his help. They suspected Fowler might have helped the man and searched his ranch, but no one was found. It was learned several months later Fowler had switched the bank robber back on his trail to Aragon, where a rancher agreed to let him ride inside his covered wagon until they reached Magdalena.

When the outlaw reached Magdalena, he bought a ticket to El Paso, where he crossed the border into Mexico. There were a number of checks among the money he had robbed from the bank, and when he got to Mexico, he mailed them back to the bank cashier at Clifton. He attached a letter of thanks, explaining that the checks were of no value to him.

During most of 1914 the Kemp well rig stood idle. A series of dry years had left most ranchers financially cramped. Through a coincidence this happened to be in Ben Kemp's favor.

Charley McCarty, a friend living near Reserve, New Mexico, grazed cattle on forest land. Because his land was overstocked, the United States Forest Service requested that he move some of his cattle. When McCarty learned of Kemp's ranch at the Mesa Redondo, he made a deal to place two hundred cows on the range on a shares basis. An application was sent to the cattle sanitary board, asking them to record a brand, Slash-T7, with which the increase was to be branded.

Kemp equipped a chuck wagon and selected a scant remuda out of the few head of horses he owned. For cowhands he selected his sons, Benny and John Stephen, and his nephew, John Damron. His daughter Mary was chuck-wagon cook. The chuck wagon was driven to Reserve, and with his small crew Kemp helped McCarty gather two hundred cows and eight bulls, most of them so wild it took some tall riding to get them out of the rough, mountainous country over which they ranged. When McCarty saw Kemp's small remuda, he loaned him three outlawed saddle horses, which furnished excitement in bucking exhibitions for the next few years. They sunned Benny and John Damron's moccasins several times, but the boys kept trying until they could ride them.

After the cattle were counted, Kemp started trailing the herd

264

to the Mesa Redondo. The first night camp was made on Apache Creek, and the next morning it took three hours to drive the small herd of cattle out of this deep canyon.

Because of the time lost in climbing out of Apache Creek, Kemp was forced to pitch camp in an open pine glade about a quarter-mile south of Hardcastle Gap. It was not a choice location, because the glade was in the bottom of a draw about 150 yards wide with rocky, timbered slopes on either side. There were only three men to stand guard. Kemp took first guard from nine o'clock until midnight. John Damron was assigned graveyard from midnight until two. Benny was to take over from two o'clock until daylight.

When Kemp returned to the chuck wagon a few minutes after midnight, he said that he thought the cattle would be all right, be-cause most of them had "turned" and would probably not get up until daylight. He picketed his night horse and crawled into bed, but in less than ten minutes he heard a tremor and rumble followed by the blast of two pistol shots. The herd was wildly stampeding down the draw.

Kemp and Benny catapulted out of bed, jumped on their night horses, and left the wagon at a dead run. In the short time it had taken them to hit saddle leather, the lead cattle had run a quarter-mile down the draw.

In the mad race to reach the lead cattle it was a miracle someone wasn't killed. The cattle were running over ground that was cov-ered with rabbit brush taller than waist high and eroded with ditches, some of them ten feet wide and eight feet deep. Chasing them over this kind of terrain on a dark night was an extremely dangerous undertaking.

Luckily there were a few calves in the herd, and when they got separated from their mothers, they began to bawl. This slowed down the mother cows, and within a mile the lead animals reached open country where they were stopped.

When a count was made the next morning, three cows were miss-ing, and part of the morning was taken up trying to find them. This delay resulted in a short drive, and camp was pitched in Valle de Uva, an open valley four miles north of Johnson Basin.

265

When the cattle left their bed ground at daybreak the next morning, Kemp headed them north up the road. By sundown the herd reached the ranch at the Mesa Redondo. This ended a four-day drive over the mountainous country between Kemp's ranch and the John S Corrals on Tularosa Creek.

20.
The Adams Story

A short time after the cattle were trailed to the Mesa Redondo, Frank Jones, the youngest son of Washie Jones, arrived at the ranch. He was interested in making a trip to the Navaho and Zuñi Indian reservations to look for a fabulously rich placer-gold mine known as the Adams Diggings. He wanted the Kemps to go with him, and they were interested. Mrs. Kemp had met Adams when he stopped by her father's ranch on Cox Canyon in 1884. Adams had told her father there was a rich deposit of placer gold in plain sight along a small canyon.

On his second trip to search for his lost mine in 1892, Adams stayed at the Jones home in Reserve. He told Washie Jones all the incidents leading up to the discovery of the rich placer and the tragic events that followed. Although Frank was just a child at the time, the Adams story was so exciting it remained a vivid memory.

Adams claimed that in 1865 he was hauling supplies for troops stationed along the old Butterfield Trail in Arizona. One night Indians stole his work teams, and he was forced to leave his wagons and walk to the nearest fort. The government managed to get his horses back from the Indians, but when he returned to his wagons, he found them burned to the ground.

Adams returned to Pima Villa on the Gila River. While he was there, he met five men who were on their way to the California gold fields. He had decided to go with them, but a half-breed, Mexican-Indian scout for the army told the party they were foolish to go so far when he could show them all the gold they could want only a few miles away.

The men were skeptical and thought the scout was trying to lead them into a trap, but he kept on talking until they finally decided to go with him. They warned him that if he was telling them a lie, they would kill him. The scout, who did not doubt that he could show them the gold, made them promise to give him six horses and the first day's panning for leading them to the location.

Adams sold all of his work horses except those needed for saddle horses and pack animals. The six men were excited over the possibility of their trip, and one of them suggested they buy a small keg of whisky to celebrate their find when they got there.

When all was ready, the party left Pima Villa and traveled in a northeasterly direction. The first settlement they reached after leaving the Gila River was Fort Apache. They rested there a day and then rode on to Round Valley. When they reached Round Valley, they crossed to the east side and camped at a rancher's cabin, two miles east of the present location of Springerville, Arizona.

Evidently Adams either tapped the whisky keg or drank too much of a supply he might have bought at Fort Apache, because his mind was in a daze for the next two days. The only thing he could remember was that they traveled over a high, open, rolling country and crossed many small draws and open canyons. The first day after leaving Round Valley they were forced to make a dry camp. The second day about mid-afternoon they reached an open canyon, which had some warm water springs surrounded by a grove of cottonwood trees. The water from these springs flowed northwest. Adams said it was a beautiful spot. Since there was an abundance of good grass, they pitched camp and stayed there until about ten o'clock the next day.

After leaving this spring, they rode up a long ridge running northeast, and about two o'clock that afternoon they came to an open, beaten trail that ran north and south. They turned north up this trail and followed it to the south side of a deep, wide canyon, in which the waters flowed west. There was a rimrock along the south wall of this canyon, and the only way of descending into it was down a trail, which was cut through the rimrock in a series of steps that resembled a stairway. On reaching the bottom of the canyon, which was nearly three miles wide, they turned east up

268

the canyon and passed within sight of an Indian village and some small plots of farming land.

A few miles east of this village the canyon narrowed down, and a black rock formation almost closed the canyon. Because it was almost sundown when they reached this point, they decided it was time to look for a suitable place to camp. Since they had just passed a village and didn't know what the Indians' attitude might be, the party decided against camping in the main canyon, and they turned north up a ridge along the east side of a narrow box canyon.

It was almost dark before they found a break in the canyon wall, where they could slide down a steep incline into the bottom. As soon as a suitable place could be found to pitch camp, part of the men started to unpack, and one of the party took a shovel and walked down to the creek bed, where he dug a hole in the sand to make a pool from which they could dip water for camp use.

The party felt safe, since they doubted that any of the Indians from the village had followed them. It was sunup the next morning before they started to cook breakfast. Since the water pail was empty, one of the men picked it up and walked down to the water hole they had dug the night before. He stooped down to dip up a pail of water, but suddenly stopped and called to the men in camp, "Come here, quick." The rest of the party, wondering what was wrong, rushed down to him. When they arrived, the man pointed at the sand and said, "Look."

Adams said they couldn't believe their eyes. The sand looked like it was half gold. Everyone in camp, except the half-breed scout, went wild. They worked along the small creek, which ran about as much water as a large spring, until dark.

That night the scout reminded them of their promise of the first day's panning and six head of horses. He told them this was not the creek he was taking them to and that the richest placer was in the next canyon. But they told him this was good enough for them, and the next morning they gave him the first day's panning and six head of horses. He rode away at sunrise after warning them to leave within a few days. If the Indians found them, they would kill every one of them. The scout was never heard of again, and it

269

was Adams' opinion that he was killed before he could reach Fort Apache.

At first everyone was so excited over the rich diggings that all they could think about was panning gold. But after a while the nights began to get cold, and they discussed building a log cabin. All agreed on this except one man, who was Dutch. All he cared about was panning gold. The other five went to work on the cabin and soon had it finished. To add to the comforts of home, they built a fireplace in the back end of the cabin and selected a large flat rock for a hearthstone. After the cabin was completed, they dug a hole under the hearth rock, where they kept their gold hidden. Adams estimated that they had about eighty thousand dollars in gold the last time he checked this cache.

By the time the cabin was completed, their supplies were running low. Four of the party decided to go to Fort Wingate (now San Rafael) after a fresh supply. Since they were short on horses after giving the half-breed Indian scout his share, they decided to take Adams' and the Dutchman's saddle horses for pack animals and leave the two men to take care of camp while they were gone.

The trip to Fort Wingate and back required four days. When five days had passed and no one had showed up, Adams and the Dutchman began to worry. They were afraid to walk very far from camp on foot, but on the sixth day their anxiety was so great, they ventured out of the box canyon to a high ridge on the east side, in the direction from which their companions were to return.

Adams said that this vantage point provided a good view of the surrounding country, and he noticed some miles to the east an expanse of open country. He and the Dutchman decided to walk there before returning to camp. Before leaving the high ridge, they took note of all the main landmarks.

Several miles to the southeast Adams could see three mountain peaks that sat on a high plateau. The peaks resembled sharply topped haystacks and had a dull, reddish glow in the late afternoon sun. To the south was a large, timbered mountain, and to the north a high, reddish, rimrock mesa. The box canyon in which the cabin was built headed into this mesa. Several miles to the northeast was a large, timbered mountain several miles long with a deep saddle across the middle of its length. To the west there was a vast expanse of rolling ridges, most of them covered with a stand of piñon and cedar timber.

Adams said it was nearly five miles to the open country east of them, and it was nearly sundown when he and his partner reached the edge of the timber. There they found the bodies of their four companions. Indians had massacred all of them and scattered their equipment over the ground.

Adams and the Dutchman were badly frightened by this gruesome sight, and their first thought was to hurry back to their camp. When they reached the east rim of the box canyon overlooking the cabin, they discovered the Indians had found it and set it on fire.

Their main concern then was to put as many miles between themselves and the Indians as they could before daylight overtook them. Adams said they travelled all night and came to an elevated plateau before daylight. They could see a high mountain far to the south, which they thought was Escudilla Mountain east of Round Valley. That was the last white settlement they had passed on their way to the canyon, and they decided to try to make it back there.

Since they were afraid to travel by day, they hid until dark. Traveling at night without food or water most of the time caused them to lose their sense of direction. Several days later they were found by a detachment of U.S. Cavalry traveling from Fort Wingate to Fort Tularosa.

Adams and the Dutchman were so weak from starvation and exposure they were out of their minds and unable to talk. The troopers took them to Fort Tularosa, where they recuperated enough in a few days to tell what had happened.

They did not want to return to Fort Wingate, but were told they would have to. Finally they agreed to accompany a troop of cavalry back to the fort, and on reaching there, they directed a burial detail to the scene of the massacre and helped bury the bodies of their four companions.

271

Adams and the Dutchman were thoroughly terrified by what had happened, and any thought of going back to the placer until the country became more civilized was forgotten.

After a few days at Fort Wingate they fell in with a detachment of cavalry headed for Post Ojo Caliente, seventeen miles northwest of the present town of Monticello, New Mexico.

At this time the army had a quartermaster sergeant named James Patterson stationed there. He was issuing supplies to the Indians. Patterson talked to Adams and examined a pouch of coarse gold that Adams claimed he had panned out of his placer. Patterson said one of the nuggets was as large as his thumb, and there were several as large as number-one buckshot. Patterson was convinced that Adams was telling the truth about his rich placer, and he hunted for it the rest of his life, but never found it or anything that even slightly resembled it.

Adams claimed he went from Post Caliente to Los Angeles, California, where he married and raised a family. During this time he had a severe attack of typhoid fever and nearly died. He lost his memory, and he said if it had not been for his wife and children, he might not have been able to recall anything about his trip to the rich placer. They had heard him repeatedly describe the route he had taken, the surrounding country, and the unbelievable amount of placer gold that lay in the bed of the small box canyon. As they repeated what he had told them, his memory slowly returned until he once more had a clear vision of what had happened.

When Geronimo, the last Apache war chief, was captured, Adams decided it would be safe to return and look for his lost mine. He formed a party of several men and went to Pima Villa. He thought that by starting there, he would have a better chance of finding the placer. Adams showed his men every camp his original party had made from Pima Villa to Round Valley. The rancher where Adams had stayed overnight was still living in Round Valley and remembered the men coming to his cabin. From there Adams was completely lost and had no idea of the route they had traveled. While trying to follow the route taken by his first party, he came to the head of Tularosa Creek, but none of that country looked familiar. His mind had been so unclear when the soldiers had taken him back to Fort Wingate that he doubted he could find the mine from there.

Adams was getting along in years and knew he would never be able to return to look for his rich placer again. Frank Jones said the feeble old man presented a pathetic figure as he sat in the flickering firelight, weeping and trying to describe the country near his rich placer mine in hopes that Washie Jones might know of or have heard of a place corresponding to his description.

Washie Jones showed Adams the Gila hot springs, but the water flowed southeast instead of northwest, and the country was too rough. After several such trips, Adams gave up and sold his saddle horse to Charley McCarty, Washie Jones's son-in-law. Then he left for Los Angeles, never to return.

Ben Kemp was not a man to get very excited over lost gold mines. But he needed some saddle ponies, and Emiel Kiehne, a friend living at the Frisco Plaza, had told him he might be able to find horses around Zuñi or Ramah. So he decided this would be a good time to make a trip up there to buy a few horses and some Navaho blankets and look the country over for the landmarks that Adams described.

Kemp left the Mesa Redondo with Benny and Frank Jones and drove to Ramah. At this small Mormon town he was told that the best place to buy blankets was on the Gallup-Zuñi road at a trading post run by a man named Charley McKittrick.

When they reached the trading post, McKittrick was buying sheep from a Navaho. The procedure he used was amusing to Kemp's party. Instead of buying a herd of so many head, he bought the sheep one at a time, using silver coins to make his purchase. He would place a dollar and a quarter on the store counter and tell the man in Navaho, which he spoke fluently, how much a dollar and a quarter would buy in the post's commissary. If the Indian was not interested, he would stare straight ahead and not say a word. Then McKittrick would add another quarter and go through the same rigmarole. When he had put down about as much as he would pay, the Indian would grunt and pick up the money, and the sheep was sold. Then McKittrick would go out to the Indian's flock, which was being held by his squaw near the commissary door, and select a sheep, which was taken out of the herd and placed in a pen with other sheep he had bought. It would take all day to buy twenty head, but McKittrick was making a profit of a dollar a head and figured he was well paid for his trouble.

While the wagon was camped at the trading post, Kemp and his son decided to ride into Gallup. Kemp saddled one of the outlaw horses McCarty had loaned him. The horse, a large black called Cole Younger, was tricky and leaped ten feet away from Kemp as he swung into the saddle. Then the outlawed horse put on an exhibition of bucking that astonished McKittrick, who remarked that it was amazing that a man Kemp's age could put up such a ride.

When the Kemps reached Gallup, they met Purdy, the Santa Fé Railway yardmaster; Smaulding, president of the McKinley County Bank; Bob Roberts, McKinley County sheriff; and Lock Carmichael, a former V + T cowboy. Purdy and Smaulding had made a trip to the head of Toriette Canyon, south of the Mesa Redondo, a year earlier, and Benny had been their guide. They had promised the Kemps a good time if they ever came to Gallup.

Ben Kemp had known Sheriff Bob Roberts and his family when they lived in Texas. The Kemps stayed over until noon the next day, and were shown a most enjoyable time. No horses were found, but a wagonload of fine Navaho blankets were bought at sixty cents a pound.

A survey of the country indicated that Adams had been through there. No one could have described the landmarks as he did without having seen them.

Ben Kemp never made another trip into the Zuñi country looking for the lost mine. But Benny and John Damron made a trip into the reservation in the spring of 1915. They covered most of the country from the point of *mal país* west to Ojo Caliente, then north to a point near Manuelito, a station on the Santa Fé Railway.

They followed Adams' trail from Ojo Caliente northeast to an old trail that ran north to the edge of a rimrock, which had steps cut into the rock. They found the Indian village that Adams had

274

described and the black rock which was a lava flow that cut the canyon. They located the three peaks which were volcanic cones. In fact, they found every thing he described but the gold. They panned in the canyon the Indian scout said was the richest, and the first shovel of sand they turned over looked as though it were half gold, but it was iron pyrite. Not a trace of real gold was found.

Several years later Ben Kemp's cowboy friend, Bob Lewis, learned that one of the soldiers who accompanied Adams and the Dutchman to help bury their companions was still living in one of the eastern states. A trip was made to the old trooper's home, and he was brought to Magdalena. The old soldier took Bob Lewis' party to the exact spot where the four men in Adams' party had been killed and showed them how they had disposed of their bodies.

He said that the bodies were badly decomposed by the time the burial detail arrived, because they had been lying on the ground for nearly three weeks. The massacre had taken place at the foot of a sand-rock point, about twenty feet high, which had a number of fissures. Instead of digging graves, they had thrown the corpses into these cracks and placed loose stones on top of them to keep coyotes from carrying off their bones. Lewis' party dug into the sand-rock fissures and found the bones of four men and the buttons from their clothes.

They were convinced they were near the placer-gold mine, because Adams had said it was within five miles of where his companions were killed. An intense search was made of the surrounding country for ten miles in every direction, but there was no box canyon or any other landmark such as Adams described. What was more puzzling, the skeletons found by Lewis' party were found several miles east of the point of the *mal país*, south of Zuñi Mountain, which is thirty-five miles southeast of where Adams claimed his four companions were killed. So Adams Diggings remain as much a mystery today as they were one hundred years ago.

After McCarty's cattle were brought to the Mesa Redondo, Benny took full charge of the well rig. The cattle tried to stray back to their old range during the first year, and Ben Kemp was in the saddle nearly every day, rain or shine.

Two of his mounts were sorrel horses named Charley and Dan Patch. Charley was used as a pack horse, because he would follow Dan Patch without being led. When a bunch of wild cattle were jumped on a heavily timbered section of the range, it was easy to tell which direction they were going, because Charley would follow at a run, neighing every jump. The noise made by the kyacks and his neighing as he dodged through the timber could be heard a mile away.

The Mesa Redondo ranch, which was located on the main road leading south from the salt lakes, had its share of transient visitors. When Ben Kemp and his son returned from riding the range late one afternoon, they found the family in a state of excitement. A wild-looking man with two dogs following him had come by the ranch about mid-afternoon and asked for something to eat. They had cooked him a meal, which he devoured as though he were a wild animal. They said he was medium height and had a full beard and piercing blue eyes.

Kemp and Benny, who wondered what such a character could be doing in this section of the country, asked their family what direction the man had taken when he left the ranch. They said he had followed the road to Johnson Basin, and Benny and his father took the man's trail and followed it to a point about two miles southwest of the ranch house. His tracks quit the road there and led to some arroyos, about five feet deep, which ran parallel along the west side of the road. When they reached these ditches, they heard a dog growl. Immediately the head of the bearded stranger appeared above the bank, and he crawled out of the ditch. Ben Kemp asked him his name, where he had come from, and where he was going. The man said his name was Ben Lilly. He had been up near Zuñi on a lion hunt and was on his way back to Reserve.

The Kemps had heard of the lion hunter and his peculiar habits. There was a cold raw wind blowing out of the southwest, and Lilly had no bedding. Ben Kemp invited him back to the ranch, but Lilly turned the invitation down, saying, "No thank you. The dogs and I will be quite comfortable here in the ditch." Although the Kemps

276

were not surprised, they rode back down the road, shaking their heads and wondering what kind of person this man could be.

On another occasion Charles Ilfeld came to the ranch and stayed overnight. He was checking Salt Lake to see if it was a suitable location for a store. He soon decided against it and returned to Albuquerque. Frank A. Hubbell later established a commissary, which he maintained for a number of years.

Hauling salt from the salt lakes at this time was a freighter, who lived near Springerville, Arizona. Kemp noticed that on his return from Salt Lake he always camped on the southwest corner of Fowler's pasture, which was near the road and about three hundred yards west of Fowler's house and cow corrals.

Kemp, who was riding the range regularly, noticed that every time the freighter camped there, a cow would disappear off the range. Most of the cows belonged to Fowler's former ranch friend, but occasionally they belonged to someone else. Three or four ranchers had cattle grazing on the open range around Fowler's ranch, and it was an easy task to round up a small bunch on short notice.

One night when the freighter camped near Fowler's ranch, Kemp notified the cattle inspector at Springerville and asked him to search the freighter's wagons when he arrived in town. The wagons were loaded with loose salt, which had been shoveled into the wagon from the stock pile at Salt Lake. When the wagons reached Springerville, the inspector searched them and found four quarters of beef buried a foot beneath the surface of the salt in one of the wagons.

The wagons were searched late at night, and the inspector left in a car before sunup the next morning for the Mesa Redondo. The freighter's son, a boy about fourteen, dodged the inspector and arrived at Fowler's ranch about thirty minutes before the inspector reached the Mesa Redondo. The boy had covered a distance of forty-two miles on horseback in less than six hours.

When the boy arrived, Fowler quickly saddled a horse and left on the run. The Kemps saw him leave, but since the inspector had not arrived, they were not sure that the beef had been found. Ben

Kemp had horses saddled and ready when the inspector arrived. Since they did not know what they might encounter, the inspector asked Benny and John Damron to go with them. The approach to the Fowlers' house was across an open flat, and anyone in the small rock building would be fully protected. Since there was no other way to get to the building, the four men rode up to the house and dismounted. Ben Kemp walked to the door and pushed it open with the muzzle of his rifle. Only one of Fowler's associates was in the building, and he offered no resistance.

The cattle inspector and Ben Kemp stayed at Fowler's ranch to search for evidence. They found the offal of a cow that had been recently butchered in Fowler's corral. Kemp was sure he knew who owned the cow. On the afternoon the freighter had camped near the corral, he had ridden by a small bunch of cattle grazing near Fowler's cabin. Among them was a brindle cow belonging to Fowler's former ranch friend. The cow was dry and rolling fat. About dusk that same evening Fowler was seen driving this bunch of cattle towards his corral.

Ben Kemp and the inspector stayed at Fowler's cabin the rest of that day and night. The next morning about ten o'clock they saw Fowler approaching the cabin across a valley to the east. When he rode up to the house, they stepped out of the door and ordered him to raise his hands. When Fowler saw the inspector, he grabbed for his shirt pocket, but both men raised their rifles and would have killed him if he had pulled a gun. After making this foolish move, Fowler quickly raised his hands, and they searched him and found a .25-caliber automatic pistol in his shirt pocket.

When they examined his saddle, they found fresh blood stains where he had carried the hide of some animal. When they asked Fowler what he had done with the hide to the animal he had butchered in the corral, he said he had dropped it in a ditch on the east side of the valley. Then they rode to the east side of the valley, where Fowler showed them a hide. But the hide belonged to a red, bald-faced cow bearing another rancher's brand.

Later it was learned that a month earlier he had bought this cow

278

from the rancher and left her on the rancher's range. When Fowler heard that the freighter's wagon had been searched, he hurriedly rode to the rancher's range and hunted until he found the cow. He butchered the cow and brought the hide back to his ranch.

Later, while talking to Fowler's former ranch friend about his cow, Kemp asked him why he didn't prosecute Fowler. "Mr. Kemp," the rancher said, "you know we were partners, and I can't go to law with him. He knows too much on me. But I'm going to stop the son of a bitch from stealing my cattle, and that's for sure."

One day a young man from Utica, New York, arrived at the Mesa Redondo. His main ambition was to be a buckaroo and ride a bucking bronco. At the time he arrived, the Kemps were breaking a few ponies for saddle horses. The New Yorker insisted on riding one of them, and they finally agreed. Rather than having him thrown by one of the broncs they were breaking, they roped out a stocky bay mare. The animal was saddled and eared down while the easterner mounted. When he was seated in the saddle, he was asked if he was set.

"Yep," he answered, "let her buck."

The boys holding the animal released her with a yell and threw their hats under her. The little mare leaped high into the air, throwing her rider so high above her back that he landed on his feet behind her when he hit the ground. Then the bronc kicked with both hind feet, and a foot passed on each side of the New Yorker's head. This scared the boys who had saddled the animal. Although they asked him if he wanted to try again, they did not rawhide him into it when he refused.

Another New Yorker who came to the ranch took a number of spills, but he was game and kept on trying until he became a fairly good rider.

Albert Finch dissolved his partnership with Jim Davis and started working for the Frank A. Hubbell Sheep Company as their windmill man. A few years later, in 1916, he quit and filed a homestead at the north end of Slaughter Mesa, eight miles east of the Mesa Redondo ranch.

The Kemp well rig was used to drill a well on his land, with the

279

understanding that it could be used as a watering place for the Slash-T7 cattle. Several threats were circulated about what was going to happen to Finch and the Kemps for establishing a ranch at this location.

One night about ten o'clock the clip-clop of a horse's feet could be heard coming down the trail west of the well-rig camp. When the rider came into camp, there was no one in the circle of light made by the campfire. He pulled his horse to a halt, and Albert Finch called from his obscure position outside the light circle and asked the man his name.

"Un hombre," he answered. Then Finch addressed him in Spanish, but he refused to answer.

This seemed suspicious, so he was disarmed and held under guard in camp for the rest of the night. Then next morning his horse, saddle, and six-shooter were returned, and he left camp, headed in the direction of Salt Lake. Three hours later Ben Kemp learned that the horse, saddle, and six-shooter claimed by the mysterious visitor had been stolen from a rancher near Brights Lake, a few miles south of the present Pie Town station on Highway 60.

Kemp saddled a horse and headed north, cutting the horse thief's trail west of Salt Lake. The thief was making good time, and Kemp had to run him fifteen miles inside the Arizona line before he overtook and captured him.

On November 16, 1916, Clara Kemp married a cowboy named Oda Gann, and they left the next morning for the Pat Gann ranch on Apache Creek. Pat Gann, a second cousin of Oda, had been killed in a gun fight a few years earlier. Oda's father gained title to the ranch, and a few years later he died, leaving the property to Oda.

Ben Fowler continued to live on his homestead a mile down the valley northeast of the Mesa Redondo. During the latter part of 1915 a man, his wife, and five children moved into the Salt Lake community. The oldest daughter of this family, a girl of sixteen, was soon captivated by Fowler's dashing ways, and within a few months they were married. After the marriage all of her family moved to Fowler's ranch to live.

280

Albert Finch built a cabin on his homestead and stocked his range with a bunch of cattle he got on shares from Henry Coleman, another rancher living near Quemado. On the evening of June 7, 1917, he and Beulah Kemp were married. The following morning they mounted their saddle horses and rode to the Slaughter Mesa ranch.

On the same morning that Albert and Beulah left the ranch, Benny and John Damron hitched four horses to a wagon and headed for Steve Kemp's ranch on Mogollon Creek, 120 miles south, in the Mogollon Mountains. The dry years had forced their uncle to seek a better range for his cattle, and he decided to move them to Salt Lake. Since he needed some assistance, he wrote a letter asking them to help trail his cattle through.

Although the Mesa Redondo and Slaughter Mesa wells were not affected by the drought, the windmills failed to pump enough water for the four hundred head of cattle. The two ranches had only one gasoline engine and pumpjack, which had to be switched back and forth in order to furnish a sufficient supply of water.

When water ran low at Slaughter Mesa, Albert Finch hitched a team to a wagon and drove to the Mesa Redondo, where the gasoline engine and pumpjack were loaded. Ben Kemp told him he would come out to the ranch early on the morning of the seventeenth to help him set up the engine and pump. Late that afternoon Albert returned to Slaughter Mesa.

The morning of June 17 was bright and clear, and Kemp started early for the Finch ranch. He crossed the valley east of the ranch along the road that ran north of Sierra Pomo to the Slaughter Mesa ranch. When Kemp arrived, he found Albert working with the engine and pump, so he stayed and helped him until mid-afternoon.

After Kemp left the Mesa Redondo, his son John Stephen rode to the Salt Lake post office after the mail. About nine o'clock that morning Mrs. Kemp and the children at the Mesa Redondo ranch house saw Fowler and one of his brothers-in-law driving a small bunch of cattle and horses up the east side of the valley. They never gave the incident a thought, because they had seen him driving his stock to a shallow well and seep spring on Cottonwood

Canyon for a month. The spring and well were on a school section leased by Fowler's former ranch friend and partner.

About two hours later they saw a man on horseback emerge from the mouth of Cottonwood Canyon and ride like the wind down the east side of the valley towards Fowler's ranch. He was waving his arms and uttering horrible sounds audible to the family at the Mesa Redondo ranch house more than a mile away. When the rider reached Fowler's cabin, a work team was hurriedly wrangled out of the pasture and hitched to a wagon. Fowler's father-in-law loaded all his family into the wagon and headed back towards Cottonwood Canyon as fast as the team could travel.

Mrs. Kemp and the children sensed that something terrible had happened, and they were frightened. When John Stephen returned from the post office, they told him what they had heard and seen. He was in a quandary over what he should do, and before he had decided, a friend by the name of John Graham arrived at the ranch. Graham was told about the mysterious actions of Fowler's in-laws, and after some discussion he and Stephen decided to ride out and learn what was causing all the disturbance.

They rode across the valley and followed the wagon tracks up Cottonwood Canyon. About fifty yards below the shallow well and spring, they saw Fowler's horse lying dead alongside the trail, and when they reached the brush fence that enclosed the well, they saw Fowler's in-laws gathered in a group around the body of a man whom they recognized as Fowler. He had been shot and killed.

They tried to question Fowler's brother-in-law, who had helped him drive the stock to the well. They also talked to a schoolteacher, who lived with a Mexican family about three hundred yards up the canyon from the well. He had been the first to arrive at the scene of the shooting. Since neither of them knew who had killed Fowler, Stephen and Graham returned to the Mesa Redondo.

Late that afternoon Ben Kemp returned from Slaughter Mesa and learned about the killing at Cottonwood Spring. The Kemps always wondered who killed Fowler, but they never knew because the crime was never solved.

Benny and John Damron met their uncle Steve on Little Dry Creek. He had started out before they could reach Mogollon Creek, and he was having trouble trying to drive 120 head of cattle and ten saddle horses by himself.

They left Little Dry Creek the next morning for the Mesa Redondo. Because the cattle were poor and weak, travel was slow, and they were forced to make one camp in Saliz Canyon, where feed was short. There Steve Kemp's best work horse got into a sack of grain and ate so much that he foundered. Bad luck seemed to be riding with them. When they reached a steep hill where the wagon road left Saliz Canyon, the right front wheel on Steve Kemp's wagon hit a rock and shattered into a dozen pieces.

Montague Stevens' sawmill was the nearest habitation. Benny drove his wagon to the mill and asked Stevens to loan them a wheel until they could get theirs repaired. Stevens had been a rancher for years. He knew the predicament they were in and readily loaned them a wheel. That night camp was pitched about a half-mile north of the present Pine Lawn station on Legget Canyon, and half an hour later the foundered horse died.

From Stevens' sawmill the cattle were driven to Reserve, where they rested for two days while the broken wagon wheel was being repaired. The small trail herd left Reserve on the morning of June 20 and reached the Mesa Redondo in the late afternoon of the twenty-third.

21.
The Last Divide

Benny was inducted into the army on September 19, 1917. After nine months of intensive training at Camp Kearney, California, he was transferred overseas to France where he was assigned to Company A, 109th Infantry, 28th Division. Benny was wounded twice during the war, and he returned home in poor health after he was discharged from the army at Camp Bowie, Texas, on February 13, 1919.

When Benny came home, he found that a drought had hit the country a year earlier, and cattle were dying by the hundreds. His family was suffering from a severe attack of flu, and no one had been able to take care of the starving cattle.

After watching a number of cows starve to death, Benny could stand by no longer. He hitched a team of horses to a light buckboard and drove over the snow-packed road to Springerville, where he ordered nine thousand pounds of barley (cottonseed cake was unavailable) to be delivered to the Mesa Redondo ranch.

Julius Becker, the merchant from whom he ordered the grain, told him it would be impossible to haul it over the snow-packed roads, but Benny was adamant. Six large horses were hitched to a wagon loaded with three thousand pounds of grain, and after three days of agonizing travel the teamster reached the Mesa Redondo.

About one out of every ten cattle that got down was saved, and the calf tally for 1919 was less than 10 per cent of what it had been the year before. In 1918, Jess McCarty and Stephen trailed 150 head to Beaver Creek, but the cattle were not used to the rough range, and nearly half of them died.

In January, 1920, Mary Kemp married Louis Charlton, who was foreman of the Cross Bar Cattle Company, which had ranches near Springerville, Arizona. Charlton was a champion cowboy and had worked with Tom Mix in the days of silent movies. He was a man of steel nerves and called the hand of some of the toughest characters in the Salt Lake community. He was a rodeo fan and won several calf roping contests. Charlton was also an expert at whittling, and his work is on exhibition at the old governor's mansion at Prescott, Arizona.

In the fall of 1920, Ben Kemp trailed two hundred cattle to Beaver Creek, and Lou took charge of them. The remaining two hundred head were kept at the Mesa Redondo.

During the war and directly after, there was rampant unrest in the west end of Socorro County. Within forty miles of Salt Lake ten people died from gunshot wounds. None of Ben Kemp's family were killed, but they went through some trying times and witnessed many unjust acts.

After Benny returned from the army, Elfego Baca, who was a friend of the Kemps, was elected sheriff of Socorro County, and some of the pressure against the Kemps was relieved.

In 1924 the ranch and cattle were sold. Kemp paid off his debts and moved to Apache Creek, where the family lived for a year. After the ranch and cattle were sold, Benny started working for the United States Forest Service. His first job was with a trail crew at Eagle Peak. Charles Denton was trail foreman.

In the fall of 1925, Ben Kemp decided to move to Arizona. He decided to try Phoenix first, and if this was not satisfactory, to range north. He loaded a wagon and a Ford truck with household equipment, then he, Mrs. Kemp, and three of their children, John Stephen, Lila, and Jess, and a friend named Walter Steen left Oda Gann's ranch on Apache Creek on the morning of October 2, 1925.

Ben Kemp drove the wagon, Stephen the truck, which also served as a chuck wagon, and Jess and Walter Steen drove the remuda, which contained about twenty saddle horses. Their route was by way of Springerville, Fort Apache, Oak Creek, and Globe. They reached the desert west of Superior on the afternoon of October 17.

Evidently Ted, the family dog, thought the family had lost their

285

minds venturing out onto this vast expanse of desolate-looking country, because he tried desperately to stop them. He would run ahead of the wagon, stop in the road, and turn to face the team. Then he would jump up and down and bark until the lead team almost stepped on him. He would leap out of their way and race back down the road in the direction from which they had come, and when he was a hundred yards behind the wagon, he would sit down and howl mournfully.

He kept this up all afternoon. When camp was pitched near what is now Florence Junction, he refused to eat and gave the impression of being sad and dejected. The next morning he was gone, and four days later he arrived at Oda Gann's ranch on Apache Creek—weary, footsore, and gaunt, but otherwise unharmed.

When the Kemps reached Mesa, they were almost on the town's main street before they knew it. The median in the street had just been completed and planted with grass. The ground was soft, and the horses plowed through it in several places. This caused quite a disturbance, and it is likely this was the last remuda to be driven down the main street of Mesa, Arizona.

After passing through Mesa, Ben Kemp headed his wagon north to Cave Creek, where the family stayed for a week. Then they moved on to Camp Creek. Jobs were scarce, but they found work at an onyx mine.

During this time Kemp noticed hundreds of bees around camp. He decided a little honey would be a welcome treat, so he and Walter Steen trailed some of the bees to their hive in a cave. When they reached the caves, which were in some cliffs on the side of a rough canyon, they discovered two large rattlesnakes at a cave's entrance. They killed the rattlers and threw them over the next cliff.

Kemp sent Walter Steen back to camp after some extra pails in which to gather the honey. After Walter left, Kemp started examining the bee cave. He tripped on the rocky mountainside and fell over the cliff below him, landing on top of the two rattlers. Luckily he did not come in contact with their poisonous fangs. He was badly bruised from the fall, but not seriously injured.

During the late fall of 1926, Benny, who was working for the

Forest Service on the Datil National Forest in New Mexico, was placed in charge of a telephone construction crew in the San Mateo Mountains. He hired his brother Stephen as straw boss of the crew. When the job was finished in late October, Benny called his brother Ed, who was working at the Ocean to Ocean Garage in Magdalena.

The three brothers met at Chloride, where they made plans to go to Arizona. They left Chloride about the first of November. With their aunt Mrs. Armour and her two children, they drove to Hardt Creek in Tonto Basin, where the family had moved after leaving the onyx mine.

After they arrived, Ben Kemp decided to make a trip to Menard, Texas, to visit his mother and sister Mary. At the same time he was going to look for the lost Bowie mine. This was the old mine shown on the map that the ancient Mexican miner had given the Bradberrys. The map indicated that it was located near the Mission San Saba. Although Kemp was almost sure he could find the mine, he and his son never found any indications that it existed. James Bowie had been the last white man to visit the mine. Since his death at the Alamo, no other man has been able to find it.

How the Bowie mine disappeared so completely is a mystery that has never been solved. There is no doubt that such a mine existed. There are records of it in the archives at Mexico City. After Indians showed James Bowie the location of the mine, they covered it up. They even scraped up the ashes from campfires near the mine and threw them into the shaft. It was erased from the face of the earth, and no one has been able to find it again.

After Kemp and Benny failed to find the Bowie mine, they drove to Honey Creek, south of the town of Llano. They found the old Spanish mine Kemp had discovered when he was a boy. According to Will Roberts, Kemp's boyhood pal who had lived at Honey Creek Cove for the past fifty-seven years, the mine had been worked out and not a trace of gold or silver was found.

After returning to Hardt Creek, Ben Kemp and his sons discussed plans for starting an apiary. There was a large number of bees around Tonto Basin, and they thought that with the proper

287

equipment swarms of them could be caught and placed in hives.

At this time Ben Kemp's half-brother was working in an oil field at Best, Texas. He wrote the Kemps a letter, which stated that work was plentiful and wages high. Since no work was available in Tonto Basin, the four Kemp brothers, Benny, Stephen, Ed, and Jess, drove to Best. To their surprise jobs were scarce, and they were forced to take any work they could find. For nearly a month Benny drove a run-down delivery truck for a lumber dealer. His brothers worked on any job available.

One day Benny received a letter from Fred McCament, forest ranger in charge of the Jewett ranger district north of Reserve, New Mexico. He wrote that he had a job for Benny as administrative assistant. Early the following morning Benny left the oil field in a cloud of dust, promising himself he would never return.

After Ben Kemp lived at the Hardt ranch for a year, he built his own home a mile up the canyon west of the Hardt place, where he lived for the remaining years of his life.

Although a hundred hives were purchased, less than a dozen were ever occupied by bees. The dream of an up-and-going apiary never materialized. Benny continued to work for the forest service, and in December, 1927, he married. The next year John Stephen married, and two years later Ed married. Jess was the only one of the boys left at home. Because other work kept him busy, he had little time to work with the bees.

Everyone that knew Ben Kemp in Tonto Basin was his friend. It had been that way in every community where he had lived, except Salt Lake. He was a man highly respected by law-abiding citizens but roundly hated by law violaters.

Since he was a rancher and lived miles from any settlement most of the time, he could not attend church. But he lived a Christian life and raised his family who adored him.

For several years he had suffered from a stomach ailment, and on August 5, 1932, he became seriously ill. He asked to be taken to Reserve, and his wish was granted. At Reserve he was placed under a physician's care, but his health grew steadily worse.

On the morning of August 22 he died. He was laid to rest in the

288

little cemetery, which overlooks the San Francisco River Valley at Reserve, among the friends who had come there with him in 1885. His grief-stricken family and friends, who knew the good example he had set in life, believed that when he passed over the last divide to the home range of eternity, he must have been welcomed by the Supreme Boss with the words "well done."

Appendix

The following items from *The El Paso Times* are taken from microfilm at the El Paso Public Library.

The El Paso Times under date of September 8, 1884, reported that T. J. Stevens, who was working for Irvin and Co., was escorted to the Munday brothers' ranch by a man named Hall. Stevens intended to buy some cattle. He had five hundred dollars in his pocket, wages he had saved from his work at Irvin's. He borrowed a horse from Col. Marr to accompany Hall. They were to meet a man named Delany and a Mexican boy at the ranch.

Stevens was expected back in El Paso by Monday or Tuesday night, September first or second. He did not return and Mr. Munday went to the ranch to see what had happened. He found the ranch abandoned, the cattle scattered, and the saddle horses stolen. Fearing something serious had befallen Stevens, he notified Captain Baylor, and he with a squad of his rangers went to the ranch eight miles up the Río Grande north of El Paso into New Mexico, where they found Stevens' body buried in a shallow grave and straightway took up the trail of the horse thieves and murderers.

Captain Baylor's letter to the Munday brothers, printed in *The El Paso Times*

Deming, New Mexico
Sept. 9, 1884

Munday Bros.
El Paso, Texas

Gentlemen:
After leaving the Lanark Station, I learned the two Americans

and the Mexican boy were seen at Alton Station, and I went at once to that point, and the wife of the station agent, or rather section boss, told me that the parties had come in there and got water for ten animals and got breakfast very late (11 o'clock). They said they were horse traders from Old Mexico and had been two days without water. She and the children described the party exactly. The children said they had two watches, one silver and one gold. They had gone towards the Portello, but had not found water, and I saw where they had come back to the railroad on the old road near the lava rocks, just one-half mile beyond Alton Station. I then followed their tracks to Aden where the station keeper and his wife described Delaney exactly. Hall and the Mexican boy did not get down. They did not water their stock, but filled their canteens and went on towards Cambray Station. The agent said they had two horses with saddles, not packed, one horse white or gray. They also left a brown or bay horse with a blazed face back five or six miles. They ran him away from the railroad for fear the cars would kill him. They told a Mexican about the horse, and I think he took him away.

I got on the cars and came on here to see what I could learn and saw a young man by the name of Woods, half Mexican, whose father lives in Las Cruces. He says there is a stray white horse at his ranch near Tres Hermanas (Castillas, I believe, is the name) that has been there for five or six days, branded "O" on the neck. I think this may be your gray horse, and if so, the murderers turned off at Cambray and took a trail through the Tres Hermanas Mountains to this ranch and have gone on towards Eureka or Tombstone.

I telegraphed Corporal Kemp to come on up to Cambray and wait until he heard from me. I have seen a young man in charge of the train just from Conalitas, and he saw nothing of the party. I am waiting to see if I can learn more before the train leaves to-night and will instruct Kemp to see which way the trail goes from Cambray Station, and if it goes towards Tombstone, to follow it, and if towards Hillsboro, to telegraph me from the railroad. They will cross at Florida or Nutt station. I will go on to Benson in the morning and to Tombstone and keep a lookout for them and get

291

the authorities after them. I am looking for the custom house officer, who has been in Tombstone and may have seen these men.

Have telegraphed Florida and Nutt stations and no such men have been seen there, so am inclined to think that they have gone on the route south of the railroad to keep away from telegrams and railroad.

The customs house officer has come in, but saw nothing of our men. I will send down a young man tonight to join our squad, who knows well every trail and watering place between Cambray and Tombstone. He can ride my horse. I will go on the morning train and write again from Tombstone. I saw a man who knows Hall well and went on to Benson yesterday and promised to look out for him.

Yours,

Geo. W. Baylor
Capt., Co. A, Tex. Rangers.

Report in *The El Paso Times*, October 1, 1884

Col. Baylor arrived this morning from the search after the murderers of Stevens. Col. Baylor separated from the rangers by going ahead by rail to Tombstone, Arizona, leaving the rangers to follow the trail. The supposition was that the murderers would strike for the Sonora line and escape by way of Guaymas and hence the importance of getting ahead of them. Col. Baylor first went to Tombstone, remaining there hidden for several days, then organized a party consisting of Andy and Pete Behan, who knew the whole country. With this party he went to the Chiricahua Mountains, Arizona. From there to San Simon Valley, thence southwest to San Bernallia ranch on the Sonora line. From there to Arroyo Aliso, Sonora, then east to Cajon Bonito, and for two days traveled near the Chihuahua head in the Sierra Madre, from the Animas Valley in New Mexico. At this point Col. Baylor met some stockmen called line riders, who were well informed as to all strangers. While at the Le Roy, a ranch occupied by an American of the same name, some Mexican guards captured a band of

292

smugglers with several thousand dollars of American goods. On the seizure there may be a continental question, as it is claimed that Le Roy is on the American side of the line.

After leaving Le Roy, Col. Baylor's party went to Walnut Creek, New Mexico, where there is a ranch occupied by a Texas stockman. No information could be obtained up to this point, and Col. Baylor sent the two men, Ames and Behan, back to the Chiricahua Mountains to go to the Guadalupe Mountains.

Colonel Baylor returned from Walnut Creek by the Hatchet Mountains, Eureka, Cedar Grove, Victorio, and struck the railroad at Gauge, where he telegraphed to find out about his men the rangers, but could not learn their whereabouts. From Gauge, Col. Baylor went to the Mimbres and down that to Deming. There he met Mr. Graham, who gave information about the rangers as follows:

Started from Cambray and followed trail towards Deming, found one horse dead four miles from Cambray. The rangers went on to Deming, losing the trail. From Deming the rangers went to Tres Hermanas, from there to a ranch in Chihuahua. Becoming satisfied they were not going in the right direction, returned to Eureka and Separ. At this point they telegraphed to Tombstone that their horses were broken down and were instructed to rest until further orders, but they started out again, and crossing the Gila River, struck the trail again, going nearly due north towards Arroyo San Francisco. On the trail they found Munday's white horse killed, and following on, they found the pony the Mexican boy had been riding tied to a tree, where he had evidently been for three or four days. They also found the rigging used by the boy near the old shaft, with the appearance justifying the conclusion that the boy had been killed and thrown into the shaft.

Following the trail, the horses gave out a second time, and a halt was necessary. Then Corporal Kemp and Private Atkinson took the two best horses and followed on the trail up a canyon into the mountains.

Sgt. Baylor and McFarland came back with the broken down stock. This is as far as information has been obtained. It will be seen that there has been a most thorough search, which is still being

293

pushed by two different parties. The trail was leading towards the Atlantic and Pacific Railroad, the robbers having been turned away from their original purpose of going to Mexico.

An immense amount of travel and hardship have been endured by the pursuing party, while the robbers' party have lost five head of their horses on the trail.

Entry in *The El Paso Times*, October 31, 1884

Col. Baylor's company of rangers leave tonight for Murphysville on the G. H. & S. A., where they will be permanently located in the future.

Index

Adams (prospector): finds placer gold, 267–73; graves of companions found, 275

Adams Diggings, New Mexico: 267, 275

Ake, Bob: 132, 190

Alexander, Ab: 156, 160, 173, 175–76, 189

Allen (killer of Buck Powell): 175

Allen, Charles: 181–82

Allen, Milt: 198

Alpine, Texas: 57–58, 60–61, 77–78, 91, 101–103, 108, 110–15

Anderson, Charley: 190, 214–17, 219

Anderson, Maude: 178–80

Apache Kid: 139, 186; escapes from officers, 136–38; raids of, 155; searchers eluded by, 189; head of, 212, 224; slaying of, 214–24

Arizona's Dark and Bloody Ground: 233

Armijo, José: 228–29

Armour, Julia Cox (Mrs. Walter): 118, 179, 287

Armour, Walter: 191

Atkison, Private (Texas Ranger): 50–55

Baca, Anastasio: 241

Baca, Elfego: 24, 285

Baca, Nicasio: 251

Baldwin, Fred: 227

Baldwin family, the: 99

Baldy Socks (horse): captured in horse roundup, 149; stolen by Black Jack Ketchum's men, 168; sales of, 189–90; stolen from Charley Anderson, 214; discovered in canyon, 216–17; brought to Chloride, N.M., 219; death at Mesa Redondo, 250; thief of revealed, 253

Barnes, Dick: 209

Bartlett (Magdalena citizen): 104–105

Bass, Sam: 58

Baumbec, Fred: 138

Baxter (murder victim): 74

Baylor, Captain George W.: 18–19, 22–27, 29–30, 35, 41, 46–50, 55

Bean, Jack: 156

Beaver Creek, New Mexico: 125, 129–32, 139–40, 143, 149, 153, 155–56, 159–60, 163, 167–68, 175, 186–87, 191, 195, 198, 202ff., 226, 229–30, 233, 237–40, 345–46, 284–85

Becker, Julius: 284

Bellah, Ed: 181

Bennett (in Alpine fight): 112–13

Bennett (troublemaker): 141–42

Bess, Jack: 103–104, 221

"Beulah Land, Sweet Beulah Land": 226

Blum, Jake: 153, 186

Bodenhammer, Billy: 156, 173–75

Bonney, William H. (Billy the Kid): 74

Booger, Ed: 90

Bowie, James: 65, 287

Bowie mine: 65, 287

Bradberry (homesteader): 64–65, 287

Bradberry, Mrs. (homesteader's wife): 64–65, 287

Bradford, Mary: 65, 117, 287

Bradford, William: 65, 111–12, 117, 287

Bronco Bill: 94

Broncobusting: 4–5, 94, 194ff., 279

Brown brothers: 11

Bullis, Captain John L.: 138

Bullware, Bob: 140

Byrnes, General (stagecoach passenger): 14–15

Callahan, Bill: 117

Campbell, George: 18–20

Campbell, Johnny: 209–10

Candelario, Alfredo: 185

Cantrell, Dave: 134, 138–39, 177

Carmichael, Lock: 274

Carson, Kit: 176

Carter (cattleman): 249–50, 253

Casey, Shep: 251–52
Cash, Jim: 263
Chadwick, Charley: 252–53
Chandler, Jack: 167
Chandler, Mrs. Jack: 162
Chapman, Edith: 36
Chapman, Gilford: 3–5, 143, 145
Chapman, Nancy Kemp (Mrs. Gilford):
   3, 173
Chapman, Jim: 117
Chapman, Tim: 143ff., 146–47, 152, 168,
   177–78
Charlton, Louis: 284–85
Charlton, Mary Lily Kemp (Mrs.
   Louis): 117, 120, 128, 140, 152, 159–
   60, 206, 226, 246, 248, 264
Chastain ranch, Texas: 111
Chavez (cow rancher): 232
Chavez (sheepman): 233
Chisholm, Mrs. (hotel proprietress): 104
Chisum, John S.: 175
Chloride, New Mexico: 135, 178–91, 195,
   208, 212–14, 219, 224, 230, 233, 287
Chuck wagons: 58, 78, 104, 126, 135,
   144ff., 156, 166, 174–75, 197, 264, 285;
   at Datil, N.M., 91, 97; Gila wagon, 91,
   96, 123
Claxton, Al: 241–42
Cleaveland, Agnes Morley: 205, 225
Clements, A. L.: 145, 220–21
Coleman, Henry: 221
Collins, John: 73–74, 160; *see also* John
   Graham
Conklin, A. M.: 24
Cooney, J. C.: 126–27, 177
Cox, Barry: 236
Cox, Erwin: 14, 74
Cox, Henry: 13, 91, 122–23, 134, 160,
   177ff.; on Cox Canyon, 73, 107–108;
   rancher on Negrito Creek, 74–77;
   moved to Fairview, 77; accident of,
   118, 125; death of, 191
Cox, Mrs. Henry: 118, 122–23, 191
Cox, Ike: 109
Cox, Josephine: *see* Josephine Cox Kemp
Cox, Julia: *see* Julia Cox Armour
Cox, Martha: *see* Martha Cox Emmerick
Cox, Sarah: 118, 179
Cox, Tabitha: *see* Tabitha Cox Graham
Crawford ranch: 98
Cunningham (lumber buyer): 249
Curley Bill (outlaw): 49, 233

Damron, John: 117, 155, 240, 246, 250–51,
   257, 263–65, 274–75, 281–83
Darling (hotel owner): 78, 112
Darling, Mrs. (hotel manager): 108
Datil, New Mexico: 91, 97–101, 205,
   225–26, 252
Davidson, Pap: 140
Davison, Frank: 144
Davis, Jim: 279
DeGarnett, Frank: 22
Delaney (ranch hand): 47–50
Deming, New Mexico: 22, 48–50, 62, 234,
   257
Denton, Charles: 285
Dines, Johnny: 150–51
Dodd, Billy: 234–35
Duncan, Dick: 58–60
Dunnigan, Carl: 144, 156
Dyer, Miles: 221

Earp, Wyatt: 44
Edison (miner): 184–85
Ellis, Bill: 117
El Paso, Texas: 18–22, 41ff., 83, 108, 144
Emmerick, Martha Cox (Mrs. Nat):
   107–108, 121
Emmerick, Nat: 107–108, 192
Estado Land and Cattle Company: 58,
   78, 82
Eton, Colonel: 123
Evans, Dub: 163

Fairview, New Mexico: 77, 152–55, 161,
   166, 175, 181, 186, 191, 214, 233
Farr, Dave: 206
Ferguson, George: 177
Fields, Nels: 195–96, 229–31
Finch, Albert: as well driller, 202–205.
   207–208, 211; as rancher, 279–81;
   marriage of, 281; *see also* Jim
   Thompson
Finch, Beulah Kemp (Mrs. Albert): 117.
   120, 128, 140, 196, 226, 281
Fitch (Socorro lawyer): 231
Ford (team driver): 249
Forrest, Earle R.: 233
Foster, George: 156, 173
Fowler (G-4 ranch hand): 86
Fowler, Ben: 250, 264, 280–82; tangles
   with law, 251–54, homestead filed by,
   263
Freeland, Rufe: 157

Freight hauling: 117, 123, 132, 277
Fullerton, Will: 209, 226
Fullerton ranch: 189, 209–10
Futch, Ike: 161, 234, 236–37
Futch, Mrs. Ike: 235–36

Gann (an outlaw): 33
Gann, Clara Lue Kemp (Mrs. Oda):
    139, 280
Gann, Oda: 280, 286
Gann, Pat: 280
García, David: 241
García, José: 202–203
García, Juan: 202–203
García, Ramon: 241
Garrett, Pat: 74
Garrett, Tommy: 192
Gates, John: 256–58
Gaoud, Bill: 112–14
Gentry, Charley: 142–43
Gentry, Mrs. Charley: 142
Geronimo: 74, 77, 272
Gibson, Mose: 153–54
Gila River: 50, 61, 74, 137, 160, 175, 177,
    195–96, 206, 240, 242, 267–68
Gillespie, Bob: 240
Gillett, James: 15, 29, 58, 78–82, 85, 91,
    103; as a Texas Ranger, 19, 24–25,
    30–33, 55; as a law enforcement officer,
    41, 112
Glaze brothers (ranchers): 199, 209
Glaze, Ollie: 199, 209
Goesling, Henry: 245
Goodnight, Charles: 175
Graham, Abe: 146
Graham, Henry: 146, 158, 177–78, 221,
    229, 248–49, 254–56, 282
Graham, Hosea: 146
Graham, John: 145–46, 148–50; *see also*
    John Collins
Graham, Tabitha Cox (Mrs. John): 74
Grahams and Tewksburys (in Tonto
    Basin War): 134
Greer, John: 258–61
Grizzly bears: 60, 73, 177; Starkweather
    grizzly, 66–71; Beaver Creek grizzly,
    211
Guage (rancher): 88–89
Gutierrez (sheepman): 226

Hagan, Al: 233, 239–40
Hale, John (ranch manager): 19

Hall (companion of J. T. Stevens):
    47–50
Hall (a deputy): 260, 262–63
Halley's Comet: 240
Happy Jack (wagon boss): 157
Hardy (ranch hand): 105–106
Hartshorn, Larry: 183–84
Havell, George: 149–50
Hearn, Walter: 150, 214–15, 217–18
Henderson, Tom: 123, 134, 139, 142, 156
Herdin, Jake: 191
Hickok, James Butler (Wild Bill): 103
Higgins, Maggie: *see* Maggie Higgins
    Lewis
Higgins, Patrick: 127
Hiler, Jim: 214, 216
Hill, Jeff: 240–41
Hill, Tommy: 135–36
Holland (hotel proprietor): 112
Holliday, Frank: 92, 96–100
Holmes, Hunkadory: 136–37
Homesteading: 115, 129–32, 245, 250,
    253, 263
Honey Creek, Texas: 11–13, 287
Hubbard, Mrs. (a widow): 252–53
Hubbell, Frank A.: 192, 277
Hughes (Texas Ranger): 21
Humphreys (horse buyer): 189
Hunting: 27–28, 60 ff., 81, 118, 175–76,
    195–96, 210–11, 229, 276
Hutchinson, Bill (Sourdough Bill): 156,
    161–63

Ignacio, Don: 82–83
Ilfeld, Charles: 277
Irvin (merchant): 55
Isacks, Bill: 80–81

Jackson (cowboy): 259
Jackson, John M. (Humpy): 138
Jackson, Pegleg: 6, 10
Jackson, Rebecca: 151
James brothers: 189–90
James, Eddy: 214
James, Emiel: 256–57
James, Harry: 214–15, 217–18
James, Johnny: 150, 214, 216, 236
Johnson, Bill: 19
Johnston, General Joe: 18
Jones, Billy: 92, 96, 249
Jones, Frank: 267, 273
Jones, Louis: 249

Jones, W. J.: 61, 246
Jones, Washie: California bound, 61; at Milligan Plaza, 63, 66, 71, 107, 267, 273

Keene, Bill: 132, 135, 143, 145, 150, 212; Apache Kid's death narrated by, 214–24
Keene, Clara (Mrs. Bill): 135–36, 139, 144–45, 160
Kelly, Ed: 156, 161–63
Kelly, Jerry: 156, 174
Kemp, Ben: 13–15, 61–63, 65, 73ff., 78, 81–84, 111–15, 125–31, 151–55, 160–63, 174–75, 177, 212, 246–51, 254–57, 264–65, 275–78, 280–81; boyhood of, 3–12; with Texas Rangers, 18–34, 38–57, 233; as bullwhacker, 35–36; as cowhand and rancher, 36–37, 57–60, 80, 87–88, 101–103, 108–11, 121, 131–32, 139–50, 155, 167–68; hunting grizzlies, 64, 66–72, 121; with the V-Cross-T Cattle Company, 91–100, 103, 107, 123–25, 156–59, 165; drilling water wells, 117, 192–93, 198, 203–11, 225–26, 228–33, 237, 240–43, 245, 263; jobs in Chloride, 178–91; as freight hauler, 246, 249, 253; trade with Indians, 273–74; in Arizona, 285–86; death of, 288
Kemp, Benny: 111, 120, 128, 130–31, 144–46, 149, 151, 153, 173, 177, 181, 185, 199–201, 204–205, 211–12, 225–28, 233–38, 246, 248–57, 263–65, 276–78, 281, 283; as prankster, 186–88; wrangler for V-Cross-T, 191–92, 197; water well drilling of, 198, 203, 206–207, 229, 231–33, 240–42, 263, 275; on Adams mine hunt, 273–75; army service of, 284; with U.S. Forest Service, 285–88
Kemp, Beulah: *see* Beulah Kemp Finch
Kemp, Boss: 240, 245–46
Kemp, Clara Lue: *see* Clara Lue Kemp Gann
Kemp, Ed: 287–88
Kemp, Jess: 285, 288
Kemp, John Stephen Timothy: 173, 264, 281–82, 284–85, 287–88
Kemp, Joseph: 56
Kemp, Josephine Cox (Mrs. Ben): 74, 77, 115–29, 139–40, 152–53, 159, 178, 195, 254, 267, 281; marriage of, 107–108; at Nine Points, Texas, 108–10; at Beaver Creek, 132–59; at Mesa Redondo, 245–46; in Arizona, 285
Kemp, Julia Jane: *see* Julia Jane Kemp McCarty
Kemp, Lila: 285
Kemp, Lue: 139
Kemp, Mary Lily: *see* Mary Lily Kemp Charleton
Kemp, Ollie: 126, 128–29
Kemp, Pearl: 152, 246, 248
Kemp, Steve: 11–12, 57, 88, 125–26, 128–29, 177, 281, 283
Ketchum, Black Jack (*also* Tom Ketchum): 153, 170; in Mogollon Mountains, New Mexico, 165–66; Hillsboro. New Mexico, bank robbed by, 167–68; train robbed by, 171; capture of, 172
Kiehne, August: 73
Kiehne, Emiel: 189, 273
Kilpatrick, Ben (Big Ed): 153–54, 166–67
Kline, Charley: 152
Kosterlitsky, General: 138
Krempkau, Gus: 19

LaBaum, Charley: 134–36
Landavaso, Jesus: 206
Lewis, Bill: 142–43
Lewis, Bob: 92, 96, 127, 142, 177, 275
Lewis, Maggie Higgins (Mrs. Bob): 127
Lilly, Ben: 277
Llano, Texas: 12, 57, 125, 287
Llano County, Texas: 11, 36, 112
Long, Will: 143–44
Lyons, Tom: 126

McAughan, Patrick: 235
McCament, Fred: 288
McCarty, Charley: 264, 273–75
McCarty, Jess: 206–208, 230–31, 233, 236, 284
McCarty, Julia Jane Kemp (Mrs. Jess): 112, 120, 128, 206, 230
McClure, Walter: 214–15
McDaniels, Polk: 246–48
McDonald, William C.: 256
McFarland (warehouseman): 201
McFarland, Bill (Bill Mac): 60–64, 66, 73, 78, 80–81, 87–88, 101–102, 110, 118
McKittrick, Charley: 273–74
McTavish, Becker: 196, 201, 253
Mackenzie, Ranald Slidell: 138

Magdalena, New Mexico: 52, 94, 96–101, 103–104, 106, 108, 123, 132, 138, 144, 150, 156, 161, 193, 195–209, 226–30, 237–38, 240, 251–53, 275, 287
Magoffin, Joseph: 19
Manning, Doc: 20
Mansfield, Arthur: 241–42
Manuel, Don: 229, 231
Marr, Colonel: 47
Martin, Sam: 92, 97, 141–42
Ma-sai (companion of the Apache Kid): 138
Maxwell, Pete: 74
Mesa Redondo: 257, 266–67, 273–74, 279–85; description of, 243–45; homesteading on, 245–46, 253, 263; drilling at, 245–46, 254ff.; ranchers on, 249–55, 263–65, 275–77
Meyers (Texas rancher): 6, 11
Meyers, August: 154
Meyers, Mrs. (mother of August): 154
Meyers, Pauline: 154
Miles, General Nelson A.: 77
Miller brothers (Buck and Gail): 118–23, 125
Milligan (bear hunter): 71
Milligan Plaza, New Mexico: 52, 61, 63, 65–66, 70–74, 103, 107, 249; *see also* Reserve, New Mexico
Mills, Red: 222, 224
Mix, Tom: 285
Monday, Johnny: 92
Moore, Bear: 177
Morley, Mrs. Ada: 204–205, 226
Morley, Mrs. Ray: 226
Morley, Ray: 205, 226
Moses (mine employee): 259
Munday brothers (ranchers): 47

Narrango, Gregorio: 256
Nations, Lee: 190
Neil, Bob: 186
Neil, Minnie (Mrs. Bob): 186–88
Nephew, Walter: 156, 191
New York Times: 161
Nine Points, Texas: 58, 101, 103, 107, 110, 112, 115, 125
No Life for a Lady: 205

Olson (ski expert at Datil, N.M.): 99–101
Oswald, Leo: 257–58
Otto, Jerry: 242

Owens, Ed: 237–39, 242
Owsley, George: 156

Page (deputy sheriff): 41
Page, George: 57–58
Patrick, Hank: 185
Patterson, James (rancher): 63
Patterson, James (quartermaster sergeant): 272
Payne (miner): 185–86
Payne, Johnny: 226, 228–29
Payne, Mrs. Johnny: 225–26
Payne, Tom: 229
Pérez, Juan: 19
Peterson, Len: 19
Petrie, Cantrell and Moore Cattle Company: 134
Pfotenhaur, Oscar: 138
Phelps (companion of McFarland): 101–103
Plains of San Augustín, New Mexico: 63, 66, 76, 91, 98, 189, 192ff., 231 ff.
Pollock brothers: 157
Porter, Henry: 142, 156
Portwood (rancher): 259
Pounds, Dr.: 61, 64–66
Powell, Buck: 175
Prospectors and prospecting: 36, 118, 138, 177, 267–73, 275
Purdy (Santa Fe yardmaster): 274
Putnam, Bob: 181, 190

Quemado, New Mexico: 241, 251–52, 281

Railston, Cole: 156–58, 173, 191, 197, 202
Red River Land and Cattle Company: 61, 91, 103, 123, 134, 156, 193, 209; *see also* V-Cross-T Cattle Company
Reed (potato seller): 182–83
Reserve, New Mexico: 150, 193, 195, 229, 246, 249, 264, 267, 283, 288–89; *see also* Milligan Plaza
Reynolds, Glen: 136–38, 189
Río Grande: 14–15, 19, 24, 28, 30–31, 33, 47, 55–60, 62, 82, 115, 119, 123–24, 221
Roberts, Bob: 274
Roberts, Will: 13–15, 18, 287
Rouse, Joe: 3
Russell, Jack: 73

Sanchez, Juan: 82–85
Sanchez y Vijil, Juan: 211, 240–41

Satan's Paradise: 205
Satathite, Benton: 233, 237, 239–40
Satathite, "Grandma" Matilda: 238
Satathite, Sam: 233
Saturday Evening Post: 205
Sauceer, Johnny: 165–66
Saunders (rancher): 222, 224
Scarborough (law officer): 170–71
Schales, Thomas: 154–55
Schmidt, Eddy: 185
Schreiner brothers (sheep ranchers): 37–38
Scotton, Ed: 41–44
Sellman, Frank: 123–25
Sieber, Al: 136
Silver City, New Mexico: 63, 161, 177
Simmons, Shack: 175
Six Years with the Texas Rangers: 29
Slaughter, Pete: 38–39, 41, 175
Slinkard, Bert: 214–15, 218, 236
Smart (ranch hand): 156
Smith (cattle buyer): 177
Smith, Chancy: 181
Smith, Charley: 182–83
Smaulding (banker): 274
Smothers (New Mexico ranger): 260, 262–63
Socorro, New Mexico: 64–66, 123–24, 209, 231 ff., 251, 256ff.
Sorrels, Dave: 233
Sorrels, Sebe: 215, 218
Southern Pacific Railroad Company: 20, 46, 48, 57, 112, 114
Spackman (grocer): 205
Springerville, Arizona: 52–53, 60, 204, 268, 284–85
Steen, Walter: 285–86
Stevens, J. T.: 47–48, 55
Stevens, Montague: 52, 71, 150, 249, 283
Straw, Nat: 92, 170, 175–77
Stoudenmire, Dallas: 18–20, 41
Sullivan, Mike: 146, 214–15, 218
Sully (payroll carrier): 258–59
Swift Packing Company: 212, 224

Tarvin, Jim: 88, 103, 108, 110
Taylor, James: 161, 234, 236–37
Taylor, Mrs. James: 236
Tays, Lieutenant: 119
Texas Rangers, Company A: 18, 35; 61 ff., 82, 109, 123; missions in El Paso, 18–20, 29–31, 41–44; holdups foiled by,

20–22; Indian raiders pursued by, 25–29; battles with cattle thieves, 31–34; Tombstone outlaw captured by, 44–45; murderers pursued by, 45–56; company disbanded, 57
Thompson (Kemp visitor): 177–78
Thompson, Jim: 199–202; hired by V-Cross-T Company, 197; in incident at Magdalena, 198; as drilling partner of Kemp, 198; real name revealed by, 202; *see also* Albert Finch
Thompson, Mark: 182
Tige (Kemp dog): 149–53
Toyah, Texas: 61–62, 119
Trading, Indian: 273–74
Tucker, Tom: 49, 233–35
Turner, Ralph: 220–21

Uvalde, Texas: 11, 13, 109

Van Horn, Texas: 14, 35
V-Cross-T Cattle Company: 91–94, 106–107, 123, 127, 134–35, 142–43, 156–57, 161, 165–67, 173, 175, 191–92, 194, 198, 206, 211, 220, 274; *see also* Red River Land and Cattle Company
Victorio (Apache chief): 15, 126

Walde, Ed: 14–15
Wallace, Big Foot: 206
Ward, Jack: 88
Ware, Dick: 39, 58, 79
Weatherby family, the: 126
Well drilling: 112, 117, 155, 192–93, 204–207, 225–26, 228–31, 237ff., 263, 275
Welty, Mrs. Lou: 216
Welty ranch: 215–16, 233
West brothers (ranchers): 256, 263
West, Bud: 245, 253–54
Wiegmann, Dr.: 135, 142, 183–85
Winn, Fred: 159, 194–97
Winston, Frank H.: 153–54, 167, 231
Wilson, Billy (cowhand): 92
Wilson, Billy (theft suspect): 134–35
Woodley, Charley: 91–95, 103, 107, 156
Woods (Deming resident): 48
Woods (mine superintendent): 179
WS Ranch, New Mexico: 50–51, 60–61

Ysleta, Texas: 18–19, 24–25, 28, 30, 35, 41
Yaples, Charley: 153, 168, 170, 214–15, 218–19

UNIVERSITY OF OKLAHOMA PRESS
NORMAN